OXFOR

TH   T0066576

RUMI, known in Iran and Central Asia as Mowlana Jalaloddin Balkhi, was born in 1207 in the province of Balkh, now the border region between Afghanistan and Tajikistan. His family emigrated when he was still a child, shortly before Genghis Khan and his Mongol army arrived in Balkh. They settled permanently in Konya, central Anatolia, which was formerly part of the Eastern Roman Empire (Rum). Rumi was probably introduced to Sufism originally through his father, Baha Valad, a popular preacher who also taught Sufi piety to a group of disciples. However, the turning-point in Rumi's life came in 1244, when he met in Konya a mysterious wandering Sufi called Shamsoddin of Tabriz. Shams, as he is most often referred to by Rumi, taught him the profoundest levels of Sufism, transforming him from a pious religious scholar to an ecstatic mystic. Rumi expressed his new vision of reality in volumes of mystical poetry. His enormous collection of lyrical poetry is considered one of the best that has ever been produced, while his poem in rhyming couplets, the *Masnavi*, is so revered as the most consummate expression of Sufi mysticism that it is commonly referred to as 'the Qur'an in Persian'.

When Rumi died, on 17 December 1273, shortly after having completed his work on the *Masnavi*, his passing was deeply mourned by the citizens of Konya, including the Christian and Jewish communities. His disciples formed the Mevlevi Sufi order, which was named after Rumi, whom they referred to as 'Our Lord' (Turkish 'Mevlana'/ Persian 'Mowlana'). They are better known in Europe and North America as the Whirling Dervishes, because of the distinctive dance that they now perform as one of their central rituals. Rumi's death is commemorated annually in Konya, attracting pilgrims from all corners of the globe and every religion. The popularity of his poetry has risen so much in the last couple of decades that the *Christian Science Monitor* identified Rumi as the most published poet in America in 1997. UNESCO has designated the commemoration of the 800th anniversary of Rumi's birth in 2007 as an event of major international importance.

JAWID MOJADDEDI, a native of Afghanistan, is currently Assistant Professor of Religion at Rutgers University. Dr Mojaddedi's translation, *The Masnavi: Book One* (Oxford, 2004), was awarded the Lois Roth Prize by the American Institute of Iranian Studies. His previous books include *The Biographical Tradition in Sufism* (Richmond, 2001) and, as co-editor, *Classical Islam: A Sourcebook of Religious Literature* (London, 2003).

OXFORD WORLD'S CLASSICS

*For over 100 years Oxford World's Classics have brought
readers closer to the world's great literature. Now with over 700
titles—from the 4,000-year-old myths of Mesopotamia to the
twentieth century's greatest novels—the series makes available
lesser-known as well as celebrated writing.*

*The pocket-sized hardbacks of the early years contained
introductions by Virginia Woolf, T. S. Eliot, Graham Greene,
and other literary figures which enriched the experience of reading.
Today the series is recognized for its fine scholarship and
reliability in texts that span world literature, drama and poetry,
religion, philosophy, and politics. Each edition includes perceptive
commentary and essential background information to meet the
changing needs of readers.*

OXFORD WORLD'S CLASSICS

═══

JALAL AL-DIN RUMI

The Masnavi

BOOK TWO

═══

Translated with an Introduction and Notes by
JAWID MOJADDEDI

OXFORD
UNIVERSITY PRESS

OXFORD

UNIVERSITY PRESS

Great Clarendon Street, Oxford OX2 6DP

Oxford University Press is a department of the University of Oxford.
It furthers the University's objective of excellence in research, scholarship,
and education by publishing worldwide in

Oxford New York

Auckland Cape Town Dar es Salaam Hong Kong Karachi
Kuala Lumpur Madrid Melbourne Mexico City Nairobi
New Delhi Shanghai Taipei Toronto

With offices in

Argentina Austria Brazil Chile Czech Republic France Greece
Guatemala Hungary Italy Japan Poland Portugal Singapore
South Korea Switzerland Thailand Turkey Ukraine Vietnam

Oxford is a registered trade mark of Oxford University Press
in the UK and in certain other countries

Published in the United States
by Oxford University Press Inc., New York

First published as an Oxford World's Classics paperback 2007
Reissued 2008

British Library Cataloguing in Publication Data

Data available

Library of Congress Cataloging in Publication Data

Data available

ISBN 978-0-19-954991-7

14

Typeset by Cepha Imaging Private Ltd., Bangalore, India
Printed in Great Britain
on acid-free paper by
Clays Ltd, Elcograf S.p.A.

To Dr Javad Nurbakhsh

ACKNOWLEDGEMENTS

I SHOULD like to express my gratitude to my immediate family, my friends, and all of the teachers I have studied under. I am also very grateful for the comments and criticisms offered by readers of initial drafts of this translation, especially Julie Scott Meisami, Dani Kopoulos, Daniel Abdal-Hayy Moore, and Dick Davis. Once again, I have been very fortunate to work with an editor as supportive and cooperative as Judith Luna. I alone am responsible for any remaining flaws.

CONTENTS

THE MASNAVI
BOOK TWO

INTRODUCTION

Book Two of the Masnavi

Rumi's *Masnavi* is probably the longest mystical poem ever written by a single author from any religious tradition. It consists of about 26,000 verses, divided into six books. The current volume is a translation of the second book of the *Masnavi*, and follows Book One, also published in Oxford World's Classics.[1] Although Books One and Two are component units of the *Masnavi*, they are also complete poems in themselves.

Much has been written on Rumi and his *Masnavi*. However, one point which has not been explored extensively is its organizational framework. Would Rumi have had an overall framework in mind when he compiled this long and complex poem? The richness of the *Masnavi* makes it very hard to draw any definitive conclusions. On the one hand, that Rumi divided his poem into six books of roughly equal length, each with its own distinct introduction, may suggest an overall framework of some kind. On the other, Rumi's many digressions, as well as his emphasis on the divine origin of his poetry,[2] can give the impression that he did not feel constrained by any particular framework.

A comparison of the first two books of the *Masnavi* reveals first of all that they are very similar in form. The poetry is divided into numerous sections by means of rubrics. These rubrics range from a single word to several lines, which occasionally incorporate an interpretation of the poetry that follows. Each book can also be roughly divided into about a dozen major stories, and they are usually distinguished from one another by virtue of the major stories that they contain.[3] These major stories differ from the more numerous shorter stories because they

---

[1] Rumi, *The Masnavi: Book One*, tr. J. Mojaddedi (Oxford, 2004).

[2] See further J. Mojaddedi, 'Rumi', in A. Rippin, ed., *The Blackwell Companion to the Qur'an* (Oxford, 2006), 362–72.

[3] Concerning the importance of the story for performance of the *Masnavi*, see M. Mills, 'Folk Tradition in the *Masnavi* and the *Masnavi* in Folk Tradition', in A. Banani, R. Hovannisian, and G. Sabagh, eds., *Poetry and Mysticism in Islam: The Heritage of Rumi* (Cambridge, 1994), 136–77.

are made up of many sections, which represent not only the consecutive parts of the narrative, but often also commentaries and elaborations (sometimes in the form of further shorter stories), which break up the main narrative.[4] If one were to consider the dozen or so major stories of this kind in each book to be Rumi's main building-blocks, then, by analysing their functions, one may be able to decipher the rationale behind Rumi's division of the poem into books, and the order of the major stories in each one.

While there is substantial overlap between the two books—at times almost identical verses are used—each book can be seen to focus on a different aspect of Sufism. Like many previous works of the Persian mystical *masnavi* genre, the order of presentation of the major stories of the first book sketches the progress of the mystic on the Sufi path. Book One begins with the well-known 'Song of the Reed' (I, vv. 1–18), which describes the longing of a reed to return to the reed-bed from which it has been cut, and this is usually interpreted by commentators as representing the birth of the human being into this world and his longing to return to his original spiritual nature in God's presence. The final major story in Book One depicts the Prophet Mohammad's disciple Ali as a mystic who has reached the end of the path. He throws away his sword when an enemy soldier, whom he is about to slay, spits in his face (I, vv. 3735–4004). This action is explained as a sign that he has returned to subsistence in God after self-annihilation, since his every action is now determined by God and not by his own will.

Although the content of each book of the *Masnavi* is too rich and diverse to be neatly categorized, one can none the less observe a logic to the selection and order of the major stories. For instance, those of Book One seem to be presented in the order of progression on the Sufi path as far as the climax represented by the aforementioned final story about Ali. This can be shown most clearly by considering the position of the story about the encounter between a Byzantine emissary and the Caliph Omar (I, vv. 1399–556) in relation to the other major stories. This story is interpreted by commentators as a depiction of the disciple's first meeting with the master of the path, and would therefore represent a major turning-point in any depiction of the Sufi path.

---

[4] The use of indentation in the Contents pages is a simplified representation of this multilayered structure.

It is perhaps no accident that the major stories which precede it focus on the problem of the carnal soul (*nafs-e ʿammara be's-su*; literally the 'soul which commands to evil'), which dominates human beings like a terrorizing lion (e.g. I, vv. 904–1398) or a devious vizier (e.g. I, vv. 325–730). By contrast, the major stories following that about the meeting between Omar and the Byzantine emissary describe awakenings to the mystical path (the parrot fleeing its cage, I, vv. 1557–922) and the increasingly lofty stations reached by those who seek proximity to God in various ways, such as through pious devotion (e.g. the old harpist: I, vv. 1923–2233) and self-annihilation in God (e.g. the lion, the wolf, and the fox: I, vv. 3026–136), until the climactic story about Ali's return to subsistence in God.

As one might expect of any writing designed to instruct Sufi disciples, Book Two also describes aspects of the Sufi path, especially the struggle against the self. However, this is not its main focus. Instead, the major stories in Book Two are primarily concerned with the challenge of discerning the true nature of people behind appearances, in order to identify with whom one should associate so as to progress on the mystical path. The extensive exordium introduces these specific issues to the reader from the outset (II, vv. 19–41). The first few of the major stories in Book Two consider this issue by describing the fates of those who completely lack the necessary discernment. One of the most memorable of these stories is that about the travelling Sufi who leaves his donkey in the care of a servant. The servant falsely reassures him about how well he will look after it without needing to be told what to do. However, the Sufi later finds his donkey has almost died through neglect (II, vv. 157–272). Another such story concerns the foolhardy man who trusts a bear against the advice of others, laying the basis of what has since become a popular proverb in Persian about ill-judged friendships (II, vv. 1936–2145).[5] The man rescues a bear from a dragon and then correctly perceives that the bear sincerely loves him. Nevertheless he is inadvertently killed by that bear when it tries to help him—it uses a huge rock to swat a fly which is perched on its master's face while he is sleeping. Thus the reader is shown most vividly that one needs to be wary not only of false friends, but also of well-meaning but ignorant associates.

[5] The Persian expression '*dusti-ye khala khersa*' (the friendship of 'Auntie Bear').

Not all the major stories in Book Two describe the failure of individuals lacking discernment. In fact, subsequent ones are more positive, since they describe the successes achieved by more discerning individuals in identifying harmful influences and defeating them, such as Mo'aviya's success in seeing through Satan (II, vv. 2614–803) or the Prophet seeing through his enemies, 'the hypocrites' in Medina (II, vv. 2836–3037).[6] In the first of this pair of stories, the Caliph Mo'aviya manages to see through Satan's seemingly helpful act of waking him in time for the dawn prayer. Mo'aviya is depicted here as too shrewd to believe that Satan genuinely wants to help him, and so he succeeds in making Satan confess his ulterior motive. The second story tells of the Prophet Mohammad's ability to see through divine inspiration the real intention of the builders of a new mosque in Medina. They pretend to be pious devotees working for the good of Muslims, but God reveals to the Prophet that they actually wish to destroy his mission.

The most important association for an aspiring Sufi is his relationship with a true master of Sufism, such as that between the sick companion and the Prophet Mohammad (II, vv. 2146–613). In Book Two, following the story about the Prophet Mohammad's inspired vision, the reader finds further stories as well as homilies about the spiritual nature of the Sufi master, or 'saint', who receives similar divine inspiration (e.g. the section entitled 'How divine light is bestowed on a mystic', II, vv. 3251–313). In keeping with the general theme of Book Two, the discussions of the nature of the Sufi master here are concerned primarily with the challenge of recognizing his spiritual rank from his outward appearance (e.g. the dervish falsely accused of stealing, II, vv. 3493–520) and his actions (e.g. the shaikh who was seen drinking wine, II, vv. 3314–438). Thus, while the stories towards the start of Book Two illustrate, in turn, failures and successes in distinguishing between appropriate and harmful associations and influences, approximately the last fifth of Book Two focuses on the difficulty for ordinary people of recognizing the saints from whose company they might benefit.

The concentration towards the end of Book Two on the theme of the discernment of the spiritual reality of Sufi masters beyond

---

[6] The term 'hypocrites' is a technical Qur'anic classification of enemies of the Prophet Mohammad who pretended to be devout followers.

appearances generates discussions of more general hermeneutical issues, which are particularly valuable for an understanding of Rumi's composition of the *Masnavi*. Rumi responds here to the literalist objection that his stories are irrational and therefore of no value (II, vv. 3617–36), by stressing that they are designed to fulfil the function of conveying mystical teachings effectively, just as the model sentence 'X struck Y' serves the function of teaching the rules of Arabic grammar. That is to say, questioning the credibility of Rumi's stories is as absurd as becoming disturbed that X struck Y, and demanding to know why X should have done such a thing (II, vv. 3645–51).

Rumi also belittles the significance of narratives in relation to the teachings that they convey towards the beginning of Book Two, in a short section entitled 'Relating the meaning of the tale was halted because of the inclination of the audience to listen to its outward form' (II, vv. 194–202). Here he expresses frustration at having to return to complete the story from which he has digressed, because of the reader's desire to find out what happens next to the main character. He therefore implies that he would much prefer to continue discussing the mystical theory which the story illustrates. Such remarks corroborate the traditional explanation that Rumi wrote the *Masnavi* after being urged to do so by his deputy Hosamoddin, who reported that his disciples preferred to read poems of the *masnavi* genre to the prose writings of Sufi theory which he had assigned them. That is to say, it suggests at face value that he used narratives to convey his teachings only reluctantly, as a concession to the needs and predilections of his readers. It is worth pointing out that Rumi's inclusion of comments about the function of his stories towards both the beginning and the end of Book Two is an example of his tendency to round off his poetry. The popular translator Coleman Barks has already observed how the very first and the very last stories in the six volumes of the *Masnavi* have much in common,[7] and a new study by Seyed Safavi and Simon Weightman has taken this much further, by arguing that the *Masnavi* as a whole was carefully designed by Rumi using ring composition. According to Safavi and Weightman, not only the work as a whole, but also its six component books and their component 'discourses'

---

[7] C. Barks, *The Essential Rumi*, new expanded edition (New York, 2004), 225.

have been arranged with extraordinary precision, and only appear to be disorganized on the surface.[8]

If there is unity in the *Masnavi* as a whole in addition to its component books, it is in spite of the fact that Book Two was started after a delay, rather than immediately after Book One. This delay is referred to in both the prose introduction and the first nine couplets of the exordium, each of which gives a different reason. The explanation of Rumi's biographers that the delay was due to the passing of Hosamoddin's wife, for whom the latter grieved at length, appears to be based on the exordium's explanation that the work could not continue until Hosamoddin's return from an absence (II, vv. 1–9; it is described more like a mystical retreat than a period of mourning, perhaps owing to the context in which it is presented). Since Books One and Two can be read as independent and complete volumes in their own right, one might be tempted to suggest that there may originally have been no plan to write more than one book. However, the ending of Book One of the *Masnavi* strongly implies that the poem will be continued (I, vv. 4016–18). Even if a continuation had not been planned, it could still have been possible for Rumi to continue his work in a way that would produce a six-volume poem that is complete, balanced, and neatly rounded off with allusions after 26,000 verses to the first few hundred of them. A more precise ring structure would probably have required a plan in advance for the whole work.

Rumi and Sufism

Rumi has long been recognized within the Sufi tradition as one of the most important Sufis in history. He not only produced the finest Sufi poetry in Persian, but was the master of disciples who later, under the direction of his son and eventual successor Soltan Valad, named their order after him. Moreover, by virtue of the intense devotion he expressed towards his own master, Shams-e Tabriz, Rumi has become the archetypal Sufi disciple. From that perspective, the unprecedented level of interest in Rumi's poetry over the last couple of decades in North America and Europe does not come as a total surprise.

---

[8] This new study by Simon Weightman and Seyed Safavi is due to be published in 2007 by the State University of New York Press as *Rumi's Mystical Design*.

Once his poetry finally began to be rendered into English in an attractive form, which coincided with an increased interest in mysticism among readers, this Sufi saint who expressed his mystical teachings in a more memorable and universally accessible form than any other began to become a household name.

Rumi lived some 300 years after the first writings of Muslim mystics were produced. A distinct mystical path called 'Sufism' became clearly identifiable in the late tenth and early eleventh centuries with the compilation of the manuals and collections of biographies of past Sufi saints. The authors of these works, who were mostly from northeastern Persia, traced the origins of the Sufi tradition back to the Prophet Mohammad, while at the same time acknowledging the existence of comparable forms of mysticism before his mission. They mapped out a mystical path, by which the Sufi ascends towards the ultimate goal of union with God and knowledge of reality. More than two centuries before the time of the eminent Sufi theosopher Ebn ʿArabi (d. 1240), Sufis began to describe their experience of annihilation in God and the realization that only God truly exists. The illusion of one's own independent existence had begun to be regarded as the main obstacle to achieving this realization, so that early Sufis like Abu Yazid Bestami (d. 874) are frequently quoted as dismissing the value of the asceticism of some of their contemporaries on the grounds that it merely increased attention to themselves. In this way, most Sufis began to regard love of God as the means of overcoming the root problem of one's own self, rather than piety and asceticism.[9]

The Sufi practice discussed most in the early manuals of Sufism is that of listening to music, commonly referred to as 'musical audition' (*samaʿ*). Listening to poetry being sung to music, while immersed in the remembrance of God and unaware of oneself, induced ecstasy in worshippers. The discussions in Sufi manuals of spontaneous movements by Sufis in ecstasy while listening to music, and the efforts made to distinguish this from ordinary dance, suggest that this practice had already begun to cause a great deal of controversy. Most of the Sufi orders that were later formed developed the practice of surrendering to spontaneous movements while listening to music,

---

[9] Translations of representative samples of the key texts of early Sufism are available in M. Sells, *Early Islamic Mysticism* (Mahwah, 1996).

but the whirling ceremony of the followers of Rumi, the Mevlevi order, is a unique phenomenon.[10] Although it is traditionally traced back to Rumi's own propensity for spinning around in ecstasy, the elaborate ceremony in the form in which it has become famous today was established only by the seventeenth century.[11]

The characteristics of the Sufi mystic who has completed the path to enlightenment is one of the most recurrent topics in Sufi writings of the tenth and eleventh centuries, but students of Sufism at the time would tend to associate with several such individuals rather than form an exclusive bond with one master. By the twelfth century, however, the master–disciple relationship became increasingly emphasized, as the first Sufi orders began to be formed. It was also during this century that the relationship between love of God and His manifestation in creation became a focus of interest, especially among Sufis of Persian origin, such as Ahmad Ghazali (d. 1126) and Ruzbehan Baqli (d. 1209).[12] The former's more famous brother was responsible for integrating Sufism with mainstream Sunni Islam, as a practical form of Muslim piety that can provide irrefutable knowledge of religious truths through direct mystical experience.[13]

In this way, by the thirteenth century diverse forms of Sufism had developed and become increasingly popular. Rumi was introduced to Sufism by his father, Baha Valad, who followed a more conservative tradition of Muslim piety, but his life was transformed when he encountered the mystic Shams-e Tabriz. Although many of the followers of the tradition of his father considered Shams to be totally unworthy of Rumi's time and attention, he considered him to be the most complete manifestation of God. Rumi expressed his love and utter devotion for his master Shams, with whom he spent only about two years in total, through thousands of ecstatic lyrical poems. Towards the end of his life he presented the fruit of his experience of Sufism

[10] Concerning the contrast between the Mevlevi *sama'* and other forms of Sufi *sama'*, see J. During, 'What is Sufi Music?', in L. Lewisohn, ed., *The Legacy of Medieval Persian Sufism* (London and New York, 1992), 277–87.

[11] See further C. W. Ernst, *The Shambhala Guide to Sufism* (Boston, 1997), 191–4.

[12] See further C. W. Ernst, tr., *Teachings of Sufism* (Boston, 1999), 82–94, and A. Ghazali, *Sawanih: Inspirations from the World of Pure Spirits*, tr. N. Pourjavady (London, 1986).

[13] The chapter of Mohammad Ghazali's autobiography which describes his experience on the Sufi path is available in translation in N. Calder, J. Mojaddedi, and A. Rippin, eds. and trs., *Classical Islam: A Sourcebook of Religious Literature* (London, 2003), 228–32.

in the form of the *Masnavi*, which has been judged by many commentators, both within the Sufi tradition and outside it, to be the greatest mystical poem ever written.

Rumi and his Times

The century in which Rumi lived was one of the most tumultuous in the history of the Middle East and Central Asia. When he was about 10 years old the region was invaded by the Mongols, who, under the leadership of Genghis Khan, left death and destruction in their wake. Arriving through Central Asia and north-eastern Persia, the Mongols soon took over almost the entire region, conquering Baghdad in 1258. The collapse at the hands of an infidel army of the once glorious Abbasid caliphate in Baghdad, the symbolic capital of the entire Muslim world, was felt throughout the region as a tremendous shock. Soon afterwards, there was a sign that the map of the region would continue to change, when the Mongols suffered a major defeat in Syria, at ʿAyn Jalut in 1260. Rumi's life was directly affected by the military and political developments of the time, beginning with his family's emigration from north-eastern Persia just two years before the Mongols arrived to conquer that region. Although the family eventually relocated to Konya (ancient Iconium) in central Anatolia, Rumi witnessed the spread of Mongol authority across that region too when he was still a young man.

In spite of the upheaval and destruction across the region during this century, there were many outstanding Sufi authors among Rumi's contemporaries. The most important Sufi theosopher, Ebn ʿArabi (d. 1240), produced his highly influential works during the first half of the century. His student and foremost interpreter, Sadroddin Qunyavi (d. 1273) settled in Konya some fifteen years after his master's death and became associated with Rumi (he is said to have led Rumi's funeral prayers, shortly before his own passing). This is one possible channel through which Rumi could have gained familiarity with Ebn ʿArabi's theosophical system, although his poetry does not suggest the direct influence of the latter's works.[14]

---

[14] On the relationship between the theosophy of Ibn ʿArabi and the poetry of Rumi, see W. C. Chittick, 'Rumi and *waḥdat al-wujūd*', in A. Banani, R. Hovannisian, and

The lives of two of the most revered Sufi poets also overlapped with Rumi's life: the most celebrated Arab Sufi poet, Ebn al-Farez (d. 1235), whose poetry holds a position of supreme importance comparable with that of Rumi in the Persian canon;[15] and Faridoddin ʿAttar (d. 1220), who was Rumi's direct predecessor in the composition of Persian mystical *masnavi*s (see below), including the highly popular work which has been translated as *The Conference of the Birds*.[16] It is perhaps not surprising that the Sufi poet Jami (d. 1492) should want to link Rumi with ʿAttar directly by claiming that they met when Rumi's family migrated from Balkh; ʿAttar is said to have recognized his future successor in the composition of works in the mystical *masnavi* genre although Rumi was still a young boy. ʿAttar died soon after this meeting, and is traditionally believed to have been killed by the Mongols during their conquest of Nishapur.

As the Mongols advanced westwards, Anatolia became an increasingly attractive destination for the inhabitants of central parts of the Middle East who wished to flee. A number of important Sufis and influential scholars chose this option, including Hajji Bektash (d. *c.*1272), the eponym of the Bektashi order, which became one of the most influential Sufi orders in Anatolia in subsequent centuries, and Najmoddin Razi (d. 1256), whose teacher, Najmoddin Kobra (d. 1221), the eponym of the Kobravi order, had been killed during the Mongol invasion of Transoxiana.

From shortly after his death, many works have been written about Rumi's life in Konya, but contradictions in these sources, and the hagiographic nature of most of the material compiled, mean that a number of important details remain uncertain. The recent landmark study by Franklin Lewis, *Rumi, Past and Present, East and West* (Oxford, 2000), has considered this problem at length. By examining the sources critically, Lewis has sought to clarify what precisely can be learnt from them and what still cannot be confirmed beyond any doubt.

G. Sabagh, eds., *Poetry and Mysticism in Islam: The Heritage of Rumi* (Cambridge, 1994), 70–111; and O. Safi, 'Did the Two Oceans Meet? Historical Connections and Disconnections between Ibn ʿArabi and Rumi', *Journal of Muhyiddin Ibn ʿArabi Society*, 26 (1999), 55–88.

[15] See further T. Emil Homerin, *From Arab Poet to Muslim Saint: Ibn al-Farid, His Verse, and His Shrine* (Columbia, SC, 1994).

[16] Tr. A. Darbandi and D. Davis (Harmondsworth, 1983).

His study is therefore indispensable for any serious academic inves-
tigation, and is likely to inspire many revisionist accounts in the
future. None the less, the general outline of Rumi's life seems to be
presented relatively consistently in the sources, and remains helpful
for putting the *Masnavi* into context.

Rumi was born in September 1207 in the province of Balkh, in what
is now the border region between Afghanistan and Tajikistan.[17] His
father, Baha Valad, was a preacher and religious scholar who also led
a group of Sufi disciples. When Rumi was about 10 years old his family
emigrated to Anatolia, having already relocated a few years earlier to
Samarkand in Transoxiana. This emigration seems to have been moti-
vated primarily by the approach of Genghis Khan's Mongol army,
although rivalries between Baha Valad and various religious scholars
in the region may also have played a part. Instead of moving westwards
directly, Rumi's family first made the pilgrimage to Mecca, and it was
only a few years after arriving in Anatolia that they decided to settle
permanently in Konya. By this time, Rumi had already married (1224)
and seen the birth of his son and eventual successor in Sufism,
SoltanValad (1226).

In Konya Baha Valad found the opportunity, under the patronage
of the Seljuk ruler Alaoddin Kay Qobad I (r. 1219–36), to continue
his work as a preacher and to teach students in a religious school. Baha
had been grooming Rumi to be his successor, but died only a couple
of years after settling in Konya, in 1231. Although the original reasons
for his arrival remain unclear, it seems that one of Baha Valad's students, called Borhanoddin Mohaqqeq, arrived in Konya from north-
eastern Persia soon afterwards to take over the management of his
school. He also took responsibility for overseeing the continuation of
Rumi's education and training. Within a few years, Borhanoddin sent
Rumi to Aleppo and Damascus to continue his education in the religious sciences. It is possible that during his stay in Damascus Rumi
may have heard the lectures of Ebn ʿArabi, who was living there at the
time. Rumi returned to Konya in around 1237 as a highly accomplished
young scholar, and took over leadership of Baha Valad's school from
Borhanoddin.

---

[17] Concerning the precise location of Rumi's birth, see F. D. Lewis, *Rumi, Past and
Present, East and West: The Life, Teachings and Poetry of Jalal al-Din Rumi* (Oxford,
2000), 47–8.

After his return to Konya, Rumi's reputation as an authority on religious matters became firmly established there, and he reached the peak of his career as a scholar, achieving what his father seems to have hoped for him. In November 1244, after seven years of excelling as a respected religious teacher, Rumi experienced a challenging encounter that would prove to be the most significant event of his life. As one would expect, an event as important as this has generated many competing accounts.[18] However, most versions share the same basic element. According to one popular and relatively simple account, Rumi is asked about his books by an uneducated-looking stranger, and responds by snapping back dismissively, 'They are something that you do not understand!' The books then suddenly catch fire, so Rumi asks the stranger to explain what has happened. His reply is: 'Something you do not understand.'

Rumi was immediately drawn to this mysterious figure, who turned out to be a wandering mystic called Shamsoddin from Tabriz (known popularly as Shams, or Shams-e Tabriz) in north-western Persia. The two began to spend endless hours together in retreat. What was shared by the pair during this time remains a mystery that can only be guessed from the volumes of poetry that it inspired. Even in the *Masnavi*, where Rumi makes painstaking efforts to communicate his teachings as clearly as possible for the benefit of his students, he none the less expresses his unwillingness to disclose anything about his experiences with Shams, despite the persistent requests from his deputy at that time, Hosamoddin Chalabi. Rumi explains that those experiences were beyond the capacity of others to understand: 'Please don't request what you can't tolerate | A blade of straw can't hold a mountain's weight' (I, v. 140).

What is reported consistently about the period of about a year and a half that Rumi spent with Shams is that it provoked intense jealousy and resentment among his disciples, who also feared that their highly respected master was risking his reputation by mixing with someone so unworthy in their eyes. These disciples eventually drove Shams away, but, on hearing reports of sightings of him in Syria, Rumi sent his own son, SoltanValad, to ask him to come back. Although Shams did return a year later, in 1247, he soon disappeared forever.

[18] For translations of all the main descriptions of this meeting, see ibid. 154–61.

According to tradition, Shams was killed by Rumi's disciples after they had seen that driving him away had failed to separate him permanently from their master, but, as Lewis has pointed out, there is little external evidence to substantiate this claim.[19]

Although Rumi was already a respected religious authority in Konya and had trained in a tradition of Sufi piety under his father, he was led by Shams to a far loftier level of Sufi mysticism. His poetry, for instance, emphasizes the importance of love in transcending attachments to the world, and dismisses concerns for worldly reputation, literal-mindedness, and intellectualism. From dry scholarship and popular piety, Rumi turned his attention to mystical poetry, and he became known for his propensity to fall into an ecstatic trance and spin around in public. It is clear that Rumi recognized Shams as a profound mystic, the like of whom he had never encountered before, and that for him Shams was the most complete manifestation of God. Rumi innovatively named his own collection of *ghazal*s, or lyrical poems, as 'the Collection of Shams' (*Divan-e Shams*) rather than as his own collection, and also included Shams's name in place of his own at the end of many of his *ghazal*s, where by convention the poet would identify himself. This can be seen as Rumi's acknowledgement of the all-important inspiration that Shams had provided for him to write such poetry.[20] Rumi chose a plain, descriptive name for his *Masnavi* (*masnavi* is the name of the rhyming couplet verse form used; see further below), which he started composing some fifteen years after Shams had disappeared, but it is not long before he digresses to praise of Shams, at the mention of the word *shams*, which means 'sun' in Arabic (I, vv. 124–42).

After the final disappearance of Shams, Rumi remained in Konya and continued to direct his father's school. However, he chose to appoint as deputy a goldsmith called Salahoddin, whose responsibility was to manage many of the affairs of the school in his place. Like Shams, he was disliked by many of Rumi's disciples, who considered him uneducated. A colourful story about the first encounter between the two describes Rumi as falling into ecstasy and whirling, on hearing the rhythmic beating of Salahoddin at work in his market stall.

---

[19] See Lewis, *Rumi*, 185–93.   [20] See further ibid. 329–30.

After Salahoddin's death in 1258, Rumi appointed Hosamoddin Chalabi in his place. At the time when Hosamoddin had become a disciple of Rumi he was already the head of a local order for the training of young men in chivalry. He had brought with him his own disciples, the wealth of his order, and the expertise he had acquired in running such an institution. However, the most important contribution of Hosamoddin was serving as Rumi's scribe and putting the *Masnavi* into writing as Rumi recited it aloud. Rumi praises Hosamoddin profusely in the introduction of the *Masnavi*, indicating the vital importance of his role for this work.

In addition to Rumi's poetry, three prose works have also survived. They reveal much about aspects of his life that have been neglected by most biographers. The collection of Rumi's letters testifies to his influence among the local political rulers and his efforts to secure positions of importance for his disciples through letters of recommendation. This contradicts the popular image of Rumi withdrawing from public life after the disappearance of Shams. His collection of seven sermons attests to the fact that he was highly esteemed by the local Muslim population. It reveals that he delivered sermons at the main congregational mosque on important occasions, and that he used such opportunities to give Sufi teachings, albeit within the rigid constraints of a formal sermon.[21] Rumi's most important prose work, however, is the written record of his teaching sessions, which was compiled after his death by his students as seventy-one discourses. This work, called 'In it is what is in it' probably on account of its diverse and unclassified contents, has been published as 'Discourses of Rumi' and 'Signs of the Unseen' (see the Bibliography). It provides intimate glimpses of Rumi as a Sufi master. The content of this work is comparable to his didactic poem, the *Masnavi*, in that it contains many of the same teachings. A reference to a specific verse in the second book of the *Masnavi* confirms that the discourses represent Rumi's teaching activity towards the end of his life.[22] However, a relatively long time-span seems to be represented in this work, for another of its component discourses refers to the opposition faced by Salahoddin when he was serving as Rumi's deputy.[23]

[21] One of Rumi's sermons is provided in translation in ibid. 130–33.

[22] Rumi, *Signs of the Unseen: The Discourses of Jalaluddin Rumi*, tr. W. Thackston, Jr. (Boston, 1999), 205.

[23] Ibid. 99–101.

Rumi died on 17 December 1273, probably very soon after the completion of the *Masnavi*. Tradition tells us that physicians could not identify the illness from which he was suffering, and that they suspected he had decided to embrace his physical death, fulfilling sentiments often expressed in his poetry. His death was mourned not only by his disciples but also by the large and diverse community in Konya, including Christians and Jews, who converged as his body was carried through the city. Many of the non-Muslims had not only admired him as outsiders, but had also attended his teaching sessions. The 'Green Dome', where his mausoleum is found today, was constructed soon after Rumi's death. It has become probably the most popular site of pilgrimage in the world to be visited regularly by members of every major religion.

Hosamoddin Chalabi served as the leader of Rumi's school for the first twelve years after Rumi's death, and was succeeded by Soltan Valad. Rumi's disciples named their school 'the Mevlevi order' after him, for they used to refer to him by the title 'Mevlana' (in Arabic *Mawlana*, meaning Our Master). It became widespread and influential especially under the Ottoman empire and remains an active Sufi order in Turkey as well as many other countries across the world. The Mevlevis are better known in the West as 'the Whirling Dervishes' because of the distinctive dance that they perform to music as the central ritual of the order.

The Masnavi

Rumi's *Masnavi* holds an exalted status in the rich canon of Persian Sufi literature as the greatest mystical poem ever written. It is even referred to commonly as 'the Qur'an in Persian'. As already mentioned, the title Rumi himself chose for it is simply the name of the form of poetry adopted for it, the *masnavi* form. Each half-line, or hemistich, of a *masnavi* poem follows the same metre, in common with other forms of classical Persian poetry. The metre of Rumi's *Masnavi* is the *ramal* metre in apocopated form ($-\breve{}- -/-\breve{}- -/-\breve{}-$), a highly popular metre which was also used by ʿAttar for his *Conference of the Birds*. What distinguishes the *masnavi* form from other Persian verse forms is the rhyme, which changes in successive couplets according to the pattern *aa bb cc dd*, etc. Thus, in contrast to the other verse forms, which require a restrictive monorhyme, the *masnavi* form enables poets to compose long works consisting of thousands of verses. Rumi's *Masnavi* amounts to about 26,000 verses altogether.

The *masnavi* form satisfied the need felt by Persians to compose narrative and didactic poems, of which there was already before the Islamic period a long and rich tradition. By Rumi's time a number of Sufis had already made use of the *masnavi* form to compose mystical poems, the most celebrated among which are Sana'i's (d. 1138) *Hadiqato'l-haqiqat*, or *Garden of Truth*, and Faridoddin 'Attar's (d. 1220) *Manteqo't-tayr*, or *Conference of the Birds*.[24] According to tradition, it was the popularity of these works amongst Rumi's disciples that prompted Hosamoddin, Rumi's deputy, to ask him to compose his own mystical *masnavi* for their benefit.

Hosamoddin served as Rumi's scribe in a process of text-production that is traditionally described as being similar to the way in which the Qur'an was produced. However, while the Sufi poet Rumi recited the *Masnavi* orally when he felt inspired to do so, with Hosamoddin always ready to record those recitations in writing for him as well as to assist him in revising and editing the final poem, the illiterate Prophet Mohammad is said to have recited aloud divine revelation in piecemeal fashion, in exactly the form that God's words were revealed to him through the Archangel Gabriel. Those Companions of the Prophet who were present at such occasions would write down the revelations and memorize them, and these written and mental records eventually formed the basis of the compilation of the Qur'an many years after the Prophet's death.

The process of producing the *Masnavi* was probably started around 1262, although tradition relates that Rumi had already composed the first eighteen couplets by the time Hosamoddin made his request; we are told that he responded by pulling a sheet of paper out of his turban with the first part of the prologue of Book One, often called 'The Song of the Reed', already written on it. References to their system of production can be found in the text of the *Masnavi* itself (e.g. I, v. 2947). They seem to have worked on the *Masnavi* during the evenings in particular, and in one instance Rumi begs forgiveness for having kept Hosamoddin up for an entire night with it (I, v. 1817).

[24] See e.g. F. 'Attar, *The Conference of the Birds*, ed. and tr. A. Darbandi and D. Davis (Harmondsworth, 1983).

After Hosamoddin had written down Rumi's recitations, they were read back to him to be checked and corrected. The crucial role played by Hosamoddin as Rumi's assistant in this process, as well as an inspiration, is highlighted by the fact that Rumi refers to the *Masnavi* on several occasions as 'the Hosam book'.

Rumi's *Masnavi* belongs to the group of works written in this verse form that do not have a frame narrative. In this way, it contrasts with the more cohesively structured *Conference of the Birds*, which is already well known in translation. It is also much longer; the *Conference* is roughly the same length as just one of the six component books of the *Masnavi*. Each of the six books consists of about 4,000 verses and has its own prose introduction and prologue. There are no epilogues.

The narratives, homilies, commentaries on citations, prayers, and lyrical flights which make up the body of the *Masnavi* are often demarcated by their own rubrics. The text of longer narratives tends to be broken up into sections by further such rubrics. Occasionally the rubrics are positioned inappropriately, such as in the middle of continuous speech, which might be interpreted as a sign that they were inserted only after the text had been prepared. Occasionally the rubrics are actually longer than the passage that they represent, and serve to explain and contextualize what follows. It is as if, on rereading the text, further explanation was felt necessary in the form of an expanded heading. According to Safavi and Weightman, however, these puzzling rubrics are of crucial importance, in that they represent the original plan of the *Masnavi* and were therefore probably organized before any of the poetry had itself been composed.

The diversity of the contents of Book Two of the *Masnavi* is representative of the work as a whole. It includes stories with characters ranging from prophets and kings to beggars and tramps, as well as animals. The citations which receive commentary are taken primarily from the Qur'an, the traditions of the Prophet (*hadith*), and the works of Rumi's precursors in Sufism. The homilies cover, in addition to specifically Sufi issues, general ethical concerns based on traditional wisdom. Rumi drew on his knowledge of a vast range of both oral and literary sources in the composition of his work,[25] as well as his

---

[25] Since most of the literary sources drawn upon for Book Two are unavailable in English, references have been provided only to the Qur'an. For further information about Rumi's sources, see Lewis, *Rumi*, 288–91.

familiarity with a wide range of disciplines, including theology, philosophy, the exegesis of the Qur'an and *hadith*, philology, literature, jurisprudence, and medicine. Most of his stories are very humorous, at least in parts, and he does not hesitate to use whatever may convey his point in as memorable a way as possible to his contemporaries, including jokes about sexuality and ethnic and gender stereotypes.

The frequency of breaks in the flow of narratives, which is a distinctive characteristic of the *Masnavi*, reveals that Rumi has earned a reputation as an excellent storyteller despite being primarily concerned with conveying his teachings as effectively as possible to his Sufi disciples. The *Masnavi* leaves the impression that he was brimming with ideas and symbolic images which would overflow when prompted by the subtlest of associations. In this way, free from the constraints of a frame narrative, Rumi has been able to produce a work that is far richer in content than any other example of the mystical *masnavi* genre. That this has been achieved often at the expense of preserving continuity in the narratives seems to corroborate Rumi's opinion on the relative importance of the teachings in his poetry over its aesthetic value, as reported in his discourses.[26] If it were not for the fact that his digressive 'overflowings' are expressed in simple language and with imagery that was immediately accessible to his contemporary readers, they would have constituted an undesirable impediment to understanding the poem. Where this leads Rumi to interweave narratives and to alternate between different speakers and his own commentaries, the text can still be difficult to follow, and, for most contemporary readers, the relevance of citations and allusions to the Qur'an and the traditions of the Prophet will not be immediately obvious without reference to the explanatory notes that have been provided in this edition. None the less, it should be evident, not least from the lengthy sequences of metaphors that Rumi often provides to reinforce a single point, that he has striven to communicate his

---

[26] In a famous passage in Rumi's discourses, he is reported to have compared writing poetry with serving to a guest something which one finds unpleasant like tripe, because that is what the guest wants (Rumi, *Signs of the Unseen*, 77–8). The main theme of the sixteenth discourse (pp. 74–80), in which this passage is found, is the relationship between form and content, and it includes Rumi's response to the charge that he is 'all talk and no action' (p. 78). The statement should therefore be understood in its proper context, rather than as evidence that Rumi disliked the art of writing poetry.

message as effectively as possible rather than to write obscurely and force the reader to struggle to understand him.

Rumi made painstaking efforts to convey his teachings as clearly and effectively as possible, using simple language, the *masnavi* verse form, entertaining stories, and the most vivid and accessible imagery possible. The aim of the present translation is to render Rumi's *Masnavi* into a relatively simple and attractive form which, with the benefit of metre and rhyme, may enable as many readers as possible to read the whole book with pleasure and to find it rewarding.

NOTE ON THE TRANSLATION

Rumi put his teachings into the *masnavi* verse form in order that, with the benefit of metre and rhyme, his disciples might enjoy reading them. I have therefore decided to translate Rumi's *Masnavi* into verse, in accordance with the aim of the original work. I have chosen to use rhyming iambic pentameters, since this is the closest corresponding form of English verse to the Persian *masnavi* form of rhyming couplets. These are numbered and referred to as verses in the Explanatory Notes and Introduction.

Book Two of the *Masnavi* consists of over 3,800 couplets, the continuity of which is broken up only by section headings. For the sake of clarity, in this translation further breaks have been added to those created by the section headings. In order for the Contents pages to fulfil their function effectively, alternative headings have been employed there, albeit at corresponding points to the major section headings in the text, which refer in many instances to merely the first few subsequent verses rather than representing the section as a whole.

Although the *Masnavi* is a Persian poem, it contains a substantial amount of Arabic text. This invariably takes the form of citations from Arabic sources and common religious formulae, but the sources for some of these passages are either unknown or oral. Italics have been used to indicate Arabic text, except in the section headings, which are fully italicized. Many Arabic terms and religious formulae have become part of the Persian language, and have therefore not been highlighted in this way. Capitalization has been used when reference is made to God. This includes, in addition to the pronouns and titles commonly used in English, the ninety-nine names of God of the Islamic tradition, as well as certain philosophical terms. The Glossary provides information both on proper names and on specialist terms.

Most of the sources of the *Masnavi* are not widely available in English, if at all, and so references have been provided in the notes only for citations of the Qur'an. Verse numbering varies in the most widely available translations of the Qur'an, some of which do not in fact number individual verses, but since this variation is very slight (maximum of a few verses) the reader should still be able to find the relevant passages without difficulty. The notes also identify those passages in the translation which represent the sayings and deeds of the Prophet Mohammad (*hadith*) without this being made self-evident in the text (e.g. by 'the Prophet said'). It should be pointed out that citations in the original *Masnavi* are very often variants of the original sources, including the Qur'an, rather than exact renderings, due to the constraints of the metre that is used. The same applies in this verse translation.

This translation corresponds exactly to the text of the second volume of the edition prepared by Mohammad Estelami (6 volumes and index, 2nd edn., Tehran, 1990). This is by far the best critical edition available, since it offers a complete apparatus criticus, indicating the variant readings in all the early manuscripts more comprehensively and transparently than any other edition. Although R. A. Nicholson's edition of the Persian text is more widely available, having been published in Europe, its shortcomings for today are widely recognized and outweigh the advantage of having his exactly corresponding prose translation and commentary to refer to.

As far as possible, the English equivalents of technical terms have been provided, in preference to giving the original in transliteration and relying on explanatory notes. Where it is provided, the transliteration of names and terms has been simplified to such a degree that no diacritics are used. It is designed simply to help the reader use Persian pronunciation, especially where this would affect the metre and rhyme.

SELECT BIBLIOGRAPHY

General Background

J. T. P. De Bruijn, *Persian Sufi Poetry: An Introduction to the Mystical Use of Classical Poems* (Richmond, 1997).

C. W. Ernst, *The Shambhala Guide to Sufism* (Boston, 1997).

C. W. Ernst, tr., *Teachings of Sufism* (Boston, 1999).

L. Lewisohn, ed., *Classical Persian Sufism: From its Origins to Rumi* (London and New York, 1993).

J. Nurbakhsh, *The Path: Sufi Practices* (London and New York, 2002; 2nd rev. edn., New York, 2006).

A. Rippin, *Muslims: Their Religious Beliefs and Practices*, 3rd edn. (London and New York, 2005).

M. Sells, ed. and tr., *Early Islamic Mysticism* (Mahwah, 1996).

Reference

Encyclopaedia Iranica, ed. E. Yarshater (New York, 1985– ; also available online at www.iranica.com).

Encyclopaedia of Islam, ed. H. A. R. Gibb et al. (Leiden, 1960–2003).

J. Nurbakhsh, *Sufi Symbolism*, 16 vols. (London and New York, 1980–2003).

On Rumi

W. C. Chittick, ed., *The Sufi Path of Love: The Spiritual Teachings of Rumi* (Albany, NY, 1983).

F. Keshavarz, *Reading Mystical Lyric: The Case of Jalal al-Din Rumi* (Columbia, SC, 1998).

F. D. Lewis, *Rumi, Past and Present, East and West: The Life, Teachings and Poetry of Jalal al-Din Rumi* (Oxford, 2000).

Rumi, *Mystical Poems of Rumi 1 and 2*, tr. A. J. Arberry (New York, 1979).

Rumi, *Signs of the Unseen*, tr. W. M. Thackston (Boston, 1994).

A. Schimmel, *The Triumphal Sun* (London, 1978).

N. Virani, '"I am the nightingale of the Merciful": Rumi's use of the Qur'an and Hadith', *Comparative Studies of South Asia, Africa and the Middle East*, 22/2 (2002), 100–11.

Editions of the Masnavi

Masnavi, ed. M. Estelami, 7 vols, 2nd edn (Tehran, 1990). The seventh volume is a volume of indices. Each of the six volumes of text contains the editor's commentary in the form of endnotes.

R. A. Nicholson, ed. and tr., *The Mathnawi of Jalalu'ddin Rumi*, E. J. W. Gibb Memorial, NS, 8 vols. (London, 1925–40). This set consists of the Persian text (vols. i–iii), a full translation in prose (vols. iv–vi), and commentary (vols. vii–viii).

Masnavi, ed. T. Sobhani (Tehran, 1994).

Masnavi-ye ma'navi, ed. A.-K. Sorush, 2 vols (Tehran, 1996).

Interpretation of the Masnavi

W. C. Chittick, 'Rumi and *waḥdat al-wujūd*', in A. Banani, R. Hovannisian, and G. Sabagh, eds., *Poetry and Mysticism in Islam: The Heritage of Rumi* (Cambridge, 1994), 70–111.

H. Dabashi, 'Rumi and the Problems of Theodicy: Moral Imagination and Narrative Discourse in a Story of the *Masnavi*', in A. Banani, R. Hovannisian, and G. Sabagh, eds., *Poetry and Mysticism in Islam: The Heritage of Rumi* (Cambridge, 1994), 112–35.

R. Davis, 'Narrative and Doctrine in the First Story of Rumi's *Mathnawi*', in G. R. Hawting, J. A. Mojaddedi, and A. Samely, eds., *Studies in Islamic and Middle Eastern Texts and Traditions in Memory of Norman Calder* (Oxford, 2000), 93–104.

M. Mills, 'Folk Tradition in the *Masnavi* and the *Masnavi* in Folk Tradition', in A. Banani, R. Hovannisian, and G. Sabagh, eds., *Poetry and Mysticism in Islam: The Heritage of Rumi* (Cambridge, 1994), 136–77.

J. Mojaddedi, 'Rumi', in A. Rippin, ed., *The Blackwell Companion to the Qur'an* (Oxford, 2006), 362–72.

P. Morewedge, 'A Philosophical Interpretation of Rumi's Mystical Poetry: Light, the Mediator and the Way', in P. J. Chelkowski, ed., *The Scholar and the Saint* (New York, 1975), 187–216.

J. R. Perry, '*Monty Python* and the *Mathnavi*: The Parrot in Indian, Persian and English Humor', *Iranian Studies*, 36/1 (2003), 63–73.

J. Renard, *All the King's Falcons: Rumi on Prophets and Revelation* (Albany, NY, 1994).

S. Safavi and S. Weightman, *Rumi's Mystical Design: Reading the Mathnawi, Book One* (Albany, NY, forthcoming).

O. Safi, 'Did the Two Oceans Meet? Historical Connections and Disconnections between Ibn 'Arabi and Rumi', *Journal of Muhyiddin Ibn 'Arabi Society*, 26 (1999), 55–88.

E. Turkmen, *The Essence of the Masnevi* (Konya, 1992).

Further Reading in Oxford World's Classics

The Arabian Nights' Entertainments, ed. Robert Mack.

The Koran, translated and edited by Arthur J. Arberry.

The Masnavi: Book One, translated and edited by Jawid Mojaddedi.

The Qur'an, translated and edited by M. A. S. Abdel Haleem.

A CHRONOLOGY OF RUMI

1207	Rumi is born in Balkh, north-eastern Persia
c.1216	Rumi's family emigrate from Persia
1219	Alaoddin Kay Qobad ascends Seljuk throne in Anatolia
1220	Death of Faridoddin ʿAttar
1221	The Mongol army conquers Balkh
c.1222	Rumi's family settle temporarily in Karaman, Anatolia
1224	Rumi marries Gowhar Khatun
1226	Birth of Soltan Valad
c.1229	Rumi's family relocate to Konya
1231	Death of Baha Valad
1232	Borhanoddin Termezi arrives in Konya
c.1233	Rumi begins his studies in Syria
1235	Death of Ebn al-Farez in Egypt
1237	Rumi returns to Konya as leader of Baha Valad's school
	Ghiyasoddin Kay Khosrow II ascends Seljuk throne in Anatolia
1240	Death of Ebn ʿArabi in Damascus
1243	The Mongols extend their empire to Anatolia
1244	Rumi meets Shams-e Tabriz in Konya for the first time
1246	Shams leaves Konya
1247	Shams returns to Konya
c.1247–8	Shams disappears
	Salahoddin the Goldsmith begins tenure as Rumi's deputy
1258	Death of Salahoddin
	Hosamoddin Chalabi begins tenure as Rumi's deputy
	The Mongols conquer Baghdad, the Abbasid capital
1260	The Mongols are defeated in Syria by the Mamluks
c.1262	*The Masnavi* is started
c.1264	*The Masnavi* is resumed after a pause on account of the death of Hosamoddin's wife
1273	(17 December) Death of Rumi in Konya

THE MASNAVI

BOOK TWO

Prose Introduction

Here is the reason for the postponement of this second volume: if all divine wisdom should be made known to the slave at once, the benefits in it would leave him unable to act, and the infinite wisdom of God would obliterate his comprehension. He would not be able to cope.

This is why God makes a little of that infinite wisdom into a toggle which can be put into his nostrils, to lead him like a camel towards the necessary action. If He were not to inform him of those benefits, he would not move at all, because knowledge of the gain to be made is what motivates human beings, who say, 'For the sake of this I will do what is right.' If He should pour infinite wisdom down on him, the slave would be unable to move, just as a camel will not walk unless a toggle is put into its nose of an appropriate size—if the toggle is too big it will just slump down: 'There is nothing, the storehouse of which is not with Us. And We only send it down in a fixed measure.'* Without water, clay cannot be made into a brick, nor can it become a brick if the water is excessive. 'He has raised the sky and He has set up the scales.'* He gives everything in the right proportion, not without measurement and calculation, apart from to those people who have been transformed from their physical forms, becoming the ones referred to when He says, 'He provides without calculation for whomsoever He chooses.'* Whoever hasn't tasted will not yet be aware.

Someone asked, 'What is a lover?' I answered, 'You will know when you become like us.' True love cannot be measured, which is why it is said to be an attribute of God in reality, and applicable to the slave only metaphorically. 'He loves them'—this is the totality; 'and they love Him'*—do 'they' exist though in reality?

Exordium

We have delayed a while this *Masnavi*—
   For blood to change to milk time's necessary:
Until the baby's born your blood won't turn
   To milk that's sweet, so listen well and learn!

The reins were pulled back by Hosamoddin
    At heaven's summit in the deep unseen;
When he went on his spiritual ascension*
    Buds wouldn't bloom without his spring's attention,
Then, from the ocean when he came to shore,   5
    The *Masnavi*'s harp-strings were tuned once more.
The *Masnavi* has burnished every heart—
    Blessed the day we opted to restart!*
The date of its resumption I'll tell you:
    It was within the year six sixty-two.*
The nightingale which left has now returned
    To hunt those mystic truths for which it yearned—
May the king's arm remain the falcon's station,
    And may His gates stay open to creation!

The bane of this world is desire, my friends—   10
    Renounce it and drink wine that never ends!*
Close tightly your mouth, and you'll clearly find
    To that world open gullets make men blind.
You vile mouth, you are nothing but hell's gate!
    This world's an intermediary state,
But next to it there is eternal light,
    As pure milk flows near blood all day and night—
Don't heedlessly step in this blood, beware!
    Your milk will turn to blood once mixed in there!
Adam took one step for enjoyment's sake   15
    And lost his seat above for that mistake;
As if he were a demon, angels fled—
    How much he wept for just a piece of bread.*
Although it was as trivial and as thin,
    His eyes were blinded by that hair of sin;
Adam saw by eternal light, but still
    Hair in his eye seemed like a massive hill.
If he had sought advice, it would have meant
    He'd not have had to beg and to repent:
When prudent intellects unite, they see   20
    How to prevent bad actions easily,

Though when the carnal soul joins intellect,
   It makes it useless due to its effect.
When due to loneliness you feel undone,
   Go to the friend's shade—you'll become a sun!
Go, seek God's friend as quickly as you can;
   Find him, then God will be your friend, good man.
The one who turned to Him while in seclusion
   Learned from His Lord that all else is illusion—
Don't turn away from friends, but from your foes;   25
   Don't wear coats when it's hot, but when it snows!
If intellects join forces that is best—
   More light shines and the path's made manifest,
While carnal souls when paired, just like the night
   Cause darkness to obscure the path from sight.
Hunter, the friend is like your eye—take care;
   Do not let straw or splinters blow in there.
Don't bring more dust with your tongue's broom, but try
   To not let any dust fall in your eye.
'Believers are like mirrors',* so his face   30
   Of such pollution doesn't have a trace;
The friend's a mirror for the suffering soul—
   Don't breathe on it, but practise self-control.
You must control your breath continually,
   So it won't cloud its face immediately.
Soil greets friends, raising flowers by the score;
   Mere soil does this—are you not worth much more?
On being joined with their friends, even trees
   Blossom all over due to their sweet breeze;
In autumn, when these trees face foes instead,   35
   Under a blanket each one hides its head,
Saying, 'A foe brings strife now, so I'll sleep—
   This is my sole recourse or else I'd weep.
I'll sleep just like the Sleepers in the Cave
   Rather than be cruel Decius's slave;*
Since Decius would waste their waking hours,
   Sleep was their source of honour and great powers.'
When filled with knowledge, sleep is wakefulness,
   While staying up with fools will cause distress.

In winter crows arrive, and from that day   40
   The nightingales stay mute and fly away;
Without the rose, the nightingales fall silent,
   As daytime ends the hour the sun is absent.
O sun, you leave our garden far from sight
   To fill *the other side of earth* with light!
The sun of gnosis has no motion, though;
   It rises in the souls of those who know,
The heaven's perfect sun especially—
   By day and night it shines, perpetually.
With Alexander, find *its rising place,**   45
   To be forever filled with royal grace;
Its rising-place will always stay with you—
   The East, in love, will seek your sunsets too!
Towards the sunset bat-like senses fly,
   Higher ones to its rising in the sky.
Rider, the sensual path is for the ass—
   Shamefully why compete with it for grass?
Besides these senses are some that are proper
   Which are real gold, while these ones are like copper.
At Judgment Day's bazaar, in place of gold   50
   Do you think that your copper will get sold?
Off darkness bodily senses have to feed,
   While sunshine's what your higher senses need.
You've brought your senses to the unseen light;
   Like Moses's, your hand now shines so bright!*
Your attributes are gnosis's bright sun,
   Which holds the heavens all in place as one.
You look now like the sun and then the sea,
   Mount Qaf,* and then the phoenix magically,
But in your essence you're none of those things—   55
   You are much more, beyond imaginings.
The spirit's linked to wisdom in some way,
   Not Arabic or Turkish—what are they!
You who appear in many forms have none;
   Anthropomorphists, monists too, You stun:
Anthropomorphism He wipes away,
   But then His forms lead monists far astray!

When drunk, Abo'l-Hasan* won't use God's name,
   But calls: '*You with small teeth and slender frame!*'
Sometimes he wrecks his own manifestation   60
   To emphasize God's All-transcendent station.
The sensual eye leads the Mu'tazilite,*
   While Sunnites* follow union's inner sight;
Mu'tazilites are slaves of outward sense;
   They act like Sunnites but it's mere pretence:
If you submit to sensual dominance,
   Your claim 'We're Sunnites' is through ignorance.
The senses proper Sunnites leave to die;
   They're led to God through wisdom's inner eye.
If bestial senses could see God, a herd   65
   Of cows and asses would see—how absurd!
If you don't know of other senses, son,
   Apart from lust, which is the bestial one,
Explain why Man was honoured specially
   And singled out to gain proximity?
Saying, 'He's formless', or 'in forms' instead,
   Is futile, if from form you haven't fled.
'In forms' or 'formless', this much I can tell:
   He's with the kernel which has left its shell.
*There's no blame on the blind,** but, if you see,   70
   You must endure, for *patience is the key*:
The medicine of patience sets aflame
   Your eyes' veils, opens up your breast the same;
And when the mirror of your heart is clear
   You'll see forms from beyond the world down here—
You'll see pure forms, and their Creator too,
   Good fortune's rug and Who spread it for you.

My idol's form's like Abraham to me:
   An idol-smasher in reality.*
Praise God that when He first chose to appear   75
   My soul saw its own image there so clear!
His threshold's dust seduced my faithful heart—
   Shame on those who still choose to stay apart!

I thought, 'If I am good, I'll earn His grace;
    But if I'm ugly, He'll laugh in my face!'
The answer's to inspect oneself before
    He laughs, 'How can I buy this from the store!'
'He's beautiful and *He loves beauty*'*—can
    An old hag be the choice of a young man?
Beauty attracts the beautiful—recite: 80
    '*Good women for good men*'* as proof I'm right!
Attraction is possessed by all things here:
    Warmth draws warm things, the cold pulls cold things near;
Eternal ones attract each other, while
    The worthless just attract the vain and vile;
Those made of fire attract just the same kind;
    Those filled with light draw their own sort, you'll find.
You shut your eyes and feel discomfort start—
    From daylight they can't bear to be apart;
While eyes are shut the pain will not subside—   85
    They yearn to join with light that is outside;
It's due to your eyes' light's attracting pull,
    Which seeks light rays as soon as possible.
If your eyes feel some pain while open, then
    Your heart's eye's shut—so open that again!
Recognize your heart's eye's appeal tonight—
    It seeks God's incomparable, pure light!
When blocked of transient light, pain fills your eyes,
    So you should open them, if you are wise;
But blocking out the everlasting light   90
    Will cause pain too—avoid this wretched plight!

When He calls me I start a self-inspection:
    'Am I fair or will my looks earn rejection?
If a fine beauty leads a beast along,
    She's only mocking what does not belong!
To see my own face can there be a way?
    Is my complexion now like night or day?'
I searched for my soul's form in everyone,
    But it did not reflect in anyone.

I moaned, 'What else are mirrors meant for then 95
    But so each knows himself from other men!'
Your mirrors show the husk and not the kernel;
    The soul-revealing mirror is eternal:
This mirror for the soul is the saint's face,
    The one who is beyond all time and space—
'Heart, seek a mirror of this type!' I'd scream,
    'Reach for the ocean, and not a mere stream!'
In this way, slaves reach God eventually:
    Pain led pure Mary to the date-palm tree.*
Your eye became my heart's eye, then I found 100
    My old heart vanished, for in you I'd drowned.
O universal mirror, I now see
    My image in your eyes so vividly!
I said, 'I've found myself at last today;
    I see in his eyes the enlightened way.'
'You're just imagining it!' my mind's doubts said,
    'Discern what's real from what's just in your head!'
My image spoke then from within your eye:
    'In union I am you and you are I.'
This eye which witnesses Truth constantly 105
    How can mere fancies enter? Answer me!
If you should see your form in others' eyes,
    Consider that as false—don't fantasize!
The kohl of false existence they've applied
    While drinking Satan's wine—they've clearly lied!
Their eyes see emptiness and mere illusion,
    Mistaking non-existents in confusion;
Since my eye's kohl is from God, I can see
    The real existents, not just fantasy.
If there's the hair of self before your eye, 110
    You'll think mere stones are pearls that men would buy;
A jasper from a pearl you can distinguish
    The day belief in your self you relinquish,
So listen to this tale, pearl-connoisseur,
    To tell what's certain from what men infer!

In the time of Omar someone imagined that
*he had seen the new moon**

The month of Ramadan, in Omar's reign,
    People ran to a hill above the plain
To greet the new moon as a hopeful sign—
    One called, 'Omar, come watch the new moon shine!'
But Omar saw no moon above, and said: 115
    'That moon's an image dreamt up in your head!
If not, explain how, with my better sight,
    I can't see any moon at all tonight.
First rub your eyebrows with a wet hand, then
    Attempt to look at the new moon again.'
The man did this, then couldn't see it there;
    He said, 'It's disappeared into thin air!'
Omar explained, 'Your eyebrow was a bow
    That shot false views at you just like a foe!'
A hair had veiled him—now he felt ashamed   120
    That vision of the new moon he had claimed:
A single stray hair veiled the sky behind—
    When your whole frame is bent, you're almost blind!
Straighten your frame through those with perfect ways—
    Seeker of straightness, don't avert your gaze.
Good weighing-scales correct the others, while
    Unbalanced ones make others mean and vile;
Whoever balances with the perverse
    Will lose his brain, bedazzled by their curse.
'*Be hard on infidels!*' the Prophet said: 125
    Renounce all things but God, as though they're dead.
Chop off the heads of others with your blade!
    Be lion-like—don't flatter them, afraid!
Don't disappoint God's faithful friends. Each knows
    That thorns are enemies of that fine rose.
Set fire to wolves like incense, don't appease.
    The wolves are Prophet Joseph's enemies.*
Beware when Satan calls you 'darling child'—
    He hopes that in this way you'll be beguiled;

He offered Prophet Adam the same bait,   130
   And thus that black rook trapped him in check-mate.
That rook moves fast—don't get caught by surprise!
   Don't watch this game of chess with drowsy eyes.
He can entrap your queen with many tricks,
   Just like the food which in your gullet sticks;
His morsel stays blocked there until you're old—
   What is this morsel? Love of rank and gold.
You fickle fool, wealth is what blocks throats up,
   So you can't down the Water of Life's cup.*
And if your wealth's been stolen by a foe,   135
   A thief has robbed a thief—you ought to know!

A snake-catcher steals a snake from another snake-catcher

From a snake-catcher someone stole a snake;
   The fool saw as success this huge mistake.
From that snake's bite its owner thus was spared—
   It killed the thief who'd now become ensnared.
The owner saw the thief as he lay dead:
   'It was my snake that took his life,' he said,
'I'd prayed to find this wretch eventually,
   To claim my snake, then take it home with me—
Thank heavens, God chose not to answer it: 140
   What I thought loss was to my benefit!'
So many prayers request catastrophe,
   But God opts not to listen mercifully.

A companion of Jesus begs him to give life to some bones

Jesus was followed by a stupid twit
   Who came across some bones in a deep pit:

'Teach me God's Greatest Name,* my friend,' he said,
   'With which you're able to revive the dead,
So I can do some good to these poor bones
   And grant them life though now they're like mere stones.'
Jesus said, 'Shut your mouth! That's out of reach: 145
   It's not designed for your lips or your speech.
It needs breath purer than the rain and light,
   And action finer than an angel's flight—
It may take longer than a century
   To make you fit for heaven's treasury.
If you should grasp this rod now, understand
   Your hand is not like Moses's pure hand.'*
He said, 'If I'm not fit for secrets now,
   You should chant over these bones anyhow!'
Jesus asked, 'What's the meaning of this, God?   150
   What is the point of a request so odd?
Despite his sickness, this fool feels no strife:
   This corpse is not concerned for his own life.
His own corpse this man chooses to neglect,
   So that a stranger he might resurrect!'
God said, 'Such fools are bad luck; all that grows
   Are thorns from what the ignorant man sows.
Those who in this world sow seeds of this kind
   Inside the rose-garden you'll never find.
A rose in their hands turns into a thorn,   155
   And as vile snakes such men are soon reborn;
Poison and snakes they make with alchemy—
   As different from the pure souls as can be.'

*A Sufi asks a servant to look after his ass and
the servant says, 'There is no strength or power
except through God'*

A wandering Sufi on his latest quest
   Stayed at a Sufi lodge once as a guest.
At the small stable he kept his ass tied,
   So he could then relax with friends inside.

With them, in meditation he partook—
    Such company can teach more than a book;
The Sufi's book's not marked with words men write,   160
    For it's a heart like snow, one pure and bright;
The scholar's work through words he writes is known;
    By footprints is the Sufi's method shown—
Like hunters he has hunted game instead:
    He saw deer tracks and followed where they led.
For several steps, on tracks he has relied,
    But now the scent of musk serves as his guide.
When he gives thanks for this source of attraction,
    Of course he will attain full satisfaction—
One stage by scent alone if you ascend,   165
    That's more than crossing scores by tracks, my friend!
For mystics, hearts where such pure moonbeams shine
    Have opened up the gates * to the Divine.
To them it is a door, to you a wall,
    To them a gem, to you a stone—that's all.
The Sufi sage much more in bricks can view
    Than you see in a mirror facing you.
The masters' souls were part of God's abundance
    Before this world was formed—this isn't nonsense!
They lived before their bodies, long ago;   170
    They gathered fruit before men learned to sow;
They could boast souls before all form and motion,
    And they bored pearls before there was an ocean;
While making Man was being still debated,
    Deep in His power's sea they celebrated;
When angels tried to stop God, disappointed,
    Such men already knew they'd been appointed.*
Man was told of the forms of every kind
    Before the spirit in form was confined;
Before the heavens, Saturn they could view;   175
    Before grains they saw bread and ate it too;
Before they had a brain they had a thought;
    Without an army wars they bravely fought.
Certainty comes to them in just one instant—
    Direct sight still unknown to those who're distant.

(You think about the future and the past—
    Escape them both and you'll be cured at last.)
Beyond all space, they still see every place;
    Before all mines they knew gold coins from base,
And prior to creation of the vine   180
    They got so drunk by drinking lots of wine.
In hot July they can see wintry days,
    And they see shadows in the sun's bright rays;
Wine in the grape's heart these men can perceive,
    And matter even when this realm they leave.
The sky drinks freely from their circle's cup;
    With gold their kindness dresses the sun up.
And if you ever come across a pair
    Of them, you'll think there's one then thousands there,
For their plurality's like waves in seas: 185
    They seem like separate forms if there's a breeze.
Like light in different windows, each man's soul
    Just seems discrete and not part of one whole;
When you look at the sun, you see one sphere,
    But those still veiled by forms claim that's not clear.
Animal spirits have divisions, friend,
    The human's though is one and has no end,
Because *God's light was sprayed on them,** and you
    Can never separate that light in two.
Companion, put your weariness aside.   190
    About His beauty mark I'll then confide.*
None can describe such beauty that we mention—
    What are the worlds? His beauty mark's reflection!
If I should breathe one word concerning it,
    My speech would cause my body then to split!
Just like an ant inside a granary,
    With joy I carry loads too great for me!

*Relating the meaning of the tale was halted because of the
inclination of the audience to listen to its outward form*

When will the one so envied by the light
    Let me choose vital teachings to recite!

Sea waves cast foam, which forms a barrier, then   195
    They draw back just to stretch ahead again.
Listen now, what precisely blocks the way?
    Perhaps it is your heart that's gone astray?
The listener's thinking of that Sufi guest;
    Absorbed with him, he wants to hear the rest,
So it is necessary to return
    To end that tale, and of his fate to learn.
That Sufi is much more than he appears;
    Walnuts have pleased you for too many years.
Our bodies are like walnuts, my dear friend—   200
    Real men beyond their bodies will ascend.
And even if you don't, God's generous grace
    Will lift you up beyond this wretched place.
Listen now to the tale, as I narrate;
    Make sure the grain from chaff to separate.

The servant agrees to look after the ass and stays behind

The session of the dervishes held there
    Soon ended and excitement filled the air.
Before their guest they then laid out a feast,
    While now his thoughts returned to his poor beast:
He told the servant, 'Go now and prepare   205
    The straw and barley for my steed with care.'
'*God give me strength!** Why tell me what I know?
    That's been my work since many years ago.'
'Moisten its barley, for it has lived long
    And its remaining teeth are not that strong.'
'*God give me strength!* Why carry on this way?
    Others are taught this task by me each day.'
'Take off its saddle first,' the Sufi said,
    'And rub some oil on both its back and head.'
'*God give me strength!* You know-all! What a bore!   210
    Thousands of guests like you I've served before,
And all of them were satisfied with me:
    "Guests are as precious as our souls"—you'll see!'

'Give it some lukewarm water—cold won't do!'
  '*God give me strength!* I feel ashamed for you.'
'Don't mix too much straw with its barley, friend.'
  '*God give me strength!* When will these orders end?'
'Sweep its space clear of stones and any shit,
  And, if the floor's wet, throw some sand on it!'
'*God give me strength!* Trust God, don't live with stress!   215
  Be like the Prophet—talk a little less.'
'Curry with a good comb the donkey's back!'
  '*God give me strength!* Shame is the thing you lack.'
The servant said this and rose to his feet:
  'I'm off to fetch some barley and some wheat.'
In truth, he left all thought of work behind;
  He'd given to the guest false peace of mind.
He joined up with some friends, and ridiculed
  The orders of the Sufi he had fooled.

After so many days of travelling   220
  The Sufi slept and dreamt the following:
His donkey with a huge wolf twice its size
  Biting off chunks of flesh from its small thighs!
'*God give me strength!*' he said, 'Am I delirious?
  Where is that servant who had seemed so serious?'
He dreamt next that his donkey walked and fell,
  First in a ditch and then deep down a well;
He dreamt all kinds of terrible affairs,
  Fetched the Qur'an and read aloud some prayers.*
He said, 'My friends have gone—what can I do?   225
  They've shut all of the doors behind them too.'
Then he thought, 'This is truly curious—
  Didn't that servant share some food with us?
I treated him with love and courtesy
  So why should he now show such enmity?
There has to be a cause for nastiness;
  Our common bond should nurture faithfulness.
But generous Adam treated Satan well,
  And yet that devil sought to give him hell;

Why then does every snake and scorpion   230
   Desire to harm men, as if just for fun?
Wolves kill—for this they are notorious;
   It's clear such creatures are too envious.
Is it not wrong to think ill of another?
   Why should I be suspicious of my brother?
But prudence means preparing for the worst—
   If you don't, then you'll soon be harmed and cursed.'
He grew distressed about his donkey's state—
   May suffering like this be our worst foes' fate!
That donkey lay in dirt, its bridle torn;   235
   All it could do was lie down there and mourn;
Exhausted by the journey, left unfed,
   The donkey lay there looking almost dead.
All night the donkey brayed as if in prayer:
   'I gave up barley! God, this isn't fair!
Have mercy shaikhs!' it spoke thus inwardly,
   'Such a vile wretch has devastated me!'
The torture that this donkey underwent
   Was like what land-birds feel when floods are sent.
It rolled from side to side throughout the night,   240
   Because of hunger and its awful plight,
Then in the morning that vile servant came
   And changed the bridle to avoid all blame,
Then like a donkey-seller struck a blow,
   Treating the donkey like a dog for show.
The donkey jumped because of the sharp sting,
   But couldn't tell men what was happening.

Members of the caravan perceive that the Sufi's donkey is sick

Each time the Sufi mounted his poor ass
   Its legs collapsed as if mere blades of grass,
And each time it was lifted up again   245
   It looked afflicted still to all the men.
One tried to twist and pull its ears with force,
   The next looked in its mouth to find the source,

One looked for stones trapped in its hooves instead,
    Another sought what made its eyes turn red.
They said, 'Shaikh, what on earth has now gone wrong—
    Did you not say: "Thank God, my donkey's strong!"?'
'The victim of "*God give me strength!*",' he said
    'Will not know how to walk, though it be led.
"*God give me strength*" was all it ate in there;   250
    It lies prostrate—last night it spent in prayer.'
Most people are like cannibals today!
    Don't trust the friendly greetings that they say.
Men's hearts are homes for demons; listen less
    To chatter from those filled with wickedness.
From them if you taste '*Give me strength!*' one night,
    Just like this donkey you'll fall in the fight.
Those tracked by a vile demon while down here,
    And by the praise of foes who aren't sincere,
Will fall head first just like a giddy ass—   255
    Islam's path and *Serat's* bridge* they can't pass.
Don't fall for flattery, but see the snare.
    Don't stroll around, as if without a care.
'*God give me strength!*' a thousand devils say—
    Adam, see Satan in the snake, and pray!
'My soul and lover!' it calls out to you,
    To butcher you and flay your skin off too.
With hot air it desires your blood; God knows
    You'll pay if you take opium from your foes.
Now at your feet it lays its head, to spill   260
    Your blood just like a butcher—it can kill.
Like lions, turn your hunters to your prey.
    From friends and strangers' praises turn away.
Base men are like this servant tragically—
    Better to have none than their flattery!
Don't settle here in their realm where there's danger.
    Do your own work and not that of a stranger.
Your body is the stranger; it is plain
    From this stems all your misery and pain—
Don't feed it sweets and greasy food, for both   265
    Will stop you seeing any inner growth.

Even if placed in musk, the body still
   Will stink the day it dies and make men ill.
Don't rub musk on your body but your heart:
   Musk is God's name—from Him don't stay apart!
The hypocrite smears musk on just for show;
   His spirit in a rubbish bin he'll throw.
God's name he chants, but all he has within
   Is the foul stench of thoughts embroiled in sin.
His chants are vain, like grass on an ash mound,   270
   A rose which on a dunghill's slope is found—
Such flowers won't stay there for very long;
   A joyful circle is where they belong.
'*Good women come to good men,*' God told you,
   '*To wicked men come wicked women*'* too.
Don't bear spite, for those whom spite leads astray
   Are buried with each other and will pay;
Spite stems from hell, including spite you show;
   It's part of hell and your religion's foe.
If you're a part of hell, take special care;   275
   Parts gravitate towards the whole—beware!
The bitter join the bitter certainly,
   But how can vain breath join the truth? Tell me!
If you're a part of heaven, though, good friend,
   You will feel pleasure that will never end.
Brother, your worth is in your thoughts alone;
   Apart from that you're only flesh and bone:
You are a rose, if all your thoughts are selfless;
   If bitter, you're a thorn that is judged worthless.
Rose water people sprinkle on their face,   280
   While urine's poured away in some foul place.
Look at the trays of the apothecary—
   Each good and bad thing placed accordingly:
Each item is displayed with its own kind,
   Such order pleases both the eye and mind.
Sugar and incense, should they mix together,
   He'll separate completely from each other.
When souls are spilled the way such trays are smashed,
   Good and bad mix like water that has splashed.

God sent the prophets with their books to earth,   285
   So He could pick the grains that have true worth;
We were all as one whole before they came;
   No one knew good from bad—we were the same,
Counterfeit mixed with genuine; our sight
   Could not discern since it was always night
Until God made the prophets' sun appear,
   And said, 'Be off, fraud! Pure one, now come near!'
Eyes now can see the colours that are shown,
   Distinguishing a ruby from a stone;
A jewel from a splinter they can tell,   290
   Since splinters make one's eyes turn red and swell.
The counterfeiters only like the night,
   While gold inside the mine longs for some light,
For daylight is a mirror which displays
   What something's worth and if it merits praise.
God said the Resurrection* is a 'day':
   Colours, like gold and red, light must display.
In fact, the hearts of saints outshine bright days—
   Daylight seems dim next to one of their rays.
The day is when the saint's soul is revealed,   295
   Eye-sealing night is when it is concealed.
This is why God swore, '*By the break of day*'*—
   The Prophet's light is what these words convey;
That God just meant the usual dawn, some claim,
   But that is His reflection all the same;
Swearing on something transient would be wrong—
   In God's speech temporal things do not belong!
Abraham '*didn't love what sets*'; tell me
   How then could God swear on what's transitory?
He said, '*I don't love those that set*'*; his Lord   300
   Could not have sworn on what he'd deemed a fraud!
And '*By the night*' means God hides from men's eyes
   The Prophet—human form was his disguise;
From yonder sky when His sun came in sight,
   '*He hasn't left you,*' it told body's night;
Through suffering, His union one can earn:
   '*He has not hated you*'* to sweets will turn.

*

Every expression of a state has told—
　　States are like hands, expressions tools they hold.
A goldsmith's tool when in some cobbler's hand　　　　305
　　Is like a seed which has been sown in sand;
The cobbler's tool for ploughmen is this way,
　　Like feeding donkeys bones and puppies hay.
Mansur's 'I am the Truth!' was purest light,
　　But Pharaoh's 'I am God!' claimed his own might;*
The rod in Moses's hand was a witness,
　　In the magicians' hands, though, it proved worthless.*
Jesus refused to teach God's greatest name*
　　To that companion, which was just the same:
He would have blamed his tools, stayed in the dark,　　　310
　　Like striking stone on clay to make a spark.
The stone is paired with iron, its true mate—
　　A true mate is required to procreate.
The one who has no mate or tools is He
　　Who is beyond doubt and plurality.

Those who use many Gods as polytheists
　　Agree there's just one God with monotheists—
Don't squint and they'll appear the same to you;
　　The polytheists assert God's Oneness too.
If you assert His Oneness, you'll spin round,　　　　315
　　Struck by His polo-stick across the ground;
Each time the king should strike them heavily
　　Such balls become more true and blemish-free.
My cross-eyed friend, heed well what you will hear,
　　Rub salve too on your weak eye through your ear!
Pure words won't enter hearts that are still blind;
　　They seek light's source and leave the blind behind.
Perverse hearts hear the devil's vile deceit,
　　Since crooked shoes are made for odd-shaped feet.
Though you respect such wisdom, you're unfit;　　　　320
　　It will evade you—you're not meant for it.
And though you write it down and count your gain,
　　Then boast that all of it you can explain,

It turns away from your vain sophistry,
 And breaks apart all chains, then starts to flee.
If one can't read, but has a heart aflame,
 Knowledge will be one's trained bird all the same;
It won't abide with any idiot,
 As peacocks won't stay in a peasant's hut.

How a king found his falcon in the home of a decrepit old woman

Unfaithful is the bird which flees its king   325
 For some old crone who sifts flour, murmuring.
While for her children she was cooking soup,
 An old crone saw a noble falcon swoop.
She clipped the falcon's wings and tied each claw,
 Then cut its talons and fed it some straw.
She said, 'Unworthy men neglected you:
 Your wings have grown too long, your talons too;
You've fallen ill through undeserving hands—
 Mother will nurse you now; she understands.'
Ignorant people's love is like this, friends: 330
 Their crooked path has many twists and bends.

The king then traced the route his bird had flown
 And saw the tent belonging to that crone;
He found the falcon in an awful way,
 Then wept and mourned that he had seen this day.
He said, 'This is for what you did to me,
 For showing me a lack of loyalty:
You fled from heaven and to hell you came—
 The people of the fire are not the same.'*
Those who flee stubbornly find this reward: 335
 To an old crone from the All-Knowing Lord!
The falcon rubbed its wings on the king's hand,
 Then said, 'I've sinned, but now I understand.
Where should the wicked creatures weep and moan,
 If, noble king, you hear the good alone?'

*

Our souls seek sin due to His liberal grace,
  For he makes beautiful each ugly face.
Do not act badly; even good you do
  Seems foul in the Most Beautiful Lord's view.
You thought your service meritorious,   340
  And so indulged in shameful sinfulness:
Prayer and remembering Him were specified,
  In doing this, though, you were spoilt by pride;
Alongside God you claimed a voice as well—
  Such unbelief made many fall to hell.
Although the king sits on the ground with you,
  Know who you are, and sit as slaves should do.

The falcon said, 'King, with deep shame I burn,
  And now repent—to true faith I return.
If someone you've made drunk walks crookedly   345
  Due to this state, hear his apology.
Although I've lost my talons, if you care,
  I will pull out for you the sun's last hair.
And though I've lost my wings, through your caress,
  The sky will make my flight so effortless.
Grant me a girdle—mountains I'll pull out;
  I'll snap the army's flag, and start a rout!
In size and strength I'm greater than a gnat,
  So Nimrod's realm my wings too can knock flat!*
Though I look weak, I'm like that flock of birds—   350
  My foe's an elephant from the wild herds.
If I drop down a pellet that is small,
  Still its effect is like a cannonball;
Although my stone is like a tiny pea,
  Each foe it hits will be killed instantly.'*
Moses came to the fray armed with a stick,*
  Then saw off well-armed Pharaoh with one flick.
Each single prophet who served God alone
  Stood firm against the whole world on his own:
When Noah asked God for a sword, He made   355
  Each wave in that huge flood sharp as a blade.*

Mohammad, don't fear armies which pass by,
  For you can split the moon up in the sky,*
Then all the stars will see and sing your praise,
  Now that it's not the moon's but your own phase.
It is your era; Moses too would pray
  That he might taste your era's grace one day:
Once he had glimpsed your era's majesty,
  Which witnesses the full theophany,
He begged, 'Lord, what an era of pure grace,   360
  In which there is full vision of Your Face!
Plunge me, Your Moses, deep inside Your sea,
  And then, in Ahmad's time, deliver me!'*
'Moses, I've shown that era now,' God said,
  'And opened up for you a path ahead,
For, though you live now, with him you belong—
  But don't expect your life to last that long!
I'm kind, and show my slaves food far away,
  So they, through longing, learn to weep today.'
A mother rubs her baby's little nose   365
  To wake him, so he feeds from her and grows;
The baby dozed off hungry, unaware,
  Now though he seeks the nipples that she'll bare:
'*I was a hidden treasure of great worth,*
  So I sent guided people down to earth.'*
Each miracle which you may now desire,
  He showed to you in order to inspire:
How many idols did the Prophet break
  His people worshippers of God to make!*
Were it not for his efforts, wouldn't you   370
  Still worship idols like men used to do?
From bowing down to idols you've been freed
  To learn His rightful claim from the true creed.
If you should speak, give thanks for this salvation,
  Gain, from your inner idol, liberation!
From idols now your head has been unchained,
  So free your heart too with the strength you've gained.
You don't give thanks for faith, it's plain to see
  That is because He gave you it for free—

Wealth's value heirs fail to appreciate: 375
  Rostam faced trials, Zal got things on a plate.*
God said, 'My mercy's moved when humans cry—
  The weeper then drinks grace which I supply.
I don't show what I don't want to impart;
  Once someone's hooked I open up his heart.
My mercy's subject to the weeper's cries—
  When he weeps, waves from mercy's seas then rise.'

Shaikh Ahmad-e Khazruya* buys sweets for his creditors through divine inspiration

There was a shaikh in debt continually,
  Because he was so fond of chivalry:
Huge loans from wealthy people he agreed   380
  And spent them on the poor and those in need.
He built a Sufi lodge with money lent—
  His life and wealth in God's way thus he spent.
God paid his debts for him across the land,
  As He made flour for Abraham from sand.*
'In each bazaar,' the Prophet used to say,
  'There are two angels who together pray:
"God give big-spenders back some extra cash,
  But make the misers' money turn to ash!"'
This fits best one who spends with his own life   385
  And gives his throat to the Creator's knife:
Like Ishmael he surrenders his neck, but
  The knife no longer has the power to cut.*
Since martyrs live on, joyful, free, and well,*
  Don't look just at their corpses, infidel!
God has bestowed eternal life, one free
  From any struggle, pain, and misery.

The debtor shaikh for years lived in this way:
  A go-between, he'd take then give away.
He sowed such good seeds till the day he died,   390
  That he might die a saint who's glorified.

When the shaikh's life approached his final breath,
   In his own being he sensed signs of death;
His creditors sat round him on that day,
   While, like a candle, he would melt away.
They all became so bitter sitting there,
   Counting the cost and feeling deep despair.
'Look at these evil-thinking men!' he said,
   'Can they not be paid back by God instead?'
They heard a boy shout 'Halva, here!' outside,   395
   To raise its price he'd praise his stock with pride.
The shaikh then told his servant: 'Go and buy
   The halva from the boy who just passed by—
My creditors can eat it joyfully,
   And, free from bitterness, then look at me.'
Immediately the servant went outside
   To buy the halva as he'd specified.
He asked the boy, 'How much does that come to?'
   'Just over half a dinar, friend, for you.'
'Don't overcharge the dervishes!' he said,   400
   'I'll give you half a dinar, boy, instead!'
The boy then placed beside the shaikh his tray—
   The shaikh's mysterious ways I'll now convey:
He signalled to his creditors to eat
   By saying, 'God has blessed this lawful treat!'
Once it was emptied, waiting still in there
   The boy said, 'Give the price agreed as fair!'
The shaikh said, 'I have no more cash to give—
   I'm deep in debt, and don't have long to live!'
The boy then slammed the tray down on the floor,   405
   And started to lament, cry out, and roar;
The boy sobbed loudly over this shaikh's trick:
   'Would that my leg had broken like a stick
Or I had walked towards a pile of trash
   Than near this Sufi thief who has no cash!
Gluttonous Sufis, greedy and spoilt brats,
   You're dogs, but falsely clean yourselves like cats!'
Due to his screaming, which was loud and wild,
   Everyone came and gathered round this child.

He told the shaikh, 'You act so cruelly;   410
   You know full well my boss will punish me!
If I go empty-handed, I'll be killed—
   Will you allow this? Will you feel fulfilled?'
The creditors could not believe their eyes:
   'What is the meaning of these tricks and lies?
You've spent our loans, and soon they'll go with you;
   Now you treat a poor child unjustly too!'
The boy stood weeping till the call to prayer,
   The shaikh just closed his eyes without a care;
Free from all worries, lying in his bed,   415
   He drew a sheet above his moon-like head;
Pleased with his fate and his own death's approach,
   Heedless of people's gossip and reproach.
If God should smile at someone once, he then
   Will not be hurt by bitter looks from men;
He whose eyes God should kiss will truly gain:
   Wrath from fate's wheel will never cause him pain.
The bright moon in the sky when it is dark—
   What does it care about the dogs that bark?
The dog is doing what it's meant to do;   420
   By spreading light around, the moon is too.
Each thing performs its allocated deeds:
   Water's not made impure due to some weeds;
Weeds float up on its surface, but the sea
   Keeps flowing, undisturbed, perpetually.
The Prophet split the moon once late at night,
   While Abu Lahab babbled out of spite;*
When Jesus the Messiah raised the dead,
   The angry Jews tore off their beards in dread.
Can the dog's barking reach the moon above,   425
   Let alone God's most favoured moon of love?
A king drinks wine to music by the stream—
   Why should he hear the frogs when he can dream.

They could have paid that boy quite easily,
   But the shaikh stifled generosity,

So none of those rich men would pay the bill—
    The power of masters can be greater still!
A servant came at the next time to pray,
    From someone generous he'd brought a tray—
A gift from someone rich and godly too,   430
    Who knew what this shaikh now was going through;
Four hundred dinars lay one side of it,
    With half a dinar lying opposite.
The servant stepped up to the shaikh, to say
    His greetings and to hand to him the tray—
When he removed the tray's lid, everyone
    Could see the miracle that had been done;
Soon gasps and sighs were all that men could hear:
    'Our shaikh of shaikhs, what's this you've made appear!
What is the secret? What sheer majesty,   435
    Great lord of lords of every mystery!
Forgive us, for we didn't understand!
    Confused, we uttered words we hadn't planned.
Like blind men we waved sticks, and heedlessly
    Broke all the lamps in our vicinity.
Just like deaf men who haven't heard a word,
    Our reasoned-out responses were absurd;*
We failed to learn from Moses's mistake,
    Shamed for his disbelief in Khezr's sake,*
Though he had such extraordinary vision,   440
    The light of which could penetrate to heaven.
With mouse-like, half-blind eyes, we stupidly
    Denied what your superior eyes could see.'
The shaikh said, 'Your reproach and clamour too
    I now forgive as lawful just for you.
I sought God's help—that was my secret way,
    And, as you saw, He rescued me today.
God had told me, "That dinar which seems small
    Requires still that the boy should scream and bawl—
Until the halva-selling boy should cry   445
    My sea of mercy won't be moved on high."'
The boy stands for your eyes, thus your success
    Depends, my brother, on your own distress—

So if a robe of honour is your aim,
    Weep wildly like a child in desperate shame.

How someone frightened an ascetic, saying:
'Weep less so as not to become blind!'

A friend told an ascetic: 'Weep much less,
    So that your eyes won't feel pain and distress.'
He answered, 'Just two things are possible:
    They'll see His beauty, or not see at all.
If they will see God's Light, why should I care?   450
    With union can these worthless eyes compare?
If they won't see God, damn them! Never mind—
    An eye so miserable is better blind.'
When you have Jesus, eyes have little value;
    Don't go astray—an inner eye he'll give you.
Your spirit's Jesus is within, so pure—
    Seek help from it, then you can feel secure!
But don't compel your Jesus-pure heart to
    Perform the work your body's meant to do,
Like that fool whom we mentioned previously   455
    Regarding Jesus and his purity—
Don't ask your Jesus for a body's health.
    Don't ask your Moses for vile Pharaoh's wealth.
From your heart keep thought of provisions out,
    Stay at the king's court—never be without!
The body is the spirit's tent, its shell,
    Or like an ark for Noah—heed this well.
That they might lose their tents why should Turks fear
    When to the royal court they are so dear?

Conclusion of the story about the coming to life of the bones
through Jesus's prayer

Jesus said God's name over all the bones   460
    Because of that young man's persistent moans;
That immature man thus, by God's decree,
    Saw bones come back to life incredibly,

But then a lion, not a man, appeared,
    And knocked him down—for his own life he feared!
It broke his skull, which fell upon the ground—
    It was an empty shell, no brain was found!
There would have been no harm if he had more
    Than just a body, but there was no core.
Jesus asked, 'Lion, why leave him for dead?'   465
    'Because he bothered you,' the lion said,
'But why not drink his blood once he's been killed?'
    'Because that isn't what the Lord has willed.'
Many like this fierce lion have moved on
    Without consuming what they'd chanced upon:
Hungry but knowing it was not their share,
    They wouldn't eat although the food was there.
You have enabled us to do with ease
    Such fruitless work—deliver us now, please!
We didn't see the hook beneath the bait—   470
    Show us how things are truly, their real state.*
The lion said, 'Messiah, killing then
    Was just a lesson for the sake of men.
If in this world I still had time ahead
    I wouldn't be right now among the dead.'
For one who finds pure water this fate's fit,
    If like a donkey he should dirty it:
Its value if he knew, he'd put his head
    Inside the stream and not his feet instead.
The donkey treats like this God's messengers,   475
    The prophets, leaders, and life-nurturers—
Why won't it die before them with this plea:
    'Revive me now, please, through the order *Be!*'*
Don't wish long life for your dog-soul, the foe
    Of your pure heart* since very long ago!
Shame on the bones which hold the good dogs back
    From spiritual goals they know they lack!
You're not a dog—how come you love bones then?
    Like leeches, why suck up the blood of men?
What kind of eyes are they which have no sight,   480
    Disgraced in tests since they get nothing right?

Opinions sometimes get it wrong, don't they?
  And your opinion's blind to the right way.
You keep on weeping for the others, eye—
  Sit down a while and for your own sake cry!
Clouds' tears make branches green and fresh as dew,
  Through tears the candle burns much brighter too.
Wherever men mourn you should also sit,
  Because to weep and moan you too are fit;
For transient things far off and missed they pine,   485
  Not for eternal rubies in God's mine.

Blind imitation locks your heart up, so
  Dissolve that lock by letting your tears flow.
Mimicry is the bane of all that's good;
  Though it seems like a mountain, it's dead wood.
It is a huge blind man who is unkind—
  Consider him mere flesh, since he is blind!
Though his speech should sound finer than a hair,
  He doesn't understand his own hot air:
He's drunk on his own words, but far apart   490
  Remains the holy wine from his lost heart.
He's like a ditch that water passes through—
  He cannot drink, so it finds those who do:
The flowing water won't remain in it
  Because the ditch does not feel thirst one bit.
Like a renowned reed-player who is vain—
  Rich customers are all he hopes to gain.
In truth, the imitator is the same
  As a hired mourner—they've one selfish aim:
He says heart-wrenching words and seems to mourn,   495
  But where's his burnt heart and clothes that are torn?
Compare the mimic's with the mystic's heart:
  Echoes and David's voice, so far apart;*
The mystic's words stem from his heart which burns,
  That mimic second-hand his discourse learns—
Don't be misled by that man's mournful speech:
  Oxen bear loads, while cart-wheels only screech.

The mimics are rewarded anyway:
    Professional mourners must receive their pay.
Infidels, like believers, shout 'God' too,   500
    But there's a difference between the two:
The beggar cries 'God!' for the sake of bread,
    The holy man so that his soul is fed.
If he knew what this means, the beggar then
    Would never think of 'more' and 'less' again.
In hope of food, he wails 'O God!' all day:
    An ass bears the Qur'an in hope of hay!
Had those words on his lips shone in his heart,
    This would have made his body split apart—
In magic, demons' names can take effect;   505
    God's name why use mere pennies to collect?

How a peasant stroked a lion in the dark, imagining it was an ox

A peasant tied his ox up one dark night;
    A lion came and ate it with one bite!
He came to see his ox, but had to look
    In every corner and each tiny nook,
And thus he felt the lion's legs and back,
    Its side and rear, but it did not attack.
The lion thought, 'If it was now more bright,
    His heart would melt, his stomach turn in fright.
For this he's stroking me courageously: 510
    He thinks that I'm his ox, since he can't see.'
God tells us, 'Blind, misled fools, have some shame!
    Did Sinai not fall crashing at My name?*
For *to the mountain if We'd sent the Book*
    *It would have trembled, split, and made all look!**
If Mount Ohod* had heard of me, its heart
    Would then have filled with blood and split apart.'
Your parents warned you of this, but instead
    You disregarded everything they said.

If you could learn it for yourself, His grace   515
    Would make you a pure voice beyond all space.
This tale is a deterrent just for you;
    It brings blind imitation's harm to view:

How the Sufis sold the traveller's ass to pay for their musical ceremony

A Sufi reached a dervish lodge one day,
    Led his ass to its stable on his way,
And fed it straw and water, cleared the floor,
    Unlike that Sufi we described before.
He double-checked his work, then shut the gate—
    What good's precaution in the face of fate?
The dervishes were poor, and '*Poverty*   520
    Can almost seem like infidelity'*—
Don't mock, rich man, because you have no cares,
    The faults of that poor man, the pain he bears!
The dervishes together all agreed
    To sell the ass because of their dire need:
They said, 'A carcass, in necessity,
    Is lawful': sins can have legitimacy.*
They sold his ass, and used some of the gains
    To buy some cakes and candles for their pains.
The dervishes expressed extreme delight: 525
    'With food and music we will dance all night!
No more endurance of the three-day fast,
    Those begging days behind us now at last!
We too are humans with souls, and we're blessed,
    Because tonight we have a special guest!'
They sowed a rotten seed thus in the earth,
    By coveting the things that have no worth.
That traveller, now exhausted by his trip,
    Found a fine welcome and companionship,
For they tried hard to please him, one by one,   530
    Like playing deviously in backgammon.

He tasted kindness and let out this cry:
  'Tonight if I don't party, when will I!'

They ate, then in *sama*ʿ* they started reeling;
  The lodge soon filled with dust up to the ceiling:
The kitchen's dust and smoke, feet like a drum
  Stamping in rapture and delirium;
Now waving arms, now stamping feet—elation
  Led them to sweep the floorboards in prostration.
Sufis will wait long for a few small bites—   535
  That's why they have enormous appetites!
Except the one who by God's light is sated—
  With begging he won't be humiliated;
Among the thousands, men like this are rare;
  The rest live off the grace that they should share.
When the *sama*ʿ had finished finally,
  The minstrel started a new melody;
The chant 'The ass has gone!' once he'd begun,
  He urged the others to join in the fun!
Stamping their feet in rapture till the dawn,   540
  They clapped their hands and screamed, 'The ass has gone!'
That Sufi sang in imitation too:
  'The ass has gone! The ass has gone!'—it's true!
The party ended at the break of day;
  They all said their goodbyes and went away.
The place soon emptied; there remained the guest,
  Clearing the space where he had meant to rest.
He took his baggage out then from the cell
  And looked for others travelling as well.
He then rushed to the stable and there found   545
  His ass was missing, no one was around:
'That servant must be feeding it,' he thought,
  'Perhaps last night it didn't drink a lot.'
The servant came, so he asked, 'Where's it gone?'
  'Who cares!' the servant snapped and sauntered on.
Enraged, he screamed, 'I put it in your care;
  I trusted you, believing you were fair.

I now want back what I left here with you—
　　Return my ass, as you're obliged to do!
Don't make excuses through theosophy—　　550
　　What I put in your care give back to me!
"The things that you acquire," the Prophet said,
　　"Must be returned before you're finally dead."
If you refuse and stubbornly won't budge,
　　You'll have to come with me now to the judge!'
The servant said, 'The dervishes passed through;
　　They mobbed me and I thought I might die too!
Who would leave offal where the wild cats nap,
　　Then look to see if they have left a scrap!
For scores of hungry men a single bite,　　555
　　One thin cat over which ten dogs will fight!'
'That they used force are you now telling me,
　　Because they wanted to cause harm to me?
Why didn't you come looking for me then
　　To tell me that my ass was with those men?
I could have seized my ass back thanks to you,
　　And they might have agreed to pay me too—
When they were here it was still valuable,
　　But now they've scattered, it's impossible!
Whom should I take now to the judge, too late!　　560
　　It's due to you that this has been my fate.
Why then did you not even try to shout:
　　"A wicked crime has just been carried out!"'
He said, 'I came so many times, I swear,
　　To tell you all about this sad affair,
But you were chanting then, "The ass has gone!"
　　With such great zeal, and you went on and on!
I went back, thinking: "He knows what occurred;
　　He's wise and still content though he has heard."'
'They chanted happily,' the guest then said,　　565
　　'The joy of chanting soon filled up my head.
I've been defeated through vile imitation—
　　May it be cursed with a complete damnation!
Especially imitation of vile men—
　　Abraham's wrath curse *those that set* * again!

The ecstasy of that group radiated,
    Then my heart felt it, and it imitated!'
Reflections from God's Friends you need at first
    In His pure ocean's depths to quench your thirst.
The first reflection cast is imitation;   570
    Once it's successive then it's realization.
Until this point don't part from His true friends—
    Don't break the shell until the pearl's growth ends!
Pure eyes, pure ears, and pure minds to acquire,
    Tear up now all the veils of base desire!
Since base desire made this man imitate,
    To his mind no pure light would radiate;
Desire for music, food, and merriment
    From knowledge was his brain's impediment—
If such desire stays on the mirror's face,   575
    Like us, that mirror must be a disgrace:
If weighing-scales for gold should feel some lust,
    How will they give a reading we can trust?
Each prophet told his people what was true:
    'I don't want payment for what I've brought you;
I'm just a guide; God is your purchaser;
    Though I'm His agent, He's your customer.*
What is my wage? Seeing the Lord one day,
    Though Abu Bakr all his wealth might pay—
His forty thousand coins is not for me;   580
    Stones can't match Aden's pearls in quality!'*

Now listen to this tale I'll share with you,
    To learn how lust can block your ears up too.
Desire makes people stammer—if some stays,
    One's heart and eye can't then receive God's rays.
The thought of gold and status harms your eyes
    Like a stray hair; to all men this applies
Except the drunkard filled with God, for he,
    Though offered massive treasures, will stay free:
This world will seem a carcass in the sight   585
    Of those who gain true vision through God's light.

That Sufi was far from true drunkenness,
   For he'd turned blind through greed and lustfulness.
One dazed by greed a hundred tales may hear,
   But not one point will enter his deaf ear!

How the announcers serving the judge spread news around town about a bankrupt

A bankrupt, homeless man in ancient times
   Was kept in gaol for all his petty crimes.
That wastrel ate the other prisoners' food
   And burdened them with his vain attitude—
No one would even dare to start their meal   590
   In case it tempted him to come and steal.
(Those not invited to God's feast on high,
   Though they be kings, gaze with a beggar's eye.)
This demon stamped on generosity,
   He made gaol hell through his dishonesty—
If you should run away to find relief,
   There also you are bound to suffer grief;
Free from wild beasts and traps there is no place,
   No peace but in retreat with God's pure grace.
The prison of this world where you must live   595
   Demands an entry-fee you have to give.
If you hide in a mouse-hole, please beware,
   For someone with cat's claws will scratch you there.
Man can escape through his imagination,
   By contemplating beauty in creation,
But should he focus on the ugly here,
   Like wax inside a fire, he'll disappear.
If you find snakes and scorpions everywhere,
   Don't worry—God will keep you in His care:
The snakes and scorpions will show amity,   600
   For His thought is the greatest alchemy.
Through optimism, patience can taste sweet,
   For then relief and joy is what you'll meet:

By faith, relief is formed inside your brain;
　　Weakness of faith brings deep despair and pain.
Patience acquires from faith a crown of gold—
　　'No patience means no faith,' we have been told:
'God has not granted faith,' the Prophet said,
　　'To him who has no patience in his head.'

That one who looks just like a snake to you   605
　　Is beautiful in someone else's view,
That he's an infidel you may surmise,
　　He's a believer, though, in others' eyes;
Both are observed in him when people look:
　　He's now a fish, and then a baited hook,
He's half-believer and half-infidel,
　　Half-greedy, half-renunciant as well.
'*Some of you are believers*', God told you,
　　And '*Some of you are unbelievers*'* too.
Just like a cow, black on one side, but white   610
　　The other side like the full moon at night—
Whoever sees the black side turns away,
　　Whoever sees the white side runs that way.
Joseph was worthless in his brothers' sight,
　　Though Jacob saw him in a better light;
Through bad thoughts, he seemed ugly in their view—
　　They didn't have the inner vision too:
Outer eyes are the inner eyes' reflection,
　　For outer eyes are under their direction.
You're in the realm of space now, but before   615
　　You were beyond space—open up that door!
In this world of dimensions, you're not free,
　　You're trapped here in check-mate perpetually!

Prisoners complain about the bankrupt to the agent of the judge

To see the judge's agent prisoners came
　　With their complaints, and to assign the blame:

'Our greetings to the great judge! Please relate
  What we endure from this man whom we hate,
Because in gaol he chooses to remain
  And he's a greedy nuisance, proud and vain.
He's there at every meal just like a fly,   620
  Though uninvited, shameless, nose raised high.
A feast for sixty to this pig seems small,
  He claims he's deaf when you say "Stop! That's all!"
Not one bite reaches any other men,
  But even if one finds a scrap, just then
The greedy demon grabs it from your hand,
  And says, "God ordered, '*Eat!*'* Heed his command!"
Please end this famine that we now endure,
  And may the judge live long and be secure!
Either throw out this buffalo who steals   625
  Or start a fund to pay for all his meals!
You are the means for all our happiness—
  We beg you, please relieve us from distress!'

The agent went to see the judge that day
  To share all the complaints he'd heard them say.
The judge then called the bankrupt from his cell
  And questioned his own officers as well.
All of the things they had complained about
  Were proven to the judge beyond a doubt.
'Pack up and leave the gaol!' the judge then said,   630
  'Return now to your own vile home instead!'
'My home's your kindness,' he said, 'Gaol's not hell
  But paradise for this blind infidel;
If you expel me I will die out there
  Of destitution—nobody will care.'
He talked like Satan, who begged, 'God be praised!
  Reprieve me till the day that they're all raised!*
I'm happy in this prison down below,
  Where I can slay the children of my foe:
If someone has faith's nourishment and bread   635
  As his provisions for the path ahead,

I'll seize it with my trickery and guile
   And make him feel regretful all the while;
I'll threaten him with abject poverty,
   Or send those who can flirt seductively.'

The stock of faith's provisions here is small
   And that vile dog is threatening it all—
If you taste faith's gift when you fast and pray,
   This wretched thief will snatch it straight away.
From Satan I beg God to rescue me;   640
   We've suffered from that devil's tyranny!
He enters millions, though he is alone;
   Each one he enters then becomes his clone:
If someone leaves you cold, know he's within—
   The devil's lurking underneath his skin.
When not in forms, he enters thoughts instead,
   So that through fancies into sin you're led—
Now thought of fun, now thought of your professions,
   Now thought of knowledge, now thought of possessions.
To beg '*God give me strength!*' you now must start,   645
   Not merely with your tongue, but in your heart.

The judge said, 'Prove you're penniless to me!'
   'The prisoners can confirm my bankruptcy.'
'What they allege can't be believed as true,
   Because they want now to be rid of you;
They want you banished somewhere far away—
   We can't accept what men like that should say!'
The people at the courthouse swore that he
   Was bankrupt and a vile monstrosity.
All of the men the judge consulted said,   650
   'Sir, wash your hands of this broke rogue instead!'
The judge said, 'Take him round the town—proclaim:
   "This is a bankrupt rogue deserving blame!"
Announce his bankruptcy and start to beat
   The drums to spread the news on every street!

Let no one give him credit at his store,
  Nor lend one penny to him any more;
And then if someone should come to complain,
  I still won't throw him into gaol again!
His bankruptcy is proven now to me—   655
  He owns no cash nor goods, as all can see.'
In this world's gaol we humans have been thrown
  So that our bankruptcy can be made known.
In the Qur'an have you not heard God tell
  That Satan is a bankrupt rogue as well?
That he's a bankrupt liar and a cheat?
  Avoid his company or taste defeat!
If you should turn to him in your distress,
  How will he help you when he's penniless?

They grabbed the camel that a poor Kurd used   660
  While selling firewood, but this man refused;
For hours, complaining, this poor Kurd then cried,
  To bribe the officers he also tried,
But still they seized the camel from this Kurd
  That afternoon, as though they hadn't heard.
On the poor camel sat the bankrupt man,
  Behind the pair the Kurdish owner ran.
They went from street to street at rapid pace
  Till everyone could recognize his face—
At every bathhouse and each market stall,   665
  This man's appearance soon was known to all.
Ten criers who could holler with loud shrieks,
  Including Turks and Arabs, Kurds and Greeks,
Announced: 'He's broke! He has no cash at all,
  So no one give him loans, however small.
He's empty outside and within, take heed!
  He is a bankrupt cheat who's ruled by greed.
Don't deal with him, for guile he doesn't lack—
  If he sells something he will steal it back!
If you then bring him to be tried, you'll fail—   670
  The judge will not send this corpse back to gaol!

He's crafty and his stomach's never full;
　　Though he pretends, he's not so pitiful:
He borrows fancy clothes he likes to wear,
　　To fool vain people who are unaware:
Wise words when spoken by a stupid man
　　Are borrowed clothes—take heed now while you can!
A thief with silk robes still can't shake your hand—
　　They've cut his hands off!* Don't you understand?'

The thief came down at the end of the day,   675
　　The owner said, 'My home is far away;
You rode the camel which belongs to me,
　　So I demand at least a modest fee.'
'What have we all been doing?' he replied.
　　'Where is your brain? Hello! No one inside?
News of my bankruptcy has filled the sky
　　But somehow you have let it pass you by;
Your ears were blocked, stuffed with false hopes of gain;
　　Hope makes blind fools turn deaf—it is your bane!
Even mere bricks heard the announcer say: 680
　　"This pimp is bankrupt, so please keep away!"'
They'd shouted this all day, but still the Kurd,
　　Immersed in vain hopes, hadn't caught a word.
'God's seal is on their hearing and their sight,'*
　　Behind their veils are forms that bring delight;
He lets your eyes see only His selection
　　Of loving glances, beauty, and perfection;
He gives your ears a share, as with your eyes,
　　Of His glad tidings, music, and deep cries.
This world has many remedies it stores,   685
　　But, first, God has to open up the doors;
Though you're now unaware, He'll make you see
　　When you feel that you need it desperately:
The Prophet said, 'Our Noble God, who heals,
　　Has made a cure for every pain Man feels.'
But you won't see a trace of your pain's cure
　　Unless He wishes—you're that insecure.

Find Placelessness, you who seek remedies,
    Like one about to die who finally sees.
This world appeared from the Dimensionless*   690
    And it has taken form from Placelessness—
From being to Non-being* now return,
    If you seek God and with divine love burn.
Non-being is where you can earn, my friend,
    But in our transient world you only spend:
Non-being is God's workshop; there's no gain
    In this realm, which holds naught but what is vain.
Teach us, Dear Friend, fine words that we can say
    To gain Your mercy every time we pray!
Both prayers and their answers come from You,   695
    Security's from You and terror too.
If we have erred, correct ways please now teach!
    You're the Corrector and the Lord of Speech.
With alchemy You can transmute what's vile,
    Transform a stream of blood into the Nile;
Your work is to perform such alchemy;
    No one else knows this special chemistry:
You mixed together water once with clay
    And moulded Adam's body in this way;
You gave him lineage, and a perfect mate,   700
    All kinds of thoughts, and every mood and state.
To some You've shown a way unto relief:
    You've let them separate from joy and grief,
And from themselves and their own families.
    You've made fair things look foul to men like these:
What senses can perceive they choose to shun,
    For they depend on the Unseen Pure One.
Their Lover's hidden, though their love is clear:
    Their Lover is beyond, their suffering here.
Escape from here! Love of forms in this place   705
    Is not for forms themselves like a girl's face;
In truth, love's not inspired by forms you see,
    Though it seems like it superficially—
Why else would you abandon forms you love
    The moment that their souls ascend above?

Their forms persist, so why must your love end?
    Find out who your beloved is, my friend!
If the Beloved were perceptible,
    For all to love Him would be possible.
Love grows through faithfulness that will not tire—   710
    A changing object such love can't inspire:
A ray of sunlight shines across a wall,
    It's just a temporary loan, that's all—
Why give your heart to a mere wall of clay?
    Seek the light's source which shines each single day!
You love your own mind and think you're superior
    To those who worship just a form's exterior—
Your intellect is one ray of God's light;
    It's gold on copper, borrowed for one night.
Beauty in humans is like borrowed gold;   715
    That's why your sweetheart turns so pale and old—
An angel suffered thus a steep descent*
    Because his loveliness was merely lent.
Such lovely beauty fades eventually,
    Just as a young shoot withers gradually:
We make him live long, then turn back to die:
    Look for the heart! Mere bones can't satisfy!
Our inner beauty's not a transient thing—
    It's nourished by the Water of Life's* spring;
He's Saqi,* Life's Draught and the drunkard too—   720
    All three become one when you're rid of 'you'.*
You can't know that One by analogy—
    Act like His slave and stop your idiocy!
For you, reality is forms in time;
    You still delight in niceties like rhyme.*
In truth, reality's what charms your soul
    And makes you see forms are dispensable;
It isn't that which makes men deaf and blind,
    Increasing love of forms in humankind:
The blind have fancies which increase frustration;   725
    True sight is vision through annihilation.

*

The literal Qur'an is for the blind;
     They've lost their ass, and grasp what's left behind:
Since you have vision, seek the ass which fled,
     And not the empty saddle left instead!
The saddle you will find too on its back:
     When you possess a soul, food you'll not lack.
Upon its back rests transient wealth and gain;
     The heart's pearl's worth much more and will remain—
Ride bareback on the donkey now, you dunce!   730
     Didn't the Prophet ride in this way once?
The Prophet did ride bareback—that is true;
     He also went on foot a great deal too.
Tether your donkey-soul with rope that's strong—
     How long will it evade hard work, how long?
Patience and gratitude your ass must learn,
     Even if it takes decades to discern.
No porter bore a fellow porter's load,
     No one has ever reaped unless he's sowed—
That is an immature hope, so grow up!   735
     Raw food that's rotten makes you soon throw up!
Don't say, 'That man found treasure suddenly;
     That's what I want—hard work is not for me!'
That was his stroke of fortune, which is rare;
     While you have strength you have to earn your share.
Work won't prevent such fortune—that's a fact;
     Don't stop your work: good luck it can attract!
Don't be a victim of 'If only . . .', brat:
     Don't say, 'If only I'd done this or that!'
The Prophet stopped men making this lament: 740
     'It's sheer hypocrisy'—by this he meant:
Sobbing 'If only . . .' with their final breath
     Gives hypocrites a most remorseful death.

Parable

A man searched for a home once hurriedly.
     A friend led him to ruined property

And said, 'If this just had a roof, you could
   Live next to me then—wouldn't that be good!
Your family would be so comfortable
   If adding one more room were possible.'
The man replied, 'Yes, that would be such fun,   745
   One can't live off "If only . . ." though, can one?'
All people are in search of happiness,
   And, due to false hopes, they feel deep distress.
Both young and old are searching hard for gold,
   But real from false can't easily be told:
When rays shine in your heart, look carefully,
   Don't guess they're gold without the means to see!
If you've a touchstone, then you can decide,
   If not, then pledge yourself to a true guide.
Inside your soul a touchstone you must own;   750
   If you don't know the path, don't go alone!
The ghouls' screams sound like calling from a friend,
   But they will only drag you to your end;
One of them screams, 'Hey caravan, come here!
   The signposts make the path to me so clear.'
The ghoul will use your name: 'Hey so-and-so!'
   To make you fall through this deceptive show!
You'll meet the wolf if you should take this bait,
   Your whole life lost, far off and getting late.
What is the ghoul's way? What should one expect?   755
   It says, 'I want wealth, status, and respect.'
Don't let these voices in, to them stay sealed,
   So that the mysteries can be revealed;
And chant God's name* to drown the ghoul's shrill cry,
   Away from this base vulture turn your eye!
Recognize false dawns from the dawn that's true,
   The colour of the glass from the wine's hue,
So that, from those eyes which see colours here,
   Restraint will make an inner eye appear:
You will see different colours few have seen   760
   And bright pearls in the place where stones have been;
What are mere pearls when you'll become the ocean
   And that bright sun with its revolving motion!

*

The Craftsman's in His workshop far from view—
    You must transcend beyond to see Him too.
Since work throws on the Craftsman its own veil,
    To see beyond the work you then will fail.
The workshop is the Craftsman's place—beware,
    Whoever stays outside stays unaware!
Enter the workshop of annihilation,   765
    To see the Craftsman and His fine creation!
Within the workshop vision is so clear,
    While all is veiled and hidden over here.
His self-existence Pharaoh kept in mind
    And to His workshop therefore he stayed blind;
That's why he felt he could change destiny,
    To make fate turn back from his door and flee,
But fate was chuckling at his schemes instead,
    Although it hid it, and could not be read:
Innocent babies by the score he killed   770
    To try to change what God Himself had willed—
So Moses wouldn't stand up to his rule,
    He murdered thousands, for he was so cruel.
Though he killed thousands, Moses thrived and learned
    How to deal Pharaoh the defeat he'd earned.
If Pharaoh had seen God decides, he'd not
    Have even thought up such a wicked plot.
In Pharaoh's house lived Moses safe and sound
    While Pharaoh killed the other children found:
He strengthened his own body, due to fear   775
    The real threat was another standing near—
'That one's a jealous enemy,' he'd claim,
    But his own body was in fact to blame,
For Pharaoh then had Moses by his side
    And yet would shout, 'Where does my foe now hide?'
Within you, your own self feels such delight
    When you attack another man through spite.

How the people blamed a man who killed his mother on suspicion of adultery

An angry man took his own mother's life
    By using his bare fists and a sharp knife.
'You are so evil!' someone said that night,   780
    'You've just ignored your mother's basic right.
Why did you kill her? Tell me if you can!
    What did she do, you evil-natured man?'
'She did the act deserving of most blame;
    I killed her, so the ground would hide her shame.'
'You should have killed the men—they should all pay!'
    'I'd have to kill a different man each day!
I killed her not to murder more instead:
    One dead is better than a thousand dead.'
Your self's the source of evil ways—beware!   785
    The wickedness of it is everywhere!
Kill it, for due to that self which is base,
    Each breath you strike a good man in the face!
The vast world seems so narrow due to it,
    And so with God you fight and foes you hit.
If you kill it, from censure you'll be free—
    You'll then not have a single enemy.
If you take issue with what I convey
    About the prophets and the saints, and say:
'Didn't the prophets kill their carnal souls   790
    Yet still face foes, though they'd fulfilled their roles?'
Now listen, seeker of what is correct,
    To answers to your doubts, and then reflect:
Prophet-rejecters were their own worst foes:
    Upon themselves they thus inflicted blows.
The ones who murder are the enemies,
    Not those who undergo more agonies.
The bat is not the sun's foe—it would fail;
    It is its own foe, blinded by its veil.
That bat is killed by radiance from the sun—   795
    How could the sun be harmed by that small one?

The one from whom comes torment is the foe,
   One who'd block rubies from the sun's bright glow:
Infidels block themselves from every ray
   The prophets, like rare jewels, shine their way—
How can this veil great mystics of this kind?
   The infidels just make their own eyes blind.
They're like the Indian slave with too much pride—
   To spite his master he tries suicide:
The slave jumps headfirst from the roof one day   800
   To make his master suffer loss this way!
If a sick man becomes his doctor's foe,
   If a child hates his teacher, it is so—
In truth it's self-abuse and robbery:
   They've robbed themselves of brain power stupidly.
If bleachers fall out with the sun's bright light,
   Or fish start fights with water through sheer spite,
Who will lose out? Who really will have paid?
   At the end of the day, whose star will fade?
If in an ugly form the Lord made you,   805
   Then don't be ugly in your nature too!
If your shoes rip, don't walk on rough terrain:
   Don't make a problem bigger—use your brain!
'I'm less than him!' you cry out jealously,
   'That man makes me feel inferiority!'
Such jealousy is a huge flaw and curse;
   Than all deficiencies this one's much worse.
The devil felt so much humiliation
   He threw himself into far worse damnation:
He wished to be superior but was cursed,*   810
   And now he sucks our blood with his deep thirst.
The Prophet one day put Bu Jahl to shame—
   He made more claims, through envy, all the same;
Bu'l-Hakam turned into Bu Jahl this way;*
   Envy makes men unworthy every day.
There's nothing better to possess, you'll find,
   Than natures which are envy-free and kind.
God made the prophets intermediaries,
   So that they would reveal men's jealousies:

Since none could feel with God a rivalry,   815
   Of God no one felt envious obviously,
But those with whom they would themselves compare
   To envy and compete with men would dare.
The Prophet's greatness now is obvious;
   No longer can a man feel envious.

There is a saint for every era, friend;
   This test continues till the very end:
Those with good natures will be liberated,
   But those with frail hearts will be devastated.
The saint is the Imam who'll rise each age;   820
   From Ali and Omar's line comes this sage;*
Seeker, he is the guide and Mahdi too,
   Both hidden and right here in front of you!*
With wisdom as his Gabriel,* he's the light;
   The lesser saint is like his lamp, less bright;
Below the lamp the niche* ranks; you might say
   The light has its gradations in this way:
God's Light has seven hundred veils, my friend—
   These veils of light are levels to ascend.
A group of saints behind each veil you'll find,   825
   Leading to the Imam, in rank they're lined.
The lowest rank, due to deficient sight,
   Are those who cannot bear more of the light;
The next rank, due to their own weakness too,
   More radiance than their limit cannot view;
That light, which for the top rank grants new life,
   To the squint-eyed brings only pain and strife.
Impaired sight can improve eventually:
   Once you've passed every veil you'll reach the sea.
How can the iron foundry's hot fire suit   830
   An apple, quince, or similar type of fruit?
Fruits ripen with a little warmth, not fire—
   A furnace's heat fruit does not require.
For iron that amount of heat's too low;
   The fire of dragons it can undergo—

This iron is the Sufi who bears trials;
 Under the hammer and the flames he smiles;
The fire's own chamberlain won't stay apart—
 Without a guard he enters the fire's heart.
Without a medium, it's impossible   835
 For you to heat your water up at all:
The medium needed is the pan you heat;
 It's like the sandals you wear on your feet,
Or the surrounding air that is so hot
 It can itself heat water in a pot.
The Sufi has no medium, nor resistance:
 The flames directly heat his whole existence;
And if the world's a body, he's its heart;
 Only through him can this world's real work start.
Without the heart how can the body talk? 840
 Without its wish to move how can one walk?
Iron is where the sparks are seen to dart:
 God is seen, not in bodies, but the heart.
Our hearts are like a body from this view
 Next to the saint's heart, which is their source too.
This needs examples or an explanation,
 But I've no faith in men's imagination,
Which might deem my good deeds depravity,
 Although my words are selfless charity—
What's best for a bent foot is a bent shoe; 845
 The beggar knocked—I've done all I can do.

How a king tested two slaves whom he had just purchased

A king bought two slaves cheaply, then one day
 Listened to what the first one had to say.
He found him clever and well-spoken too—
 From sugar lips sweet water's what flows through.
Each person is concealed beneath his tongue;
 This curtain over their soul's gate is hung,
But when speech, like the wind, pulls it apart,
 It shows the secrets hidden in the heart—

Is there a pearl or just some wheat instead?   850
    Some gold or snakes and scorpions left unfed?
Or treasure with a serpent curled around—
    Treasure unguarded who has ever found?
Without preparing this slave spoke the way
    That others can if they rehearse all day,
As if within him were a vast, deep sea,
    Which scattered pearls of wisdom constantly.
The light that shines from every pearl-like heart
    Shows how to tell the true from false apart;
The light of the Criterion* gives such vision   855
    To show the truth from falsehood with precision.
If this pearl's light should give sight to our eyes,
    You'd hear from us both questions and replies!
You see two moons due to your failing sight;
    This vision makes you question now what's right—
Correct your sight through moonbeams, to perceive
    The moon as one—the answer then receive!
Command your thoughts: 'Don't be cross-eyed this way!'
    That pearl's the light's source and the actual ray.

When answers enter your heart through your ear,   860
    Your eye tells you: 'Ignore it—listen here!'
The eye tastes union which the ear can't reach—
    Eyes see through ecstasy, ears hear mere speech;
Attributes change through what the ears can hear,
    Essences through things which to eyes appear:
If all you know of fire is what men say,
    Get cooked in flames and you'll learn more this way.
It's not true certainty until you burn—
    Sit in the fire, true certainty to earn.
When ears learn to perceive, they turn to eyes;   865
    The order '*Say!*'* is trapped there otherwise.
This talk could go on, but let's now return
    What that king did with his two slaves to learn.

The king sends away one of the slaves and
interrogates the other

When the young slave's intelligence grew clear,
   He signalled to the other to come near
(I've called him 'young' because that is endearing—
   When old men say 'my son' they are not sneering).
The second slave obeyed as slaves must do,
   He had a filthy mouth and black teeth too;
Although this made the ruler feel unwell,   870
   This slave's deep secrets he sought out as well.
'With your looks and your filthy mouth,' he said,
   'Don't sit near me, but over there instead!
For you're my scribe, and that's our only link—
   You're not a friend with whom I'd share a drink.
You'll be the patient for this skilled physician,
   Who'll try to cure your mouth of its condition.
It's wrong to burn a rug due to one flea:
   It would be wrong to shun you equally.
Now sit down with us for a while, and share   875
   Some stories, to reveal the brain in there.'
He sent the first slave to the bathhouse then,
   And said, 'Scrub well, and come to me again.'
He told the ugly slave: 'You're smart—well done!
   You're worth a hundred slaves not merely one.
You're not as bad as that slave tried to claim
   When he would jealously give you the blame,
Saying, "He's crooked and he's stolen much;
   He's bent and cowardly and such and such!"'
This slave said, 'He speaks always truthfully;   880
   No man I've met has shown more honesty.
It is his nature to tell just what's true—
   Refuting him I'm not prepared to do;
I don't think he's corrupt; grace fills his head—
   I'd rather just suspect myself instead!
Perhaps he can detect in me some flaws
   Which I can't see myself due to some cause?'

Whoever sees his own faults, if he's wise,
    Will strive in self-reform until he dies.
Most men are heedless of themselves, my brother,   885
    That's why they pick at faults seen in another:
'Form-worshipper, I don't see my own face—
    I see yours, and you see mine in its place!'
Whoever sees his true soul deep inside
    Has more light than all creatures far and wide;
Though he should die, his sight will last forever—
    His vision is the eye of the Creator;
The light with which this man sees his own face
    Is not the light we sense, but purest grace.

The king said, 'All his flaws expose to me   890
    The way he spoke about you previously,
So I can tell if you're my intimate,
    And fit to serve as my associate.'
He said, 'I'll tell you of his faults, although
    He is by far the best man that I know.
His faults are kindness, love, and loyalty,
    Deep friendship, knowledge, and sincerity;
A tiny fault is he's too generous—
    He'd give his life because he's chivalrous.'
A hundred thousand lives God will bestow;   895
    If you're not chivalrous you'll never know:
How can you be so miserly with life,
    If you have seen the light—why choose this strife?
Water is hoarded by fools on the shore
    Who cannot see the ocean offers more.
The Prophet said, 'If you knew certainly
    That your reward on Judgment Day would be
Ten times as good as what He's granted here,
    You'd constantly be generous with good cheer.'
Chivalrous men can see the change ahead—   900
    This knowledge rids them of all fear and dread.
Meanness is failure to see what's in store—
    Seeing the pearl makes divers' spirits soar;

No one should be a miser here today,
  For no one gambles all for naught away.
Thus eyes inspire all acts of chivalry;
  This realm's transcended by the visionary.

'He also lacks conceit,' the slave then said.
  'He looks for faults within himself instead:
He is his own worst critic; I have seen   905
  Him kind to all, though to himself he's mean.'
The king said, 'Don't rush to extol his ways
  And, in the process, offer such self-praise,
For I'll see him again soon all the same—
  And so you might yourself be put to shame.'

Out of sincerity and fidelity to his friend the slave swears that his opinions are true

He said, 'I swear that's not the case at all,
  By the King of this world, the Merciful,
Who sent the prophets not due to His need,
  But as an act of grace, so we'd be freed,
The Mighty Lord who out of lowly clay   910
  Created glorious heroes of the way!
He cleansed them of the nature of terrestrials
  And made them even overtake celestials—
From fire he turned them into purest light,
  Sent them above the rest and far from sight.
*That lightning flash** reached spirits from His kingdom,
  So, from it, Adam could acquire much wisdom;
What Adam missed Seth afterwards collected,
  And so as his successor was selected;
When Noah found this jewel, then joyfully   915
  He scattered pearls across the spirit's sea;
Abraham's soul, due to this powerful light,
  Walked into flames without a trace of fright;*

When Ishmael fell into its stream, he laid
  His head before his father's sharpened blade;*
David's soul warmed thanks to this pure light's glow—
  His iron loom then melted just like snow;*
To Solomon when this light union gave,
  Each demon then became his faithful slave;*
When Jacob bowed to fate submissively,   920
  Through Joseph's scent his eyes again could see;*
While moon-faced Joseph saw that sun's bright beams
  And learnt how to interpret people's dreams;*
And when the rod in Moses's right hand
  Found light, it showed how small was Pharaoh's land;*
When Jesus found it, he rose up from here,
  Like on a ladder, to the highest sphere;*
And once Mohammad had received this boon,
  In just one second he then split the moon;*
By Abu Bakr when this was perceived   925
  "Veracious" was the name that he received;*
And, through the real beloved, with his heart
  Omar learnt to tell true from false apart;*
When to Osman's eyes such light was bestowed,
  He gained two lights* from rays which overflowed;
Ali dispersed pearls once he'd seen His face,
  As God's own lion* in the realm of grace;
Jonayd saw his own army* was so vast,
  Then this great Sufi countless stations passed;
When Bayazid saw God's grace as the aim,   930
  God made "The Pole of Mystics"* his new name;
And when Karkhi watched over this deep stream,*
  He led all mystics—his soul was supreme;
Prince Ebn-e Adham rode his horse this way
  And turned into the greatest king that day;*
Once he'd traversed this path, Shaqiq became
  The sun of judgement and earned much acclaim.*
Thousands of hidden kings, who'll never die,
  Live in the other world with heads held high;
Their names are hidden through God's jealousy—   935
  Not every beggar reads them easily!

I swear by those made of pure light from Him,
　　Such men are fish which in His ocean swim
(To call Him "Ocean Soul" does not seem right,
　　I'm looking for a better name tonight).
By Him from Whom all things emerge as well,
　　A kernel next to Whom seems like a shell,
My fellow slave's good traits a hundred fold
　　Exceed this small amount that I have told.
What I know of my comrade's virtues, king,　　　　940
　　You won't believe, as they're astonishing!'

The king said, 'What are your own qualities?
　　Tell us and stop describing his now, please!
What do you have? Display your gains to me.
　　Which pearl have you discovered in the sea?
After death, sense perception is in vain—
　　Have you the soul's light, through which hearts can gain?
When in the grave earth robs your eyes of sight—
　　Do you have what can give your vision light?
And when your limbs are torn off on that day,　　　945
　　Will you have spirit wings to fly away?
When this vile bestial soul dies with no trace,
　　You'll need a soul which lives on in its place—
*Whoever comes with good deeds** will gain more,
　　If they've done good for God, not as a chore.
In essence are you human or an ass?
　　Will you reach God when all effects must pass?
Transient things, like fasting and the prayer,
　　Since they don't last, must vanish in thin air.
Such things up to the Lord you cannot raise,　　　950
　　But sickness from your essence they erase,
And by such acts your essence is improved;
　　Through abstinence diseases are removed.
Striving in abstinence can change effects—
　　The bitter mouth's made sweet, for it perfects.
Through farming, soil can turn to crops you eat;
　　Cream makes your hair curl up like fields of wheat,

While sex is just a pretext which soon ends—
   Its purpose is the child that's born, my friends:
If once a camel and a horse should mate,   955
   It's for the colt's birth at a later date;
Planting an orchard is done simply so
   The aim's fulfilled, that juicy fruit should grow;
Alchemy is a mere technique to me—
   Present the gold produced through alchemy!
And burnishing is no more than the means
   Of purifying objects when one cleans.
You claim "I did that act, beyond dispute!"
   So show us your results, the orchard's fruit.
Be silent! Showing off like that is base!   960
   Don't slay a shadow in a camel's place!'

He answered, 'King, with anguish my heart bleeds
   On hearing your dismissal of good deeds:
Dear king, despair will make your slave's heart burn,
   If the good deeds he sends will not return.'
If there's no transfer at the Resurrection,
   Our words and deeds are vain—we face rejection;
Each accident should change to a new guise
   That Hour—with new existence they should rise.
Each thing transforms to what's appropriate: 965
   For herds a shepherd seems the perfect fit.
At Resurrection all things gain new forms,
   Which are well-ordered, based on certain norms.
Weren't you an accident once just the same,
   The writhing of your parents with one aim?
Look at the buildings that men can erect—
   They're born in the mind of the architect:
This house which seemed so fine to us, whose doors
   Were well-proportioned like its roof and floors—
An accident, the architect's mere thought,   970
   The tools and all the pillars here has brought.
What then is every worthwhile thing's first source?
   It is a fancy or a thought, of course.

Each atom you see in the world today
  Was once produced by accidents this way.
First comes the thought and then the action, friend,
  The world was formed like this—please comprehend!
Fruits are just inner thoughts initially,
  Though they're made visible eventually.
After we plant a tree, it's probable   975
  Our primary aim will be made visible—
Its branches, leaves, and roots appear first, though
  They all are sent just for the fruit to grow;
And thus the secret of the heavens too
  Became known as the lord of '*But for you*'.*
This speech gives accidents a transformation,
  Just like your favourite parable's narration.
All things were accidents once, such that they
  Can show the truth of '*Has there been one day?*'*
From images all accidents come here;   980
  And thoughts made those first images appear—
This world's one thought from the Whole Intellect;
  Images are the envoys He'll select.
This world is just the place for your probation;
  That world is where you'll find your compensation.
'King, when your servant sins, that accident
  Becomes a chain and to the gaol he's sent—
So, if he serves well he can then expect
  From you a robe of honour to collect.
Thus, accident and substance, egg and bird,   985
  Produce each other—no, that's not absurd!'
The king said, 'Tell me, slave, if this is true,
  How come yours failed to hatch some substance too?'
He answered, 'Wisdom has kept it concealed,
  And to this transient world it's not revealed,
For, if the shapes of thoughts were manifest,
  All men would worship and not face a test:
If they were not veiled, but left clear instead,
  On each man's forehead they could then be read—
Who then would practise still idolatry?   990
  To mock truth who'd have the audacity?

And if the Resurrection were today,
  Who in the world would sin on Judgment Day!'
The king said, 'God has veiled what bad men meet
  From common folk, but not from His elite:
If I throw in a dungeon one emir,
  I hide this from some, but not my vizier.
God has shown me each deed's true reckoning,
  And all the images from which deeds spring.
Show me one sign, so I can clearly see;   995
  The clouds won't veil the glorious moon from me.'
The slave said, 'Then, what value is my speech?
  You know already; all's within your reach.'
The king replied, 'For this the world's been shown:
  To make completely clear what can be known;
Until He chose His knowledge to make plain,
  God didn't place inside this world deep pain.
You can't keep still a second here without
  A good or evil action leaping out,
And this demand for you to act is made   1000
  So that your inner soul will be displayed.
How can your reel-like body now keep still
  When the thread's end keeps pulling it at will?
The sign of this pull is your restlessness,
  And idleness for you is like distress.
Both worlds keep giving birth; each cause thus shares
  In motherhood—effects are what each bears.
Once an effect is born, it soon will grow
  Into a cause itself and this will show—
The generations are produced this way;   1005
  Enlightened eyes can see this clear as day!'
The king had heard enough now to decide
  Whether the slave showed signs of worth inside;
Of course, this king had the required perception,
  But more than this I'm not allowed to mention.
The first slave came back from the baths just then
  And the great ruler summoned him again,
Then said, '*May you stay healthy now you're clean!*
  You're gentle and the finest slave I've seen.

I hope that all the things he said of you 1010
    Will turn out to be totally untrue!
Whoever's seen your face has felt delight—
    More precious than the world is that fair sight.'
He said, 'Please give me a small clue, dear king,
    What that vile wretch has just been whispering.'
'He said that you're two-faced and insincere,
    That you are really poison we should fear.'
On being told his friend spoke spitefully,
    A sea of rage boiled in him violently;
He foamed and turned deep red at what he heard 1015
    And then reviled his friend with every word:
'From when he first was my associate,
    Just like a dog he was so full of shit!'
He kept on cursing due to the king's bluff,
    The king then pointed to his lips: 'Enough!
The truth's now clear and cannot be denied:
    His flaw is on his mouth; yours is inside.
You must sit with your vile soul far from me;
    He'll supervise you—serve obediently!'

'Discern real praise from mere pretence instead, 1020
    Like grass from piles of trash,' the Prophet said.
Ignore a fair face which is just a cover,
    For inner ugliness will harm its lover;
And though his face be ugly, if his state
    Is good within, before him fall prostrate!
The outward form must pass eventually;
    The inner realm survives eternally.
How long will you adore the jug's design?
    Seek water not the jug, however fine!
You saw just forms; meanings escaped your eyes— 1025
    Seek the pearl in the shell, if you are wise!
These shells of bodies, though they are alive
    Through the soul's ocean in which they can thrive,
Not all of them contain a pearl inside—
    Look carefully with your eyes open wide!

Ask 'What does it contain?' Then choose with care,
   Because a precious pearl is very rare.
Based on its size, a mountain is worth more
   Than the fine ruby hidden in its core;
Your hands, your feet and hair as well in size   1030
   Are obviously much bigger than your eyes,
But still it is quite clear to you and me
   Superior are your eyes, with which you see.

By just a single thought that's formed within,
   A hundred worlds can soon be made to spin;
The sultan's form might be one of a kind,
   So great a thousand soldiers march behind,
And yet this king's form follows the decree
   Of just one thought, which nobody can see.
Due to a single thought thus thousands pass,   1035
   Just like a flood, across the earth en masse—
That thought may seem to many very small,
   But like a flood it can control us all.
So when you see that each skill by a thought
   Was generated in this world from naught,
That houses, castles, towns in which we dwell
   And mountains, rivers, open fields as well,
The earth, the sun, the ocean and the sky,
   As fish need water, on thought they rely,
Why then out of stupidity, blind one,   1040
   Count thought an ant and body Solomon?
The mountain seems so massive in your view,
   Thought mouse-like—just that mountain frightens you.
This world is great and awesome in your sight;
   The clouds and thunder make you shake with fright.
But to the world of thought you feel immune,
   Because you're heedless—you'll regret this soon!
Since you lack wisdom and are form alone,
   You're not a human but a donkey's clone.
You think the shadow's real and feel such joy—   1045
   But what is truly real you deem a toy.

Just wait until the day when thought should spread
 Its wings, without a veil to hide its head!
Huge mountains turn to soft wool you will see,
 And this vast earth become naught instantly.
You won't see sky, nor stars, nor anyone
 Apart from God, the Living, Loving One.
A story, true or not, I'll now dictate;
 These truths I've told it will illuminate:

How a king's assistants grew jealous of his favourite slave

A king showed to one servant special grace   1050
 By granting him the most exalted place:
Forty commanders couldn't earn his pay,
 Nor his top-ranked viziers whom they'd obey!
Through such good fortune from his star's ascendant,
 Just like Ayaz he was Mahmud's attendant.*
Before the body, his soul was created,
 And it was then to the king's soul related—
Only such things which had been formed before
 Should matter—don't watch new things any more!
That which the mystic owns has worth alone,   1055
 Because he's focused on what was first sown:
Whether it is a wheat or barley seed,
 He'll notice it, and won't fail to take heed.
This world that's night-like has created naught
 But hot air—just the odd foiled trick and plot.
With tricks how can you make hearts smile and love
 When you can't even see God's tricks above?
The hunter just puts snares within a snare—
 Not even he can flee God's trap, beware!
Though countless plants should grow, then fade away,   1060
 What God has planted is what lives today:
He sows new seeds on those He sowed before:
 These seeds are transient, those for evermore;
The seeds sown first are of the perfect kind,
 The second seeds are rotten, left behind.

*

Before the one you love discard all thought,
　　Although from His thought yours have all been brought.
What God has raised has actual worth alone:
　　What grows in the end is what was first sown.
Sow for His sake whatever seeds you sow,　　　　　　　　1065
　　Since you're His captive lover—watch them grow!
Avoid the carnal soul and don't get caught
　　In its traps! All but God's work is worth naught.
The end of time may come, and, in that case,
　　That thief will meet before the King disgrace:
His stolen goods, his guile used for self-gain,
　　From Judgment Day will on his back remain.
A thousand brains may try to set a snare,
　　One different to that one which God's placed there—
His snares for them they'll strengthen through persistence:　1070
　　To a strong wind how can straw show resistance?
'What's the point of existence?' you now say,
　　Your question must be worthwhile in some way:
If it has no real worth, then why should I
　　Listen to it and not just pass it by?
And if your question has a point to it,
　　Why think the world is of no benefit?
Though from one point of view the world's worth naught,
　　From other viewpoints it is worth a lot.
Though your work seems to some inadequate,　　　　　　1075
　　Since you feel it is good keep doing it:
The world loved Joseph's beauty, even though
　　His jealous brothers felt he had to go;
Many thought David's Psalms* were very good;
　　Others judged their sound worse than banging wood;
The Nile was purer than the Draught of Life
　　And yet deniers found there blood and strife.*
Martyrdom brings new life, believers claim;*
　　Hypocrites say it's death deserving blame.
What single blessing in the world is there　　　　　　　1080
　　Of which one group is not denied a share?
Can sugar benefit the cow or ass?
　　Each has its own food—not all can eat grass.

If you find food bestowed not to your taste,
    You need good mentoring for such a waste!
Or, like a sick man, one might chew the ground
    Imagining that it is food he's found,
Ignoring his true source of nourishment
    For what brings sickness and bewilderment:
Giving up honey, poison he will eat—   1085
    He thinks this source of sickness tastes like meat.
For men, God's light is the original food;
    Animal food, for them, is far too crude.
But, due to sickness, now some men assume
    That clay and water's what they should consume:
With weak legs, a frail heart, and pallid face,
    They turn from *heaven and its paths of grace*.*
The grace of God is food for His elite;
    Without a mouth or throat such men can eat.
The sun's food comes from the light of the Throne,   1090
    While wicked men feed from the grave alone:
True martyrs *are still nourished**—that's their fate;
    Their food requires no mouth nor serving plate.
The heart feeds off supportive company;
    From knowledge it acquires more purity.
Humans are just like cups in form—few see
    The wine inside, their true reality.
Meetings with men will nourish you; you'll grow
    From your encounters, and it soon will show:
Planetary conjunctions, when inspected,   1095
    Reveal that both the planets are affected.
A child is born when couples mate; it's known
    That sparks are made when iron's struck on stone;
And after rain falls on the soil, we see
    Fruit, vegetables, and herbs grow healthily;
When men eat vegetables this doesn't cease—
    They gain contentment, joy, and inner peace.
When joy and pleasure fill your soul, then you
    Will gain beneficence and kindness too—
Our bodies will gain food that's spiritual,   1100
    If we aim higher than what's sensual.

Your blushes form when blood flows to your head,
   And blood comes from the sun which burns bright red.
Red is the best of colours: it's the one
   That comes down to us all from the Great Sun,*
But land which joins with Saturn is instead*
   Barren, infertile land that's almost dead.
Concurrence sparks potentiality:
   Demons control men of hypocrisy.

From the ninth heaven these truths have been brought   1105
   To much acclaim, though that was never sought—
The pomp of people is a borrowed thing,
   But it's intrinsic to the Lord, our King.
Men will abase themselves just for their pride,
   For pomp, and to become self-satisfied;
In hope of glory for a single day,
   They'll struggle till their thin necks waste away.
Why don't they come where I now stand, for here
   I bask in the Bright Sun's grace, far from fear?
A pitch-black tower's where your sun must rise,   1110
   The Sun of Grace, though, is beyond all skies.
He has no rising-place that's known to men:
   His essence doesn't rise and set again.
I'm like one of His motes that's left behind,
   Sunshine without a shadow you can find.
Revolving round this Sun is what I do
   And this is due to that Sun's splendour too.
The Sun's aware of all the causes, but
   From Him the rope of causes has been cut.
Good friend, I gave up hope repeatedly—   1115
   In whom? In that most generous Sun, trust me!
But don't trust me when I say I can stand
   My exile—I feel like fish on dry land!
If I lose hope, the deep despair you'll see
   Was once created by the Sun in me.
Can things be cut off from their own creator?
   His Being apart, where can existents pasture?

Existents all graze on this pasture's grass,
　　Be they Boraq,* a stud, or lowly ass.
The blind horse grazes blindly though—that's why　　1120
　　It is refused: the grass it passes by.
Not knowing movements all come from the Ocean,
　　Some change the prayer niche they face in devotion.
They drink salt water from the sweetest sea,
　　Which will make them turn blind immediately;
The sea then calls out, 'Come back! That's not right:
　　Drink using your right hand, regain your sight!'
Here 'right hand' means opinion that's correct;
　　Where good and bad come from it can detect.
The spear must learn its thrower has no trouble　　1125
　　In making it now straight and now bent double.

Through love of Shams, I'm sapped of strength tonight,
　　Or else I would give all the blind folk sight!
Hosam, Pure Light of Truth, heal one for me
　　Of blindness which is caused by jealousy,
Fast-acting, healing balm for failing eyes,
　　Darkness-destroying cure for doubts and lies!
Rubbing the blind man's eyes with your balm clears
　　The darkness of a hundred thousand years.
Heal all the blind except the envious few　　1130
　　Who jealously keep on denying you!
To those who envy you don't give new life;
　　Even if I should be one, send down strife!
Those jealous of the Sun and its pure light,
　　Resenting its existence, like the night,
Have this incurable disease, my friend,
　　Trapped deep inside this pit until the end:
They still demand the Sun should not remain
　　Though it's eternal—so they wish in vain!

The falcon is trapped among owls in the wilderness

The proper falcon will return one day;　　1135
　　The blind one will instead soon lose her way.

One strayed into the jungle, where she found
   Herself trapped by some owls who'd gathered round—
She was pure light once, the most holy kind,
   But fate, that strong commander, made her blind:
It threw a lot of sand into her eye,
   So she'd end up in ruins where owls fly.
But that mean stratagem was just the start:
   The falcon's wings these owls soon tore apart;
The owls then shouted out, 'It's obvious   1140
   To steal our home this falcon flew to us!'
They acted like a pack of dogs who block
   A dervish's path and then bite his frock.
The falcon said, 'With you I don't belong;
   I've turned down better places—you're so wrong!
I'm leaving now, for I don't want to stay;
   I will return to my great king today.
Don't fret, you owls, for I would not stay here;
   I'm going to my homeland. Is that clear?
This ruin seems so thriving to your eyes,   1145
   But the king's forearm is this falcon's prize.'
'The falcon's tricking you!' an owl then said,
   'To drive you from your homes—don't be misled!
Through cunning, from our grasp our homes she'll wrest,
   And by pretence she'll tear us from our nest.
This fraudster acts as though she is content—
   In truth, she's greedy and malevolent!
As if it's honey, she lusts after clay—
   Who'd trust a bear with sheep? She acts this way.
She boasts about the king, and his hand too,   1150
   Just to mislead mere simpletons like you.
Even if she should be the king and reign,
   Don't listen to her if you've half a brain.
Is this bird someone that a king would meet?
   Is garlic suitable for something sweet?
These words are just deceit and trickery:
   "My king will rage and come and search for me."
It's unbelievable, absurd hot air!
   This vain boast aims to catch us like a snare.

If you believe her, you're a stupid fool.   1155
  Can such a scrawny bird know kings who rule?
If one of us should crack her skull right here,
  The king's defensive forces won't appear.'
The falcon said, 'If you touch me, the king
  Will then uproot your homes with one great swing!
What is an owl? If falcons bother me
  Or try to make me suffer agony,
The king will climb up mountains, race for miles,
  And with their skulls he'll make a hundred piles.
His grace protects me, so I have no fear;   1160
  Wherever I should go, the king is near.
My image stays inside the sultan's heart—
  Without it, his huge heart would split apart.
And when the king tells me to fly away
  I soar to the heart's zenith like his ray:
Just like the sun and moon you'll see me fly;
  I tear apart the veil across the sky.
My thought gives intellects illumination;
  The sky split open due to my creation.
Even the phoenix is amazed by me—   1165
  How can mere owls perceive my mystery?
For me the king thought of his gaols again
  And freed a hundred thousand captive men.
He made me mix with owls for a short time—
  My breath turned them to falcons; it's sublime!
Happy the owl who, in my path of flight,
  Luckily of my secret catches sight!
To be exultant, cling fast to me now.
  You owls will turn to falcons—don't ask how.
Whoever is in love with such a king   1170
  Won't be a stranger while she's wandering;
And if the king's the cure for someone's pain,
  Though she has wailed much, she won't grieve again.
I rule a realm, I'm not a worthless stray.
  The king now beats the drum from far away:
The falcon drum beats out '*Return!*',* which shows
  God is my witness still despite you foes.

Though I'm not like the king, since he's the best,
  Pure light from him I still can manifest.'

Essence and form don't mean we are apart: 1175
  Water unites with soil in a plant's heart;
Wind joins with fire in substance like its food;
  Wine joins with humans and affects our mood.
Since we're not of the King's class or His kind,
  To reach Him we must leave our selves behind.
The Lord remains alone once He removes
  Our 'I'-ness, dust beneath His horse's hooves;
Souls turned to dust in which His signs are found
  As hoof-prints which His horse left on the ground.
If you become the dust beneath His feet,   1180
  Then you will be the crown of the elite.

Lest my appearance drive you far from me,
  Eat sweets before you hear my homily!
Form has caused many men to fall astray,
  Though some chased form and reached God anyway.
Body and soul are joined to some degree,
  Although they have no similarity:
The eyeball fills with light which gives it sight;
  And drops of blood contain the heart's pure light;
Kidneys house joy, the liver grief and pain;   1185
  Intellect, candle-like, lives in the brain.
Of how they're all joined we are ignorant,
  To work out why our brain is impotent.
With human souls the Absolute's connected—
  From Him, rare pearls each human heart collected.
Like Mary, we're made pregnant, through that touch,
  With the Messiah we adore so much!
Not the Messiah who walks in this place,
  But that Messiah who's beyond all space.
The soul, once pregnant with the Holy One,   1190
  Then makes the whole world pregnant too, in turn.

Thus to a second world this world gives birth,
   So resurrected souls see that world's worth.
If I discuss this till the Final Day,
   There would remain a lot more left to say.
These words themselves are really just a prayer,
   Which aims to catch a sweet breath He might spare.
Who can stay silent and not give his all
   When '*Here I am!*'* He answers to Man's call?
This '*Here I am!*' you cannot hear, although   1195
   You can still taste it clearly, head to toe!

A thirsty man throws bricks from the top of a wall into a stream

There was a high wall very near a stream—
   A thirsty man sat there; in pain he'd scream.
What blocked him from the water was this wall;
   He'd writhe, like fish placed on dry land, and bawl.
He threw a brick into the stream one day;
   To him the splash it made had much to say;
With words from the Beloved and Divine
   That splashing sound soon made him drunk like wine.
He liked this splash so much he couldn't stop—   1200
   He took more of the bricks and let them drop.
The water's splashes asked him, 'Please explain:
   From throwing bricks in me what do you gain?'
'I gain two benefits,' the man then said,
   'So I don't want to stop until I'm dead;
Of benefits from this sound, this is first:
   It sounds like a robab* to those who thirst;
And it resembles Esrafil's* deep blasts
   Which raise the dead to life that truly lasts,
Or like in spring when thunder starts to roar   1205
   And gives the garden flowers men adore,
Or like when for the poor there's charity,
   Or when a captive learns that he'll be free,
Or like the Merciful's breath from the Yemen
   Which reached Mohammad on its way to heaven,*

Or like the Prophet's scent, which intercedes
    For every sinner who repents and pleads,
And also handsome Joseph's scent, which spread
    As far as Jacob's soul from his son's head.*
From throwing bricks my second benefit   1210
    Is that near *gushing water** I can sit.
By taking bricks off till there's none at all,
    I will eventually remove this wall.'
Lowering the wall leads to a higher station,
    And its removal aids annihilation.
Prostration breaks cement effectively,
    So let's *bow down to gain proximity!**
But if the wall stands tall and proud instead,
    It then prevents the lowering of the head.
On Water of Life nobody can pray   1215
    Unless they've left their bodies made of clay.
Whoever facing this wall has more thirst
    Will manage to pull all its bricks out first;
For water's sound whoever is more keen
    Tears more bricks off the veil to the Unseen—
The water's sound fills this man up with wine;
    Others hear splashes, but perceive no sign.

How great to take the opportunity
    To pay one's debt while still so young and free,
In those prime years when one can boast good health,   1220
    Strength, power, courage, and much inner wealth;
In youth, which like a fresh, moist garden, brings,
    Without restraint, much fruit and lovely things,
While fountains of desire and strength still flow
    To feed the body's land and make crops grow,
When its high-roofed house is well-built and tall,
    Its pillars straight with no supports at all.
That is, before old age binds necks with force—
    *A halter of palm fibres** its rope's source—
When soil turns barren, weak, and crumbly too,   1225
    And plants won't grow no matter what you do;

When strength and power's waters are both drained,
   And help from other people can't be gained;
When eyebrows hang down and are almost white,
   And eyes grow moist with tears and failing sight;
When you look wrinkly like a lizard's back,
   Your teeth hang loose, the sense of taste you lack,
The day now late, the ass lame, the road long,
   The body wrecked—its functions all gone wrong,
The roots of bad traits firmly in the ground,   1230
   The strength to dig them up not to be found.

The governor tells a man: 'Dig up the thorn-bush you have planted in the road!'

A rough but clever-talking man one day
   Planted a thorn-bush straight in people's way.
Pedestrians reproached him, they would bawl:
   'Dig it up now!' He wouldn't move at all.
The more that wicked rascal's thorn-bush grew,
   The more their feet were cut and bleeding too;
The clothes of passers-by would all get torn,
   And paupers' feet would get pricked by a thorn.
The governor said, 'Dig it up, young man!'   1235
   He said, 'Okay, I'll dig it when I can.'
'Tomorrow!' he'd repeat; it wasn't long
   Before the thorn-bush grew robust and strong.
The governor said, 'Honesty you lack!
   Complete this now and don't try turning back!'
He answered, '*There's still time left*, so please wait.'
   The governor said, '*Debtors can't be late*.'
You who repeat 'tomorrow' need to know:
   Each day that passes when you are too slow
That wicked bush grows younger with more guile,   1240
   The digger, though, feels weaker all the while;
Each day the thorn-bush strengthens further still,
   The digger ages, weakens, and falls ill;

The bush grows fresher each day that goes by,
  The digger gets more withered and more dry—
While it grows younger, you keep growing old,
  So hurry, don't delay—do what you're told!
View as a thorn-bush your bad qualities—
  They wound you frequently like a disease.
And you've grown sick of them increasingly,   1245
  But now you've no more sensitivity.
If you don't feel for others' sorry fates
  Because of your repulsive, selfish traits,
Then you deserve the wounds that torture you,
  For you torment yourself and others too.
Strike with an axe now if you are a man!
  Break Khaybar's gate like Ali if you can!*
Or with the rose the thorns you must unite,
  And join your fire with the Beloved's light!
Your fire is put out by light He bestows;   1250
  This union turns your thorn into a rose.
He's the believer while you stand for hell—
  Believers can extinguish fire so well:
The Prophet said, concerning hellfire's speech,
  That it will beg believers near its reach:
'Pass quickly, please! Go back the way you came!
  Your light has stopped the burning of my flame.'
The fire's death comes from the believer's light;
  Against this opposite fire cannot fight.
Fire is light's opposite on Judgment Day: 1255
  Flames come from wrath; from grace comes each light ray.
If you would like fire's evil now to die,
  Pour grace's water into the flame's eye—
To be its spring is the believer's role;
  The Water of Life is the saint's pure soul;
Your self will try to flee him—that's its aim,
  For he's of water while it is a flame.
From water, flames will always want to flee
  As they're put out by water easily.
Your thoughts and feelings are of fire, but those   1260
  Of Sufi shaikhs are light which God bestows.

On fire, if water from such light should pour,
   The flames will leap up high and start to roar.
'Die now, in pain!' this fire must now be told,
   So that the hellfire of your self turns cold;
Then your rose-garden won't be burnt like wood,
   Nor your just nature and will to do good.
The seeds which you sow after that will yield
   Herbs, tulips, and wild roses in your field.
I have digressed again with what I say.   1265
   Return now! But where is the proper way?
You jealous man, we wished just to make clear
   Your ass is lame and home is far from here.
Hurry! The sowing season will soon end
   With nothing left but sin and shame, my friend.
The worm bored through roots of your body's tree—
   Uproot it and then burn it totally!
Traveller, beware, now that the day is late!
   Life's sun has set within the well of fate.
Hurry while strength remains and you still can   1270
   Act chivalrously like a strong young man!
Gamble away the seeds you have left, so
   In moments a new plant might start to grow!
While this jewelled lamp burns on, you must be quick—
   Pour more oil into it and trim its wick!
Don't say 'tomorrow'—life is short. Take heed,
   Don't let days pass till sowing a good deed.
The body is an obstacle for you—
   Out with the old, if you yearn for the new!
Close your lips. Open now your palm of gold.   1275
   Don't be so mean. Be generous and bold.
Chivalry means abandoning all lust,
   Which will prevent you rising from the dust.
Chivalry's from the tree of paradise;*
   He who lets go must pay a heavy price.
Abandoning lust—that is *the firmest rope*;*
   This rope will draw your soul above—have hope!
Act well, so chivalry will thus begin
   To take you up, back to your origin.

You're handsome Joseph, this world is your well;*   1280
   The rope is trust in God's will—can't you tell?
Joseph, the rope has come now, so cling fast.
   Don't miss it, for the time has almost passed.
Thank God this rope was lowered down to you,
   And grace and mercy have mixed with it too,
So you might see the world with a new soul,
   One manifest but still invisible.
This non-existent world looks real to you,
   Only because the real world you can't view.

The dust is carried by the wind, to play   1285
   Illusion tricks and make veils in this way—
That dust in motion is the husk, of course,
   The Hidden One its kernel and its source.
In the Lord's hands the dust is like a tool,
   While wind is lofty, noble, fit to rule;
Mere human eyes see dust alone in front—
   The eyes which see the wind are different.
Each horse knows other horses of its kind;
   Each rider knows what's on a rider's mind.
Your eye's the horse, the rider is God's light—   1290
   Riderless horses are a sorry sight,
So train the horse in the way of perfection
   Or else it will deserve the King's rejection.
By the King's eyes the horse's eyes are led;
   Without His eyes its eyes are filled with dread.
Unless you lead your horse towards some hay,
   It neighs 'No!' and refuses to obey.
Thus God's light must mount sensual light, before
   The soul can yearn to go to God once more:
Riderless horses cannot find the way;   1295
   A king who knows the path they must obey.
Follow your senses when His light's their rider—
   His light controls them then like an insider.
God's light makes earth's light beautiful and bright—
   This is what's meant by *Light on top of light*:*

Earth's light will pull you to the world you see;
   God's light takes you beyond miraculously.
Perceptibles are from a lower sphere:
   God's light's the sea, the senses one small tear—
But you won't see that rider, other than   1300
   Through worthy deeds and righteous speech, good man.

Even mere sensual light is kept from you
   Inside your pupils, where you cannot view.
How will you see that holy man's pure light
   When you can't see the earth's with your poor sight?
That sensual light is hidden from your eyes;
   More hidden is that light beyond the skies.
Like straw which by a heavy wind is blown,
   This world is helpless next to the Unknown:
It spins it high, then brings it back down low,   1305
   Repairs it now, then breaks it like a foe;
Sometimes to left, sometimes to right it's borne;
   It makes a rose-garden, then makes a thorn.
The hand is hidden but the pen can write:
   The horse trots, though the rider's out of sight;
The arrow flies; the bow remains unseen—
   The Soul of Souls no human's ever seen.
Don't break the arrow—from a king it came,
   From one aware; it has a certain aim.
God said, '*When you threw then you did not throw,*'*   1310
   God's acts have precedence, as life will show.
Don't break the arrow but your rage—it's blind,
   If it thinks milk and blood one of a kind;
So kiss the arrow, which you ought to bring
   Moist with your bloodstains to the Glorious King.
What can be seen is feeble, helpless, chained,
   While what's unseen is fierce and unrestrained.
We are the prey—to whom belongs the snare?
   We're polo balls—who is the batting player?
He tears and then He sews, but where is He?   1315
   He blows and burns like fire, but we can't see.

Now He may make a saint an infidel,
   Then turn an atheist to a monk as well.
The seeker is in danger of the snare
   Until he's purged of self, clear as the air;
And on this path fierce brigands lie in wait—
   You'll need God's help to flee from a grim fate.
Not a pure mirror yet, the aspirant
   Has not caught the prized bird at the king's hunt;
Once he completes the path, then he'll be free,   1320
   Safe in a station of security.
No mirror turns to iron in retreat;
   No bread returns to being stacks of wheat;
Ripe grapes don't turn to the disliked sour type—
   Once grapes are ripe, they don't become unripe!
When ripe, far from the realm of change, take flight!
   Like Borhan-e Mohaqqeq* turn to light!
Escape yourself and you'll be proof today;
   A slave becomes a sultan in this way.
For those who wanted to perceive it here,   1325
   Salah* would open eyes and lead them near;
Every eye blessed with God's own light could see
   In this man's face deep mystic poverty.
Like God, the shaikh will teach without a tool;
   Without words his disciples he will school.
Like soft wax in his hands the heart's the same;
   Sometimes his seal brings fame, and sometimes shame.
His seal brings up a seal-ring in my mind;
   Of what then does the bezel's form remind?
The goldsmith's image this sends to my brain,   1330
   Like one more part of a connected chain.
Whose voice has filled the mountain of the heart,
   Which wasn't full but silent at the start?
He is the sage, wherever he may be—
   May his voice fill my heart perpetually!
One mountain *doubles voices*, and I'm told
   Another echoes them a hundredfold.
The mountain gushes at that voice's sound
   A hundred thousand pure springs from the ground;

When grace pours from the mountain like a flood,   1335
    The mountain's water will turn into blood:
For Moses's sake Sinai changed this way,
    With rubies covering it straight away.*
Wisdom and life mere stone came to possess—
    My people, are we humans then worth less?
From our souls no such springs have yet been seen,
    Nor are we, like the angels, dressed in green.*
I still have not heard longing's passionate roar,
    Nor seen a Saqi with pure wine to pour.
Where are the longing men who with an axe   1340
    Can cut through mountains like the softest wax?
Perhaps the moon some beams might radiate
    Which through the mountain might just penetrate?
Each mountain is uprooted from its place
    At Resurrection—who can stop this grace?
This inner resurrection is supreme—
    That one's a wound, this one a soothing cream;*
Whoever's seen this salve will feel no pain:
    Those who see goodness good traits too will gain.
The ugly one near beauty feels so blest,   1345
    But beauty fades if it is Autumn's guest;
When bread becomes life's close associate,
    It gives new life to those who feed on it;
When wood joins fire and then is set alight,
    The darkness disappears and all is bright;
When a dead donkey falls in a salt-mine,*
    It gains new life, no longer asinine.
*The colour of God** is His dyeing vat:
    All things become one-coloured mixed in that.
If you tell one who's fallen in, 'Arise!'   1350
    '*Don't blame me*, I'm the vat itself!' he cries,
Just like that saint who '*I'm the Truth*' once said*—
    He still was iron, but he burned bright red:
The iron's colour is effaced by flames;
    It's silent while the fieriness makes claims—
In colour when it is the same as gold,
    Without a tongue it shouts, 'I'm fire, behold!'

The fire's effect leaves iron glorified:
  'I'm fire, I'm fire!' it now repeats with pride.

I am fire too; if you have any doubt,   1355
  Test me by touching me—you'll soon find out!
I am fire too; does this claim seem untrue?
  Bring your face close to mine and I'll show you!
When Man receives God's light, the angels fall
  To bow to him, God's chosen over all,
As do those who like angels have forced out
  From their souls all rebelliousness and doubt.
What fire? What iron? Shut your mouth now please!
  Don't show off with your clever similes!
Don't dirty now the water with commotion,   1360
  Silence your tongue as you approach the ocean!
It can engulf a hundred men like me,
  But I can't keep away from this vast sea!
For it, my mind and soul I'd sacrifice!
  This mystic sea has paid my soul's blood-price.
I'll swim in it until my legs feel dead,
  And then, like ducks, I'll float on it instead!
Those present, though they may be unrefined,
  Are better off than those who've stayed behind.
Polluted body, go now to the pool!   1365
  You can't be washed outside it, stupid fool!
Even a clean man who should stay away,
  From cleanliness is bound quite soon to stray.
The purity of men's hearts is eternal,
  The purity of bodies just external,
Because the heart's a pool which secretly
  Possesses its own path towards the sea.
Your finite purity needs something more;
  Expenditure reduces what you store.
The water told a dirty man, 'Come here!'   1370
  He said, 'I'm too ashamed to stand so near!'
The water said, 'How will shame leave you then?
  How will you ever be made clean again?'

Such men who hide from water prove it's true
　　That '*shame prevents faith*'—don't let this stop you!
The heart is muddied by the body's pond;
　　The body's cleaned by the heart's pool beyond.
My son, come to the heart's pool, and beware
　　Of steps towards the body's pond down there!
Body and heart's seas clash, their waves are tossed,　　1375
　　But still *a barrier's there which can't be crossed.**
Whether you're straight or crooked, move ahead,
　　Try to run forward, don't crawl back instead!
Though there is danger near the king, don't fear.
　　Those with high aims can't bear not to be near.
The king is sweeter than sweet sugar, so
　　Towards his sweetness souls should want to go.
Fault-finder, stick to safety if you must;
　　If you seek peace you're weak and lack full trust.
My soul's a furnace, happy when it's lit;　　1380
　　To be the fire's home is enough for it.
In love there is such burning—you are not
　　A furnace if you can't feel love that hot!
When yours is dervish poverty's pure breath,
　　You've gained eternal life and have fled death;
When anguish just increases joy in you,
　　Your soul blooms roses and pure lilies too—
What others dread is your security:
　　The duck, unlike the sparrow, loves the sea.

Physician, once more I have turned insane!　　1385
　　Beloved, I am frenzied once again!
How multiform are your chain's rings which bind—
　　Each one gives madness of a different kind.
Each ring's gift is unlike the rest: in me
　　Each breath I feel a new insanity!
This proves the proverb '*madness is diverse*',
　　Especially from this prince who's glorious.
My madness crosses furthest boundaries;
　　Now madmen come to give advice to me!

How friends came to the madhouse for
Zo'l-Nun al-Mesri*

It happened thus to Zo'l-Nun al-Mesri: 1390
   Inside him was such wild insanity.
This frenzy started to intensify;
   It reached beyond all hearts, above the sky.
Mere earthbound men, don't try now to compare
   Your frenzy with that of the pure, beware!
His madness no men could endure to see;
   His fire burned their beards of pomposity.
When flames burned these men's beards, they gathered round
   To take him to the gaol, where he was bound.
There's no way one can pull back love's long rein,   1395
   Though for the path the vulgar show disdain;
Mystics fear vulgar men for they are blind,
   And so these lofty kings are hard to find.
When scoundrels rule, the likes of great Zo'l-Nun
   Will be led to the prison very soon.
The great king rides alone across the lands—
   Can this rare pearl be kept in children's hands?
This pearl's an ocean in a drop, my friend,
   A sun inside an atom, comprehend!
A sun appeared as a mere atom once,   1400
   Perceived just by men with intelligence;
All atoms were effaced in it, and then
   The world got drunk and sobered up again.
When judgment is by traitors, then for sure
   You'll see hang on the gibbet poor Mansur;*
When those in power lack intelligence
   *'They kill the prophets'** is the consequence;
Through folly, to the prophets those astray
   Complained: *'We think you're bad luck*—go away!'
Ignorant Christians seek security   1405
   Still from that lord who was hung cruelly—
That he was crucified by Jews they say,
   So how can he protect them all today?

Pure Jesus's heart bled for them, so how
    Can *'while you're with them'** help the Christians now?
The danger to the goldsmith and pure gold
    From counterfeiting cheats is twentyfold:
Josephs hide from the people's jealousies—
    They'll jump in fires to dodge their enemies;
Josephs are in the well due to deceit—   1410
    His brothers left him for the wolves to eat;
How Joseph suffered from such jealous lies!
    Envy is like a huge wolf in disguise.
For Joseph, Jacob always used to fear,
    Especially when he knew wolves were near—
The outward wolf did not harm his fine son;
    The wolf of jealousy surpassed that one:
This wolf attacked instead in that wolf's place,
    With the excuse: *'We had gone out to race.'**
A thousand wolves don't know such trickery;   1415
    This wolf will be disgraced eventually:
Without a doubt the envious will transform
    On Judgment Day into a vile wolf's form.
All greedy, mean, and carrion-eating men
    Will be forced to take on a pig's form then.
The fornicators' genitals will stink,
    As will the mouths of all who love to drink.
Filth which before was sensed by just a few
    On Judgment Day will be so clear to view.
Man's being is a jungle, so defend   1420
    Against it if you're from beyond, my friend!
Thousands of wolves and swine exist within,
    Good traits and vile ones, pious deeds and sin—
Whichever one is stronger will take hold:
    More gold than copper makes the compound gold.
Behaviour which you now choose as your norm—
    At Resurrection you'll adopt that form:
A wolf may enter in a human's head
    Or radiant Joseph might come in instead.
From breast to breast pass gentleness and spite   1425
    Through a route which is hidden from your sight.

And from a human to a cow and ass
    Virtue and worthy knowledge too can pass:
The wild horse can be trained in how to walk,
    A bear to play, a billy-goat to talk;
For dogs to learn to lead is not that hard:
    They can be taught to herd sheep, hunt, and guard.
The Seven Sleepers' dog* gained their pure light,
    A seeker it became in its own right.
Each moment in the breast new species rise,   1430
    Demons and angels, beasts in every guise.
From that great jungle lions know of best
    There is a way towards the hidden breast,
So steal a pearl the mystics keep within,
    You who are less than a mere dog, dive in!
If you steal pearls, make sure to snatch the best;
    If you bear loads, then pick the loveliest.

The disciples understand that Zo'l-Nun has not gone mad, but has acted that way deliberately

Zo'l-Nun's friends came to see him at his cell,
    Sceptical of reports he was unwell:
'Perhaps this is deliberate from the sage,   1435
    For he's God's sign, the *qebla** of the age?
Far be it from his wisdom like the sea
    That madness should make him act stupidly!
And God forbid this moon, whose rank's so high,
    Should be veiled by the clouds now in the sky!
He's chosen to hide from the public there;
    The loathsome intellectuals he can't bear:
The shallow intellect's vile infamy
    Has led him to go mad deliberately:
"Whip me with a cow's tail now!" he has said.   1440
    "Don't question me! Come, strike my back and head,
So I'll gain life, like that corpse long ago
    Whipped hard with Moses's cow's tail* —each blow
That I receive will leave me feeling thrilled
    Like that man who in this way had been killed."'

That man came back to life miraculously,
  As copper turned to gold through alchemy.
That murdered man sprang up and pointed out
  His gang of killers, so there was no doubt:
'This group killed me,' he then said publicly,   1445
  'And now they're stirring trouble up for me.'
When this material body should fall dead
  A new existence comes alive instead,
Both paradise and hell this spirit sees;
  It knows so clearly all the mysteries;
Who its own killers were it will declare,
  And then display deceit and falsehood's snare.
This path requires the cow's death, so the soul
  Might be revived by its tail—that's the goal.
So kill the cow, your carnal soul! Don't mourn!   1450
  This way your hidden spirit will be born.

Resumption of the story of Zo'l-Nun

When those friends came to see him in the gaol,
  'Hey! Who are you? Beware!' they heard him wail.
They said politely, 'We've come from afar;
  We're friends who want to find out how you are.
How are you, sea of wisdom? Please explain
  The lies that madness has destroyed your brain.
Can smoke rise from the furnace to the sun?
  A phoenix by a crow can't be undone!
Don't hide the truth from us; explain it please!   1455
  We are your lovers and true devotees!
One shouldn't drive away well-meaning lovers,
  Nor dupe them, hiding underneath the covers.
Divulge your secret clearly, lord of grace!
  Bright moon, don't hide behind the clouds your face!
We're lovers with pained hearts, sincere and true;
  In both worlds we have fixed our hearts on you.'
He started first to utter foul abuse,
  Then gibberish as though his tongue was loose;

Next he threw sticks and stones, and they would duck   1460
    And run away, afraid they might be struck.
Zo'l-Nun then laughed aloud and shook his head,
    'Look at the hot air of false friends!' he said.
'What friends! Where is the sign that they're sincere?
    To proper friends such pain is something dear.
How can you flee a friend's pain when he yells?
    Pains are the kernels held in friendship's shells:
Isn't the sign of friendship happiness
    Though you experience pain and deep distress?
A friend is gold while pain is fire—we know   1465
    True gold feels joy inside the flame's red glow.'

How Loqman's master tested Loqman's wisdom

Loqman,* a pure slave, showed this memorably:
    He would serve day and night efficiently,
And was the best slave in his master's view,
    Who valued him more than his children too,
For though Loqman was a low slave by birth,
    He'd mastered lust, and thus increased his worth.
A king once told a shaikh, 'Hey there, good man!
    Ask me to grant you something while you can!'
He said, 'Don't you feel shame, your majesty,   1470
    To talk in such a vulgar way to me?
I have two slaves, both vile and wretched too,
    But these two worthless slaves rule over you!'
The king asked, 'What are they? Don't be unjust!'
    He said, 'The first is rage, the second lust.'
For kingship, real kings do not have concern,
    Since their light shines without need for the sun;
Treasure belongs to those with gold as essence;
    The foe of false existence boasts Existence.*
Loqman's own master was so outwardly,   1475
    But he was Loqman's slave still inwardly—
In this world such things are not a surprise:
    A pearl is less than straw in some men's eyes;

The desert *'place of safety'* some have called—
  By its false looks their brains have been enthralled;
For some, clothes tell of people's worthiness—
  They call men vulgar for the way they dress;
Some fall for false asceticism's show,
  Though light's required its actual worth to know.
Light free from imitation's harm one needs   1480
  To know a man before his actual deeds,
To enter his heart through the intellect,
  Free from all gossip, his worth to detect.
Knowers of the Unseen, God's own elite,
  Are *spies of hearts* whom you can never cheat.
Such men, like thoughts, can enter into you;
  Your secrets are unveiled for them to view.
What does the sparrow have that she should be
  Veiled from the falcon's intellect—tell me!
The secrets of God's essence are revealed   1485
  To them—how can men's secrets stay concealed?
These men can travel quickly through the sky—
  Walking on land's not hard when you can fly.
Iron became like wax in David's hand;*
  What will become of wax? Please understand!

Loqman was just in form a slave, no more;
  Slavery was simply like a badge he wore.
Some masters when they travel somewhere new
  Dress slaves in their own clothes, and they change too
Into their slaves' clothes, so men are misled   1490
  Into believing that a slave's the head.
The master walks behind as good slaves do,
  So no one looking on will have a clue.
'The seat of honour is what you must use!'
  He tells the slave, 'I'll follow with your shoes.
Be harsh and curse me, so none will suspect.
  Towards me from now on don't show respect.
Your duty now is to stop serving me,
  For here I've sown the seed of trickery.'

Like slaves such masters willingly would act,   1495
 So it's believed that they are slaves in fact.
With being powerful masters they've been sated;
 They do such work to be annihilated.
Slaves of desire though are a different kind,
 Although they claim they rule their soul and mind.
From masters come the paths to true effacement,
 From lust's slaves naught but slavery's abasement.
Compared with this world that world that's unseen
 Is topsy-turvy—you've seen what I mean!
His master understood this situation,   1500
 For he'd seen tokens of Loqman's true station.
He learned the secret and felt satisfied;
 To do his own path's duties he then tried.
He would have set him free immediately;
 To please Loqman was his priority.
Loqman desired that nobody discover
 That he was God's brave devotee and lover.
To hide your secrets from foes isn't strange,
 Hiding them from yourself, though, makes a change—
Hide from your own eyes struggles you endure,   1505
 So from the evil eye you'll stay secure;
Surrender now to His reward's great snare,
 Then from yourself steal something, unaware!
To wounded men some opium first they give,
 And then take out the blade so they might live.
One man was torn with pain the hour he died;
 His soul left while he was preoccupied:
Whatever thoughts you give your heart up to,
 That moment something will be snatched from you,
So occupy yourself with what is best   1510
 And then they'll take from you what's ugliest!
Dear prudent one, whatever you achieve,
 Once you feel safe the thief with it will leave.
A trader's goods fall in the stream, so he
 Grabs hold of the best goods immediately—
Since in the water something will be lost
 It's best to save what has a higher cost.

The excellence and wisdom of Loqman become manifest to those who wish to test him

The food for Loqman's* master that they gave
   He would immediately send to his slave,
So that Loqman could taste it first of all,   1515
   He'd then eat what was left, however small.
The master ate what he'd left and felt bliss,
   But threw out what his servant chose to miss,
And, if he ate some, it was not through lust—
   Their special bond was an eternal trust.
They brought a melon as a gift. He said,
   'Please call Loqman, my son, to eat instead!'
He passed a melon slice for him to eat;
   Loqman ate it as though it tasted sweet.
He gave more to him due to what he'd seen   1520
   Of relish in him—he ate seventeen!
With one slice left, the king said, 'That's for me!
   How sweet this melon is I now shall see.
Loqman ate them with obvious delight—
   Everyone here now longs to have a bite!'
Its bitterness burned up his throat: his tongue
   Was blistered by it; pain filled up each lung!
The king was stunned and lost his wits awhile,
   Then said, 'My soul and life, this tastes so vile!
How could you eat such poison and not mind?   1525
   How could you think the host was being kind?
What tolerance and patience I did see!
   Perhaps you feel your life's your enemy?
Why didn't you just leave the poisoned food
   And say, "Excuse me, please, if this seems rude"?'
Loqman said, 'I've now eaten from your hand
   So much that I feel shame. Please understand:
Refusing one thing bitter from you, I
   Thought shameful, kind sage whom I won't defy.
I owe all to your generosity,   1530
   Drowned in your snare and bait as in the sea.

If I complain about one bitter thing,
 Throw dirt on me and make me feel shame's sting!
Delight in your hand which bestows sweet sugar
 Became that melon's bitter taste's remover.'

Through love the bitter turns sweet, as we've told;
 Through love all copper too becomes pure gold;
Through love the goblet's dregs turn clear and pure;
 Through love the pain we feel becomes our cure;
Through love some even can revive the dead;   1535
 Through love the king becomes a slave instead.
This love results from knowledge—so how can
 The throne be taken by a stupid man?
To love, deficient knowledge can't give birth,
 But only to what's lifeless and lacks worth;
By what looks pretty it is easily stirred,
 As though the true beloved's voice is heard—
Deficient knowledge can't discriminate:
 The lightning with the sun it would equate.
The Prophet called deficient men 'cursed' once;   1540
 He meant deficient in intelligence;
The physically deficient gain God's grace,
 Therefore to curse such men is a disgrace.
Much worse than that is weakness in the mind—
 That merits cursing, being left behind.
Perfecting wisdom is achievable;
 Perfecting bodies is impossible.
Each unbeliever's infidelity
 Was due to a weak mind's deficiency;
Physical weaknesses are not the same: 1545
 God sent relief: '*For blind men there's no blame.*'*
Lightning is transient, unreliable;
 You can't tell what lasts from what's temporal.
The lightning laughs—to ask 'At whom?' one might:
 It laughs at those devoted to its light.
Such light is flawed, unlike light which is best,
 That which is far beyond the East and West:

Lightning we know will *take away men's sight*,*
   Eternal light though helps men in their plight.
To ride on foam from waves next to the sea,   1550
   Or read in lightning flashes patchily,
Is failure, for you'll fail to see the end;
   It is to mock your heart and mind, my friend.
The intellect should know what's finally planned;
   It is the self that cannot understand.
Intellect turns to self when devastated
   By self, as if by Saturn it's check-mated.*
Even misfortune you should contemplate—
   Gaze on the one who brought you such a fate.
If you reflect on the tide's ebb and flow,   1555
   You'll see how good luck often follows woe.
To different states He keeps on moving you,
   In this way opposites to bring to view:
Your deep dread of *the left side* will display
   *Hope for the right side** on the Final Day;
In this way, you'll have two wings—who'd deny
   That with one wing alone no bird can fly?

Either let me keep quiet, or instead
   Command me to complete what I have said!
If You want neither it is up to You;   1560
   About what You intend we have no clue!
Abraham's soul one needs, to gain the light
   Which can, through flames, bring heaven to one's sight,
And to climb rung by rung up to the sun,
   And not be stuck in this dominion.
Traverse the seventh heaven like God's Friend;*
   Say: '*I don't love the ones that set'* —ascend!
This carnal world we live in leads astray
   All men except those who resist lust's sway.

*Conclusion of the story about the jealousy of the king's
entourage for the special slave*

The tale about the king's slave whom some eyes   1565
   In court watched jealously, since he was wise,
Was left unfinished due to my digression—
   We must return to it for one last session.
The kingdom's blessed gardener can see
   The differences between each single tree:
The tree that will be bitter to the core
   And that tree which is worth a hundred more
He won't judge equals when each one first grows,
   Since each one's outcome he already knows,
That different fruit they'll bear eventually,   1570
   Though now they're similar superficially.
The shaikh who *sees by God's Light** is aware
   Of both the start and ending of this pair—
He shuts his eyes to this world for the Friend,
   Preferring that eye which perceives the end.
Those jealous men were like bad trees, which are
   Bitter and ruled by an unlucky star.
They boiled and their mouths foamed in jealousy.
   In secret they made a conspiracy,
For they wished to behead that slave and tear   1575
   His roots up from this world just like his hair.
His soul's the king's soul too—how could he die?
   The Lord protects his roots from those who'd try.
The king learnt of their thoughts and secret plot,
   But, like Bu Bakr Robabi,* he said naught.
He viewed the hearts of those who schemed with lies,
   But simply would applaud before their eyes:
Some devious people tricky traps prepare
   To make a king get caught inside their snare—
A mighty king who's limitless in grace   1580
   Can't be ensnared, you asses! Know your place!
To trap this king they knitted still a net;
   From him they'd learned this skill—such fools forget:

The pupil who begins a rivalry
   With his own master wretched luck will see.
With which one? With the whole world's master, who
   Both clear and hidden realms can easily view;
He sees *by God's light** all things clear as day;
   He's torn the veils of ignorance away.
The pupil's heart has holes like rugs that age,   1585
   And yet he puts a veil before that sage—
His own veil laughs at him and what he's done;
   Its mouth's a window for that glorious one.
The master tells the pupil angrily:
   'Than dogs you seem to have less loyalty!
You don't think I'm a master of that kind
   Whose rule is strong—you think, like you, I'm blind.
Haven't I nurtured both your brain and heart?
   Water won't reach you, if you choose to part.
My heart's the workshop for your fortune, son—   1590
   Would you destroy this workshop, wretched one?'
You boast you'll lead him to your fire to burn,
   But, through the window to your heart, he'll learn,
For through this window he can read your mind—
   Your heart reveals all to men of this kind.
Suppose he simply smiles and won't react,
   Because he's generous and knows how to act;
It's not your flattery that makes him smile,
   But due to your thoughts he reads all the while—
With falsehood thus his falsehood you have won: 1595
   Deal a small blow, be dealt a massive one!
If he'd smiled in approval, judged you true,
   A thousand flowers would have bloomed in you,
For when his heart approves things, then the sun
   Will enter Aries and lift everyone—
This makes the spring smile and the weather fine;
   Blossoms and meadows at this time combine,
A thousand doves and nightingales cry out
   The songs this world has had to do without.
Your spirit yellows like the leaves with age,   1600
   So how can you not sense the ruler's rage?

The king's sun in reproach's zodiac,
　　Like print in books, with shame makes faces black:
Mercury's pen* on our souls' leaves will write;
　　Each page is balanced thus with black and white,
But he'll write orders soon in green and red,
　　So that our souls flee weakness, fear and dread—
Green and red are spring's abrogating power;
　　They're like the rainbow, lovely as a flower.

How reverence for Solomon's message was reflected in the heart of Belqis, the Queen of Sheba,* by means of the wretched form of the hoopoe

May Belqis, Queen of Sheba, now be blest!　　　　　1605
　　A thousand intellects this queen possessed!
From Solomon a hoopoe brought a message,
　　A sealed note with inside it a key passage;
She read those pithy words which were so wise,
　　Chose then the messenger not to despise:
She'd seen a hoopoe form with phoenix soul,
　　Her eyes saw foam, her heart seas as a whole.
The intellect for this cause fights our senses;
　　The Prophet fought his foes for such offences:
They judged him just a human far too soon,　　　　1610
　　Not having seen the Prophet *split the moon.**
Throw dust now on your outward eye's false vision,
　　The foe of intellect and true religion!
God called the outward eye blind, mean, and low,
　　A worshipper of idols and our foe;
It sees the foam but not the waves behind,
　　Today but not tomorrow—thus it's blind.
Although Time's Master is in front of it,
　　It cannot see His treasure, not one bit!
One word from that Sun if an atom gave,　　　　　1615
　　Our sun would long to be that atom's slave;
One drop sent from the Sea of Unity
　　Bewitched our seven seas eternally;

A handful of mere earth, at His dictate,
   Was sent to make the heavens fall prostrate;
Adam was made God's deputy; then came
   The angels bowing to his earthly frame.
The heavens were all torn apart * —but why?
   An earthling opened up a mystic eye.
Like wine dregs, clay in water will descend,   1620
   So how can clay beyond God's throne ascend?
It won't receive from water such a lift,
   But from the Bounteous Source it gains this gift.
He can make air and fire sink to the ground
   And thorns surpass the finest roses found—
We know that *God does what He wills*;* He reigns;
   He can form cures out of the source of pains!
If air and fire He should one day throw down,
   And turn to dregs, which are thick and dark brown,
Then raise up earth and water very high,   1625
   And make the path above one men can try,
'*You raise up whom You will*'* will be made clear.
   He told an earthling, 'With wings fly up here!'
And He told fire, 'Turn into Satan! Go,
   Deceive men in the basest realm below!'
So, earthly man, transcend the stars. Soar high!
   Make fiery Satan in the dirt now lie!
'I'm not like the four natures and first cause;*
   I'm constant and control without a pause.
Without a reason, My deeds are correct;   1630
   They're predetermined—use your intellect!
I'm free to change, whenever, what I do,
   And, when I choose, I'll put to shame some too!
"Become filled up with fire!" I tell the sea,
   To fire "Turn to a rosebush!" I decree,
I tell the mountain, "Be as soft as wool!"
   I tell the sky, "Come down! It's possible!"
And I command the sun, "Join with the moon!"
   Then I'll change them to black clouds very soon.
I make the sun's fount turn as dry as flour   1635
   And change blood into musk through My great power.'

The sun and moon like two black clouds—no joke!
God next will place upon their necks a yoke.

A philosopher rejects the Qur'anic verse 'If your water should have seeped into the ground . . .'*

A man read from the Holy Book one day:
'*If water seeps in soil* * I've blocked its way:
The water in the soil's depths I will hide
    And make the spring like deserts I have dried—
Who can bring water to the fount but Me?
    I have no peer in grace and majesty.'
Then a philosopher with education   1640
    Passed by in earshot of this recitation,
And when he heard this man recite, he said:
    'We are the ones who dig it up instead!
With spades and axes, wells by men are found,
    Who raise the water up then from the ground.'
That night he dreamt a lion-like man came
    And punched him—blinding him was this man's aim—
Then said, 'From these light-fount eyes guiding you
    Dig up some light if what you say is true!'
He jumped up to confirm what he had feared—   1645
    His eyes were blind; their light had disappeared!
If only he had begged then for forgiveness,
    That light would have returned, for God is generous;
Seeking forgiveness isn't in our hands:
    Not every drunk sips this, nor understands.
His actions and denial blocked the way
    From his heart to repentance straight away;
His heart became then just as hard as stone—
    In stone, repentance's seed can't be sown.

Where can Sho'ayb* and his true prayer be found   1650
    To turn a mountain now to fertile ground?

Abraham's firm faith made him capable
  Of following what seemed impossible;
A Copt once begged the Prophet for his aid—
  Stony ground into fertile land he made.
In contrast, though, an infidel's rejection
  Turned gold to copper, peace to war's dejection—
It caused an ugly change thus on its own,
  Turned cultivable land to barren stone.
Not every heart's allowed to fall prostrate;   1655
  Grace won't reach all who eagerly await.
Beware then, don't do things that are depraved,
  Thinking, 'I will repent and thus be saved'!
Water and heat are needed for contrition;
  Thick clouds and lightning are a precondition:
To ripen, fruit needs water and much light;
  With clouds and lightning they will turn out right.
Without tears and bright lightning in your heart,
  How shall you put out anger's flames which dart?
How shall the meadow of His union grow?   1660
  How shall pure fountain springs be made to flow?
How shall a flowerbed tell grass what it feels?
  Or violets with jasmine trees make deals?
Or plane trees open up their palms to pray?
  Or other trees, like drunkards, lean and sway?
And how shall blossom shake off from its sleeve
  Its wealth, unless it does so by God's leave?
How shall a blood-red tulip shine so bright?
  A rose take gold from its purse that's sealed tight?
And how shall nightingales smell roses too?   1665
  Or doves, like men who search, cry out 'Koo koo!'*
How shall the stork call 'Lak lak!' friend of mine?
  What does that mean? 'The Kingdom, God, is Thine.'*
The secrets in its mind how shall earth show?
  Without the sky how shall the orchard grow?
From where were all these marvellous garments sent?
  From the Most Noble and Beneficent.
All of those marvels witness special men
  Who've soared to Him and then returned again.

They've seen the King, Whose signs delight them too,   1670
  While those who've never seen Him have no clue.
The mystic's spirit at *Alast** could see
  His Lord, and so it felt drunk instantly!
He has drunk wine, so he detects its smell;
  If he had not, would he know how to tell?
Wisdom's our camel, though it be a stray,*
  And, like a guide, to kings it shows the way.
You dream of someone with a lovely face
  Who gives this promise of a sign of grace:
'Once you see this sign, your wish will come true: 1675
  A man tomorrow will come up to you;
He will be riding at a steady pace,
  Then, once he reaches you, you'll both embrace.
Another sign is that this man will smile
  When near you, with his arms crossed all the while.
On the next day you must not share the news
  With anyone, or all I've told you'll lose.'
God ordered Zechariah: 'For three days
  You mustn't speak—this is a crucial phase!
Keep silent for three days and nights, and then   1680
  John will be born, a star among the men.
Don't breathe a word in these days to a soul,
  For silence is required to reach the goal—
Don't speak at all about this sign, beware!
  Retain it in your heart and hide it there!'*
You'll then be told of other signs in store—
  They're nothing though, as he has hundreds more:
'These are the signs designed to let you know
  That rank and power you crave God will bestow:
You will soon weep all night with sleeplessness,   1685
  And then at dawn you'll burn with neediness.
Your day will have turned dark without Him here;
  So thin your neck will then start to appear.
You will have given what you own away,
  Like those who gamble all just to obey.
You'll have forsaken both your health and sleep;
  Thin like a hair, your head too you won't keep.

For long, like incense, in flames you'll have stayed,
  And, like a helmet, bowed before the blade!'
A million acts of helplessness and need   1690
  Belong to those whose hearts forever bleed.

The morning after having had this dream,
  Through hope, triumphant your next day will seem.
You'll keep on looking to your left and right,
  Thinking: 'Where is that token from last night?'
You'll tremble like a leaf and say 'Alas,
  If I don't find it and this day should pass!'
You'll search each nook and cranny, everywhere,
  Like one who's lost a calf and feels despair.
Men will ask you, 'Why run thus to and fro?   1695
  Who is it that you've lost? How long ago?'
You'll answer, 'All is well, but nobody
  Will hear about the brilliant news from me;
If I tell you, my sign will pass me by—
  If that should vanish, then I'd rather die!'
You'll look in every rider's face, and they
  Will shout, 'Don't stare, you mad fool! Look away!'
You'll say, 'I've lost a friend, distinguished men,
  And now I aim to find that man again.
May your most noble fortune last forever!   1700
  Please pardon now and pity this poor lover!'
When you search hard it's not of no avail—
  Tradition says: 'Endeavour does not fail.'

Then suddenly a rider will appear.
  This holy man will hold you very near,
Making you lose your wits and every sense.
  The ignorant will say, 'It's mere pretence!'
What do they know of fervour of this kind?
  To union with Him and its signs they're blind.
The sign is meant for those who recognize—   1705
  How can this sign appear to others' eyes?

Each instance that from Him a sign's arrived
    The viewer's soul has always been revived,
Like thirsty fish when water is provided:
    '*These are the Book's signs*,'* by which we are guided.
The signs appearing as a prophet's share
    Are meant for just the souls which are aware.

This talk remains short of stability—
    Forgive me for my wild insanity!
How can one count all atoms? It's in vain,   1710
    Especially when love has snatched your brain.
The leaves inside the park shall I then count?
    Or calculate to what bird squawks amount?
This can't be counted, but I'll do my best
    To guide those who must undergo this test.
Jupiter's good luck, Saturn's bad luck; none
    Can calculate their power—it can't be done.
Yet aspects of these two one can explain,
    Such as how they can make men lose or gain,
So that a clue about the Lord's decree   1715
    Is made known to all people equally:
He who has Jupiter as his ascendant
    Will feel much happier and seem resplendent,
But if it's Saturn then one must beware:
    Caution will be required in each affair—
Of Saturn's fire if I don't help him learn
    The poor and helpless wretch is bound to burn.
'*Remember God!*'* He said on catching sight
    Of us immersed in flames—He sent His light.
'Though I transcend your *zekr** and piety,   1720
    And images aren't suitable for Me,
Still, when you're drunk on fancies in your mind,
    It shows your need for aids of such a kind.'
Outward remembrance is inadequate;
    Royal descriptions are too high for it—
'He's not a weaver!' one man might declare;
    About his King is he then unaware?

Moses condemns the prayer of a shepherd

Once Moses overheard a shepherd pray:
    'O God! O God!' he heard this shepherd say.
'Where do you live that I might serve you there?   1725
    I'd mend your battered shoes and comb your hair,
And wash your clothes, and kill the lice and fleas,
    And serve you milk to sip from when you please;
I'd kiss your little hand, and rub your feet,
    And sweep your bedroom clean and keep it neat;
I'd sacrifice my herd of goats for you—
    This loud commotion proves my love is true.'
He carried on in this deluded way,
    So Moses asked, 'What's that I hear you say?'
'I speak to my Creator there on high,   1730
    The One who also made the earth and sky.'
Moses replied, 'You've truly lost your way;
    You've given up the faith and gone astray.
It's gibberish and babble, stupid twit;
    You'd better learn to put a cork in it!
Your blasphemy pollutes the atmosphere
    And tears to shreds that silk of faith so sheer.
While socks and shoes might be superb for you,
    How can they fit the sun? Have you a clue?
If you don't shut your mouth immediately,   1735
    A fire will burn up all humanity!
You don't believe? Then please explain this smoke,
    And why your soul turned black when you just spoke.
If you're aware that He is God, our Lord,
    Why act familiar when that is abhorred?
Such stupid friendship's truly enmity;
    The Lord's above such acts of piety.
For relatives reserve your generous deeds—
    God has no body, nor material needs:
Milk is for creatures who must drink and eat;   1740
    Shoes are for those who have a need for feet.

Even when you address his chosen slave
   Select your words with care, don't misbehave,
Since God has said, "I'm he and he is I;
   When I was ill you never once stopped by:*
He wasn't left alone with his disease,
   That servant who *through me both hears and sees*."*
Don't talk to saints without the reverence due!
   It blocks your heart, and blots your record too.
If you address a man by Fatema's* name,   1745
   Though man and woman are inside the same,
He'll still seek vengeance for it if he can,
   Even if he's a calm and patient man—
That glorious name which women all revere
   Can wound a man more deeply than a spear.
While hands and feet are great for you and me,
   They'd just contaminate God's purity—
He was not born, nor does the Lord beget,*
   But reproducing beings are in his debt.
Those with a body were once born, and must   1750
   Remain until death in this realm of dust;
That is because we wither and decay;
   Unlike our Maker we must fade away.'
The shepherd said, 'Your words have struck me dumb.
   Regret now burns my soul, and I feel numb.'
He breathed a heavy sigh and ripped his cloak,
   Then in the desert disappeared like smoke.

God rebukes Moses for what he said to the shepherd

A revelation came down instantly:
   'You have just turned a slave away from me!
Was not to lead to union why you came?   1755
   Is causing separation now your aim?
As far as possible don't separate—
   Above all else divorce is what I hate.*
I've given each one his own special ways
   And his unique expressions when he prays;

What he thinks virtuous you deem scandalous:
    This person's meat to you seems poisonous.
I stand immune to all impurity;
    Men's pride and cunning never bother me.
I don't command for my own benefit,   1760
    But so my slaves themselves can gain from it.
For Indians their own dialect sounds best,
    But folk from Sind think theirs the loveliest.
I'm not made any purer by their praise;
    They gain in eloquence and godly ways.
And I pay no attention to their speech,
    But their intentions and the heights they reach—
I know when men's hearts have humility,
    Even if they should speak too haughtily.'

The heart's the essence, words are mere effects: 1765
    The heart's what matters, hot air He rejects.
I'm tired of fancy terms and metaphors;
    I want a soul which burns so much it roars!
It's time to light one's heart with pure desire,
    Burn thought and its expression with this fire!
How far apart the meek and well-behaved
    From ardent lovers, who may seem depraved.
Each moment lovers burn themselves away:
    A ruined village has no tithes to pay.
Don't pick at faults and call him a disgrace,   1770
    Don't wash the blood upon the martyr's face!
It suits a martyr better that he bleeds,
    And that's worth more than countless pious deeds.
Men in the Kaaba end the *qebla** rule—
    What use are boots when swimming in a pool?
You don't seek guidance from those drunken men,
    So why insist they mend their rags again?
God's lovers stand beyond all faiths, as they
    Are shown by God Himself a higher way.
A gem which lacks a seal remains a gem;   1775
    Though sorrows rain down, love's not changed by them.

A revelation comes to Moses, excusing the shepherd

Then in the depths of Moses God concealed
    Such secrets that can never be revealed;
Into his heart poured words, pure and refined,
    Transparent just like speech and sight combined. -
He lost his wits and then found them anew,
    From pre- to post-eternity he flew.
If I describe this it will be in vain;
    What lies beyond words how can I explain?
This mystery would smash your brain to bits;   1780
    When writing it the firmest stylus splits.

Once Moses had heard God's reproach, he ran
    Towards the desert, searching for that man;
He followed footprints that the shepherd laid,
    Scattering dust throughout the track he'd made.
Footprints of drunkards are a special kind,
    Distinct from those the sober leave behind:
He starts just like a rook, steps straight ahead,
    Then bishop-like diagonally instead,
Sometimes just like a wave's crest rising high   1785
    And then as if a fish has slithered by;
Occasionally he'd write his thoughts in sand
    Like fortune-tellers reading what is planned.
On reaching the poor shepherd finally,
    Moses announced, 'I bring you God's decree:
Don't bother with good manners any more,
    But let your heart express what's in its core!
Your unbelief is faith, your faith God's light;
    The world through you is also safe and bright.
Absolved by God, *Who does what He should will,**   1790
    Speak out, and don't be scared I blame you still!'
He said, 'I passed that stage right at the start;
    I'm drenched in blood now from my love-torn heart!
I've passed *that lote tree found at heaven's end;**
    A thousand spheres beyond, I still ascend.

You cracked the whip, which made my stallion vault
    Above the heavens with a somersault!
May God stay close to human beings like me,
    And may He bless your hand eternally!*
With words my current state can't be expressed;   1795
    What I have said give just a hint at best.'
The image in the mirror which you see
    Is yours and not the mirror's obviously;
The breath inside the reed its player's blown
    Is not the reed's but the reed-player's own.
Whenever you should praise God, be aware
    It's like this shepherd's crazy-sounding prayer:
Though yours seems better and more accurate,
    Still, for the Lord, they're both inadequate;
So when the veil is lifted don't protest: 1800
    'What's now revealed we never could have guessed.'

Through kindness he hears *zekr** you dedicate
    And women's prayers though they still menstruate:*
Blood makes her prayer impure, likewise in you
    Your doubts and questioning pollute prayers too;
Polluting blood is washed away with ease;
    Within you there are worse impurities,
Which, if you lack His water of pure grace,
    Will not be rubbed off from your inner face.
When you're prostrate, if only your attention   1805
    Were on the meaning of the prayers you mention.
Say, 'Just like my existence, it's worth naught;
    You give good things for bad things I have brought!'
Earth has the mark of God's great clemency:
    With dung it raises flowers seasonally.
Thus it will hide our filthy, smelly shit
    And, in return, buds start to grow from it.
An infidel saw that he was behind
    Mere soil in giving help and being kind:
From his existence flowers didn't grow,   1810
    And so to pure things he became a foe.

He said: 'I'm going backwards as days pass;
   If only I'd remained mere dust! Alas!*
If only I'd not chosen then from clay
   To change, I would still nurture seeds today!
While travelling it, my journey much has taught,
   But on returning I have brought back naught.'
His inclination was towards the earth,
   So in the journey he saw little worth.
Turning away is lust and greediness,   1815
   Turning to Him is truthful neediness.
Each plant which longs to reach above soon grows
   And flourishes with life that God bestows,
But those that bend towards the ground will be
   Sapped of their strength and wither rapidly:
If your soul longs to soar up through the sky,
   You will gain much and soon return on high,
But if your head points downwards, don't forget:
   You'll sink, and God loves not *the ones that set!**

Moses asks God about the mystery behind why oppressors prevail

Moses said, 'Generous God, remembering You   1820
   For one breath earns a life that's long and true!
In humans I've seen such deformities;
   Like angels, I've complained of forms like these,*
Saying: "Why make such forms in which to sow
   Seeds of corruption? I demand to know!
Why light the fire of tyranny and sin
   And burn things down, like mosques and those within?"
Their tears and blood are made to flow this way
   In order that they humbly beg and pray.
There's wisdom, I believe, to each decision,   1825
   But I seek certainty which comes with vision—
"Keep silent now!" my faith demands of me,
   While my desire screams, "Seek it fervently!"

Your secret to the angels You've made known,
  That honey can be worth the sting You've shown,
And Adam's light to them You made appear,
  Difficulties to them You thus made clear.'

Death's secret Resurrection Day* displays:
  The secret of the leaf its fruit conveys;
What blood and sperm make is soon known to all—   1830
  Thus great things are produced by what seems small.
The students wipe their tablets clean before
  They scribble on those tablets words once more;
He turns the heart to blood and tears, and then
  Writes all the secrets on it with His pen—
So when you wash this tablet, realize
  It will become a book before your eyes.
To make sure new foundations will be sound
  One first digs up the old ones in the ground,
And everyone must dig up mud at first   1835
  That *gushing waters** might then quench their thirst.
As it is healed a child weeps bitterly,
  Ignorant of the treatment's mystery,
While men pay healers gold that they've collected
  And welcome then the needle that's injected.
Towards the heavy case the porters run
  Before the others can pick up that one;
Over this case the porters even fight,
  As do the ones competing for Truth's light.
Huge burdens are the prelude to repose: 1840
  Bitter things lead to bounties He bestows—
Heaven's reached through things you dislike; hell's fires
  *Await those men who follow their desires.**
Your lust is a fresh, healthy branch today—
  Burn it with love and reach Kawsar* this way!
Whoever's suffering in a prison must
  Have earned this fate because of greed and lust;
Whoever lives in castles like a lord
  Through suffering hardship has earned his reward;

And those with too much gold for men to count   1845
 Must have been patient to save that amount.
With true sight one can disregard causation,
 But you must heed it till you reach that station!
With souls beyond this natural world's domain,
 Such mystics can break through causation's chain;
They see that prophets' miracles are free
 From earthly causes and dependency.
Physicians are required to heal the sick;
 An oil-lamp is dependent on its wick,
So for your lamp you change the wick each night—   1850
 The sun does not need wicks, though, to shine bright.
Your ceiling must be plastered, but the sky
 Does not need plastering, so don't you try!
Ah, Our Beloved soothed our aching hearts,
 But the retreat must end as daytime starts;
The moon's face only in the night is shown—
 You'll find Him through a burning heart alone.
Forsaking Jesus for your ass, you'll stray
 And like a donkey you'll be forced away.
In Jesus is the knowledge that's divine,   1855
 Not donkeys, you who are so asinine!
You hear the donkey and feel motherly;
 It orders asinine ways stubbornly—
Feel sympathy for Jesus, fool, instead!
 Don't let your bestial nature rule your head.
Just let that sensual nature weep all day,
 So, by this means, your soul's debt you can pay.
You have obeyed that ass for years; you gave
 Your life to walk behind it as its slave.
Your sensual, carnal soul—*put it behind.**   1860
 It must stay last while first comes the pure mind.
Just like an ass is your base intellect:
 It only thinks of straw it can collect.
Jesus's donkey gained a heart as prize,
 A station next to those who are most wise;
The self's ass weakened—wisdom thus could win:
 A heavy rider makes the ass grow thin.

But if your wisdom weakens, then that donkey
   Becomes a dragon, making you its monkey.
If life with Jesus makes your heart feel pain,   1865
   He'll give you health soon, so with him remain!

O Jesus, you have suffered for God's sake
   Because no treasure is without its snake.
Jesus, how are you coping with deniers?
   Joseph, how are you with those jealous liars?
For stupid men's sake, you bear endless strife,
   So selflessly you can replenish life.
With those sick, useless ones how do you live?
   Apart from headaches, what can such trials give?
You're radiant like the morning sun, while we   1870
   Fill our time with fraud and hypocrisy!
You're honey while we're vinegar; these two
   When mixed together form a healing brew.
We've added too much vinegar, please pour
   More honey in—don't hold back any more!
This type of action's frequent from our kind:
   Too much sand in the eye makes one turn blind.
From you the act that would be typical
   Is granting wretches something valuable.
Your heart was roasting in the tyrant's flame,   1875
   Yet '*Guide my people!*'* was what you'd exclaim.
Since you are incense, if they make you burn,
   To a sweet-scented realm this world will turn.
You're not that incense flames diminish, and
   You're not a soul trapped by depression's hand.
The source of incense can't be set alight;
   How can the wind put out your holy light?
From you the heavens gain their purity;
   Your wrath tastes sweeter than your grace to me.
Unkindness from a sage is better than   1880
   The kindness coming from a stupid man:
'Enmity born of his intelligence
   Is worth more than love due to ignorance.'*

How a prince troubled a sleeping man into whose mouth a snake had entered

A wise prince saw a snake begin to slide
    Into a man's mouth, which was open wide;
On seeing this he didn't hesitate
    To hurry there, but he arrived too late.
Not only wise, he liked to help all men—
    He hit the sleeping man awake again.
This made the man run off in dread and fear,   1885
    To hide beneath a fruit tree which was near.
A lot of rotten apples from that tree
    Had fallen off—the prince said, 'Eat! They're free.'
So many apples then he gave to him
    That they spilled out, his throat full to the brim.
'Prince, why come after me? What did I do?
    Was there a time when I had bothered you?
If you've a problem with me, raise your sword—
    Kill me immediately, my noble lord!
What bad luck to have now come to your view!   1890
    Happy are those who don't set eyes on you!
When no misdeed or crime has been committed,
    No one believes such cruelty is permitted.
With words blood gushes from my mouth as well—
    God give what he deserves: send him to hell!'
He kept on cursing him, while that wise one
    Continued beating him and shouting: 'Run!'
The blows made him run at a rapid pace
    And so he'd keep on falling on his face.
He felt weak, stuffed with food, and sleepy too;   1895
    His face and feet became soon black and blue.
The prince on horseback drove him on so fast
    By evening this man vomited at last:
Out of him came both good and rotten food
    As well as that snake which had dared intrude!

On seeing that a snake came out, he ran
   And fell prostrate before the helpful man;
Once he had seen that vicious, ugly snake,
   His pains subsided—gone was every ache!
He said, 'Are you the Angel Gabriel?   1900
   Or God Himself? You are so merciful!
Blessed the moment I came in your view;
   I then was dead—now I've gained life anew.
Just like a mother you came after me,
   And, like an ass, from you I tried to flee.
A mule flees its own master—what a fool!
   Due to his kindness, he pursues that mule;
Not due to thought of loss or benefit,
   But lest the hungry wolf should ravish it.
Happy the men who get to see your face   1905
   Or suddenly arrive near to your place!
The purest souls will sing aloud your praise;
   My previous prattle could I but erase!
O lord and king, O eminent emir,
   Ignorance spoke, not me—don't be severe!
If I'd got wind of this and found a clue,
   I wouldn't then have said such things to you.
I would have sung your praises constantly,
   If you had given just one hint to me;
But you stayed silent, frightening me instead—   1910
   Without a word you pounded on my head.
My head became so giddy, filled with pain;
   To start with it had just a little brain!
Forgive me please, you handsome, virtuous man!
   Forget my gibberish please if you can!'

'If I had given hints,' the prince then said,
   'Your bravery would have dissolved through dread.
If I had told you all about the snake,
   Sheer terror would have made your spirit quake.
The Prophet said, "If I should let you know   1915
   That in your soul you have a wicked foe,

Gall-bladders of the bravest would then burst
    And none would move or act, as if they're cursed."
Its helplessness no man's heart then would bear,
    His body wouldn't have the strength for prayer;
Like mice before a cat each man would die,
    Or lambs who see a huge wolf passing by;
No plan of action would for him remain—
    That's why I helped but chose not to explain.
Just like Robabi,* silently I smile;   1920
    Iron I bend like David all the while,*
Because my hand can do unheard of things,
    Such as provide for wounded birds new wings.
"*God's hand is over their hands*"* is well known:
    God thus declares our hands are like His own.
A very long hand He let me acquire
    Which stretches past the heavens, and much higher;
My hand displayed its skills once to the sky—
    *The moon was split** when these skills caught its eye!
My silence was because of your weak brain: 1925
    God's power to weak men one can't explain.
Lift up your head from slumber, comprehend:
    God knows what is the best course in the end.
The strength to eat enough you'd not have found
    To make you spew it all out on the ground.
I carried on; your curses I ignored;
    I prayed in silence, "*Make things easy, Lord!*"
I didn't have permission to tell you,
    But still I had to show you what to do,
And due to inner pain I prayed inside: 1930
    "*They know not, God; my people please still guide!*"'*
That man who'd just escaped from death like this
    Bowed down before him, saying: 'What sheer bliss!
May you gain your reward from God, good man!
    This wretch can't thank you in the way He can.
God will say thanks to you, my chief and guide;
    My small mouth can't contain fit praise inside!'
Hostility from sages is like this:
    Their poison will instead fill you with bliss.

An idiot's friendship, though, leads to perdition,   1935
  As shown to you by this profound tradition:

On putting trust in a bear's fawning and good faith

One day a dragon dragged a bear behind;
  A brave man came to help, for he was kind.
The succour of this world is men like these
  Who heed the shrieks of victims and their pleas;
The cries of victims everywhere they hear
  And, like God's mercy, brave men will rush near.
These props supporting this world's weaknesses,
  These healers who cure hidden sicknesses,
Are justice, mercy, and love that is pure—   1940
  Like God, they can't be bribed or made impure!
Ask one: 'Why do you help immediately?'
  He'll say, 'They're helpless and in agony.'
Lion-like men hunt chances to be kind;
  Pain is the medicine they wish to find:
Wherever pain is, there the cure will go;
  Where hills slope down the water's bound to flow—
Since you need mercy's water, bend down too,
  Get drunk from mercy's wine which flows to you!
Mercy keeps filling up your head with grace;   1945
  Don't sink for one delight to a low place!
Courageous man, ascend now like a dove
  And hear sweet *sama*ʿ* music from above!
Take out the plugs of evil whispering,
  So shouts from heaven in both ears will ring!
Remove the hair which covers now your eye,
  To see the lofty cypresses on high!
Cough up the phlegm that's blocking up your head,
  So God's wind fills your nostrils up instead!
Don't let a trace of bile and fever stay,   1950
  So you'll taste sweetness in this world today!
Don't keep it limp—insert man's remedy
  And make the women climax rapturously!

The fetters on your spirit's feet undo,
  So it can soar up as it used to do!
The shackles on your hands and neck now break—
  New fortune then from heaven you can take.
If you can't reach the Kaaba of His grace,
  Your helplessness before the Lord to place,
Then your recourse is weeping bitterly—   1955
  His mercy is the nurse and remedy.
Nurses and mothers both anticipate
  The babies' cries; to comfort them they wait.
God made your needs like babies', so He'll hear
  When you should weep; then milk He'll make appear.
'*Call upon God!*'* God said—keep weeping, so
  The milk of His kind love will start to flow.
If winds should howl and rainclouds start to pour,
  It's for our grief—be patient a bit more!
God said, '*Find in the sky your daily bread!*'*   1960
  Why cling then to this lowly place instead?
Like a ghoul's voice, your fear and desperation
  Will lure you to the pit of degradation.
The calls which beckon you beyond the sky
  Have come down for your ears' sake from on high,
But every call that beckons you to lust
  Is howling from a wolf you shouldn't trust!
Height here is not a physical dimension—
  The soul's and wisdom's peak is the intention:
Causes are higher than effects, men say,   1965
  Iron and stone than sparks they send away.
Higher than vain men sits the true fakir,
  Though next to them this great man might appear;
Nobility determines who comes first—
  The seat placed furthest from the top's the worst.
Iron and stone in action's course are prior,
  And so it seems that these two should rank higher.
That spark they send out, since it is their aim,
  Must be superior to them all the same:
Iron and stone may come before their goal,   1970
  But they're the body while the spark's the soul.

In sequence even if the spark's posterior,
　　In nature, still it is that pair's superior:
The branch precedes the fruit found on the tree,
　　The fruit's worth so much more though obviously;
Because fruit is the branch's aim, it's true
　　Fruit's first, branch last, although the branch first grew.
When that bear screamed for help, a lionheart
　　Released it, pulling those huge claws apart.
He showed such cleverness and manliness　　　　　　1975
　　To slay that dragon which had caused distress.
The dragon has much strength, but lacks a mind;
　　Above yours too there's a superior kind.
Your own intelligence you see—why then
　　Do you not see its source? Head there again!
What now is low came from above, so turn
　　Your gaze to lofty heights and you will learn
That this gives light with which to truly see
　　After a period of perplexity.
Accustom now your eyes to those light rays—　　　　1980
　　Unless you are a bat, fix there your gaze!
Seeing conclusions proves you've gained that light;
　　Feeding your lusts means that your grave's in sight.
Great men see all potential traps ahead,
　　But fools hear of just one and are misled;
That single trap makes them stray even faster,
　　Proudly each one will even shun his master:
Like Sameri,* who'd learnt one skill with pride
　　From Moses, and then vainly turned aside;
From Moses though he'd learnt his cherished skill,　　1985
　　He closed his eyes to his great teacher still.
Moses then used a new skill suddenly
　　Which stunned and left for dead vile Sameri.

Book-knowledge fills your head seductively;
　　It beckons you and seeks authority—
Don't lose your head! Be like your own foot's sole
　　And then take refuge with the Mystic Pole!*

Though you be kings, don't look down with disdain;
    Though you be honey, seek his sugar-cane.
Your thought's a form, while his thought is the soul.   1990
    Your gold's false; mines belong to this great Pole.
Now seek yourself in him, you're really he—
    Fly to him, coo as doves do constantly!
If you don't want to serve him now with care,
    You're in the dragon's jaws just like a bear.
Perhaps the teacher will deliver you
    And pull you from all harm as he can do.
You have no strength, so weep in fits all day;
    You're blind, so from the guide don't turn away!
Are you less than a bear? Cry when in pain!   1995
    The bear which cried found pain would not remain.
God, melt like wax this stony-hearted man.
    Make his cries sweet and worthy, as You can!

A blind beggar said, 'I have two types of blindness'

There once was a blind man who used to say:
    'I'm blind in two ways; pity me and pray!
Be twice as merciful and twice as kind—
    I'm stuck with this sad fate; I'm doubly blind!'
Someone said, 'One of them we all can see,
    But what's the other blindness meant to be?'
He said, 'My voice is ugly like the bray   2000
    Of donkeys, doubling blindness in this way:
My ugly voice induces so much grief
    It steals all listeners' love just like a thief.
Wherever it is heard it will create
    Much grief and rage, and it makes people hate—
Double your mercy for two blindnesses!
    Make room for one who always trespasses!'
Through his complaint, his voice's ugly sound
    Made people in compassion gather round.
Because he'd owned up, he would soon rejoice—   2005
    His heart's voice gave his tongue a lovely voice.

But if his heart's voice had been bad as well,
  Three blindnesses would have locked him in hell,
Though saints who share God's grace unselfishly
  Could then have touched him as a remedy.
When this man's voice turned soft and sweet, it then
  Could melt like wax the stony hearts of men.
The infidels' cry is an ugly sound—
  It won't find sympathy from those around;
'*Be silent!*'* has an ugly voice in mind,   2010
  That of bloodthirsty dogs among mankind.

The bear's wail draws compassion, different
  From your unpleasant and ignored lament.
With Joseph, like a wolf you have behaved;*
  Innocent blood you drank, for you're depraved!
Empty yourself of what you've drunk—be sick!
  And seal the wounds at which you'd always pick!

Completion of the story of the bear and that fool who
trusted that it would show good faith

When from the danger that bear was set free
  By that kind man who showed much bravery,
Just like the dog of Sleepers in the Cave*   2015
  It then became that man's most faithful slave.
Its master rested, for he'd struggled hard,
  And so the bear served as his bodyguard.
A passer-by asked, 'What has happened here?
  How come the bear treats you as someone dear?'
The dragon story he began to share;
  The passer-by said, 'Never trust a bear!
Friendship with fools is worse than enmity—
  It should be chased away immediately!'
'You speak from jealousy. Heavens above!   2020
  Don't focus on its wildness but its love!'

'Love from a fool is false seduction, friend—
  My "envy" will prove better in the end.
Join me, drive off this bear—leave it behind!
  Don't choose the bear, forsaking your own kind!'
'Mind your own business! I loathe jealousy.'
  'This is my business, but you cannot see.
Good man, I'm not less than a savage bear;
  Be my companion, leave that wild beast there!
My heart now trembles with concern for you—   2025
  Don't walk with such a bear as fools would do!
My heart's not stirred without a cause or aim;
  It is from God's light, not a specious claim:
A true believer, *I see by God's light*—*
  Flee this fire-temple of your sorry plight!'
The things he said had no effect at all;
  Men's ears are blocked by their suspicion's wall.
The good man took his hand; he pulled away:
  'You are no friend of mine! You've gone astray,
So leave at once! Don't show concern for me!   2030
  Meddlesome fool, stop now your sophistry!'
'I'm not your foe,' the passer-by then said,
  'It would be best to come with me instead.'
He snapped back, 'I am sleepy. Let me be!'
  The passer-by said, 'Friend, submit to me,
To sleep in the protection of a sage,
  Safe with a mystic from the wild bear's rage.'
He doubted still this passer-by's intent
  And turned away to show his discontent:
'Perhaps this liar wants to injure me?   2035
  He is a thief or beggar obviously.
Perhaps he made a bet with friends that I
  Would prove an easy man to terrify?'
Not one good thought came to his mind; confusion
  Ruled him because his mind had much pollution.
All positive thoughts he saved for the bear;
  The two belonged together like a pair.
Before a sage a bear he chose to trust—
  This fool thought it affectionate and just.

Moses says to one who worshipped the golden calf:
'What happened to your intelligence and scepticism?'

Moses stopped a deluded man to say: 2040
    'You're cynical because you've gone astray.
About my prophethood you had such doubt
    Though I had strong proof and am good throughout:
Many miraculous feats you saw me do,
    But doubts and fancies just increased in you.
The devil's whispering tricked you, so you would
    Sneer sceptically about my prophethood;
I forced apart the sea's waves perfectly,
    So that from Pharaoh's evil you'd be free.
For years from heaven manna was bestowed   2045
    And, through my prayers, from stone fresh water flowed—
These things and many more just as diverse
    Did not reduce your false doubts—you're perverse!
A golden calf once mooed through sorcery
    And you prayed, "You're my God!" immediately!
Bowing to it succeeded then to sweep
    Your doubts away—your cold brain went to sleep.
Why didn't you doubt all the lies it said?
    Before that object why bow down your head?
Why didn't you suspect its idle claim?   2050
    To trap you with its magic is its aim.
You dogs, who is that liar Sameri
    To carve a god out for humanity?
Why let his lies make you all of one mind,
    Leaving all thought of problems far behind?
Why worship a mere calf when it has lied,
    Although my prophethood you all denied?
You bow to it through sheer inanity;
    Your brain is Sameri's prey tragically.
From God's light you have turned your eyes away,   2055
    Because you're ignorant and far astray—
Your brains be damned, and what you choose to do;
    It is correct to kill vile fools like you!

What did the golden calf say when it spoke?
   The love in your hearts how did it provoke?
Much greater miracles I have displayed;
   By worthless men, though, God is not obeyed.'

Base men are smitten with stupidity,
   As futile men admire futility!
Since each one is beguiled by its own kind,   2060
   A bull and lion playing you won't find.
For Joseph can the wolf feel sympathy
   Unless through cunning, as his enemy?*
If it leaves wolfishness, it's then a friend—
   A dog can be a human in the end.*
When Abu Bakr could identify
   The Prophet, he said, '*This face doesn't lie.*'
Bu Jahl did not feel empathy one bit—
   He turned away although *the moon was split.**
We hid the truth from mystics with love's pain,   2065
   But hidden from them it did not remain.
Those ignorant, who from love's pain are free,
   Were often shown the signs but couldn't see.
One must keep clean the mirror of one's heart
   To tell the lovely and the vile apart.

*The man who gave advice leaves behind the one deluded
   by the bear after counselling him as much as possible*

That passer-by left after that attack;
   '*God give me strength!*' he said and then went back.
'I gave advice and argued—how I tried!
   But vain thoughts in his heart just multiplied.
Blocked is the way of counsel for this man,   2070
   And so "*Withdraw from them!*"* is my sole plan.'
When your cure makes the sick man's brain unsound,
   Find a true seeker and read from '*He frowned*':*

The blind man's come to seek God earnestly—
　　Don't force him off due to his poverty!
You're eager for the notables to turn
　　To Islam, so the rest from them will learn;
Mohammad, you have seen some chiefs tonight,
　　And so you're happy with the thought they might
Become supporters of your new religion, 2075
　　For they rule Arab men and Abyssinian;
To Basra and Tabuk* you hope such news
　　Will spread—*their kings' faith subjects always choose.*
That's why you turned away from one who's blind
　　But rightly guided—this upsets your mind.
'This is a chance that's very rare,' you said,
　　'You can return another day instead,
So why now while I'm busy bother me?
　　This counsel is not due to enmity.'
Mohammad, that blind man is worth much more 2080
　　To God than mighty emperors by the score!
Remember: '*People are like mines*'* —take heed!
　　One mine in worth a thousand may exceed:
One ruby or cornelian mine is worth
　　Much more than all the copper mines on earth.
Mohammad, copper here gives us no gain—
　　A breast is needed full of love and pain.
Don't shut the door! A blind man full of light
　　Has come—give him advice! It is his right.
If a few fools reject you, persevere! 2085
　　Don't be made bitter even if they jeer!
If a few fools should charge you with a crime,
　　God will serve as your witness in good time.
'I don't seek recognition now,' he said,
　　'When God's one's witness one feels no more dread.
If a bat should gain something from a sun
　　That proves the sun's not an authentic one:
The curses of such bats is evidence
　　That I'm the bright sun with true radiance;
To rose-water if beetles ever crawl, 2090
　　That proves it's not true rose-water at all;

If counterfeits for touchstones should cry out,
    That they are proper touchstones we must doubt;
The burglar longs for nights and not for days—
    I'm day not night; I shine with such bright rays.
I am discerning and act like a sieve:
    For chaff, room to pass through me I won't give.
The chaff from wheat I strive to separate,
    The differences between them to relate;
I serve as God's own weighing scales this way;   2095
    The light from heavy I make clear as day.
Calves think that cows are gods—they fantasize!
    For donkeys this is fitting merchandise.
I'm not a cow that calves may call with moos,
    Nor a rough thistle that a camel chews.
My enemy thinks that he's wounded me—
    He's wiped dust from my mirror helpfully!'

How a madman sought to ingratiate himself with Galen, and Galen became afraid*

Galen told his companions, 'Bring for me
    Such and such medicine and remedy!'
'Master of all the sciences,' one said,   2100
    'That's medicine to treat the mad instead—
Far be such drugs from your superior brain!'
    He said, 'I was stared at by one insane:
He gazed at me with joy and wouldn't leave,
    Then tried to flirt and fiddled with my sleeve!
If there were no congeniality,
    How could that wretch then turn his face to me?
He must have seen his own sort in his mind
    To have approached, and not a different kind.'
When a connection's made between a pair,   2105
    There must at least be one thing that they share—
Birds of a feather fly together, while
    Fools dig their graves by sitting with the vile.

The reason why a bird flew and fed with a bird of a different feather

A certain wise man said, 'Once I could see
    A crow content in a stork's company;
Amazed, I sought to find a telling clue
    About what was in common for these two.
I was perplexed, but when near them I came
    I noticed then that both these birds were lame!'
Would a great falcon, one of noble birth,   2110
    Keep company with owls of lowly earth?
The former is a lofty sun, while that
    Vile latter type is like a hell-bound bat.
The former, free from flaws, reflects pure light;
    The latter begs because she's lost her sight;
A moon that shines upon the Pleiades
    Next to a worm in dung beneath the trees;
A Joseph, who is Jesus-like as well,
    Next to a wolf or ass that needs a bell;
To Placelessness* while one has flown away,   2115
    The other like a donkey longs for hay.
A rose tells beetles, with a mystic tongue,
    'Disgusting stench, you smell much worse than dung!
You flee our rosebush proud of your rejection,
    But that's due to our rosebush's perfection:
Since I'm protective, I bang on your head;
    "Wretched one, keep away from us!" I've said,
"If you stay longer in my company,
    People might think that you belong with me."
For nightingales this lovely field is fit,   2120
    But beetles all belong on piles of shit.'
Since God has spared me from contamination,
    Why would He raise filth near my lofty station?
The vein in me like theirs God cut away—
    Evil-veined ones will not reach me today.
The sign of Man from pre-eternity
    Is angels bowing when his rank they see,

And Satan still not bowing down his head—
 'I am the chief and king!' he claimed instead.*
If Satan had bowed down too, then Mankind   2125
 Would have been creatures of a different kind.
Prostration, for the angels, was a trial;
 Man's witnessed also by that foe's denial—
His proof is in the angels' recognition
 And also in that petty cur's sedition.
This discourse could go on, but let's return—
 The ending of this tale we want to learn:

The outcome of the reliance of that deluded man on the bear's fawning

As the man slept, the bear pawed flies away,
 But they would whizz back there without delay;
Repeatedly it pawed them from his face,   2130
 But they kept whizzing back at rapid pace.
The bear grew angry and went off alone
 Towards a hill to fetch a massive stone;
When it returned it saw a small fly leap
 Onto the man's face while he stayed asleep—
It raised the stone and slammed it heavily,
 Hoping to force that pesky fly to flee!
It crushed its sleeping master's head instead,
 Proving the truth of what the wise have said:
'The fool's love is just like love from a bear: 2135
 His hate is love, his love hate, so beware!'
The fool's word is so unreliable;
 Believing him is not advisable.
Never believe him, even if he screams!
 Liars break oaths, and none is what he seems.
This one lies even when he doesn't swear,
 So don't fall for such oaths and lies—beware!
His brain's the prisoner, his self the chief;
 He'll swear on the Qur'an to claim belief.
Don't heed his promises! He doesn't care   2140
 If he should break them—he will easily swear!

Sometimes his ego will become enraged
    That with a serious oath you want it caged:
If prisoners shackle their own ruler, he
    Will break those shackles off immediately,
Then pound them on their skulls which lack a brain,
    And throw the oath at them with much disdain.
Don't wait for him to *honour oaths he swore!**
    Don't tell him, '*Keep your promise!*'* any more.
The one who places in the Lord his trust   2145
    Will cling to Him and shun the realm of dust.

How the Prophet visited a Companion, and an explanation of the benefit of visiting the sick

A notable Companion once was sick
    And looked so thin he seemed more like a stick.
The Prophet came to visit him one day,
    Since kindness was his nature and his way.
There's benefit in visiting sick men—
    The good will soon come back to you again:
The first is that the man who's suffering
    Might be a mystic chief or lofty king—
Lacking the heart's eye, stubborn man, how could   2150
    You tell mere kindling from pure aloes' wood?
There's treasure in this world, so don't despair!
    In every ruin you'll find treasure there.
Approach each dervish who can now be found;
    Find proof he's true, then don't stop circling round!*
Since you can't see beyond a person's skin,
    Assume that all have treasure deep within—
Though not a master, he may seek the light;
    Though not a king, he may still be a knight.
You need a fellow traveller on this course,   2155
    Whether he goes on foot or on a horse.
If he's a foe, good still comes from this act:
    Kindness turned many foes to friends you lacked,

Or it at least made their hate dissipate,
   Because it is a balm which can heal hate.
And there are further benefits, my friend,
   But it would take too long to reach the end.
The gist is: be a friend to everyone,
   Carve friends from stone just like the sculptor's done.
And if they make your caravan grow longer,   2160
   It can fight robbers off when it is stronger.

God spoke to Moses: 'Why didn't you come to visit me in sickness?'

God once told Moses off, 'You who've been blest,
   And even seen the moon rise from your breast;
With my own holy light I made you shine—
   When I was ill where were you, friend of mine?'*
Moses said, 'God, who's free from any flaw,
   What riddle is this? I am filled with awe!'
God asked him then, 'Why didn't you enquire
   About me then, as friendship would require?'
Moses said, 'Lord, You've no deficiency;   2165
   My mind's confused—explain this please to me!'
'A special slave of mine fell ill,' God said,
   'He is I:* understand these words you've read!
His weakness is as if it were my own,
   His sickness too; I don't leave him alone.'
Whoever wants to be near God must sit
   With God's saints—this has the same benefit.
If you're cut off from them, then your starved soul
   Will seem a part kept separate from the whole,
For if the devil keeps you separated   2170
   From such great people, you'll feel alienated.
If you should stay apart a little while,
   I warn you—it's due to the devil's guile!

A gardener divides a Sufi, a jurist, and a Sharif from one other

A gardener one day saw behind the leaves
   Inside his orchard three who looked like thieves:

A saint, a Sayyed,* and a jurist, who
  Each looked a knave and rascal in his view.
The gardener thought, 'I have much evidence,
  But as a group they'll give a strong defence;
Against three men I cannot cope alone—   2175
  I have to split them, trap each on his own.
I'll lead each to a different location,
  Then fool each one when he's in isolation.
To send the Sufi off he used deception,
  Then changed his image in his friends' perception:
He told him, 'Please go to the house and bring
  A rug for these friends, one fit for a king!'
And when the Sufi left, he told the others,
  'Jurist and Sayyed, listen now dear brothers:
From jurists' fatwas, we learn what to eat;   2180
  Their knowledge helps to make our faith complete.
And you're a prince of high nobility,
  A Sayyed, from the Prophet's family.
Who is that Sufi, mean and greedy too,
  To sit beside as lofty kings as you?
Split his head open when he comes this way,
  Then in my orchard as my guests please stay!
What's a mere orchard? I'd die willingly
  For your sakes, for you are so dear to me.'
With sly suggestions he beguiled the pair—   2185
  Don't split so readily from friends, beware!
They'd sent their Sufi friend to fetch a rug;
  Now after him with a stick went this thug.
The brutish gardener asked, 'Did Sufism
  Teach you to enter my land on a whim?
Was this taught by Jonayd or Bayazid?*
  Which one said, "Stroll in; to ask there's no need"?'
He struck the helpless Sufi on the head,
  Splitting it open, and left him for dead.
The Sufi cried, 'My life will quickly end;   2190
  Protect yourselves! Learn from your former friend!
Did you consider me a foreigner?
  I'm less one than this bastard murderer.

What I have drunk, for you two still remains;
    Each base wretch this reward for certain gains.
The world's a mountain and the words you say
    Are echoes which return to you one day.'

After the gardener killed the Sufi, then
    He used a pretext of this kind again:
'Dear Sayyed, please go to the house for me;   2195
    Tell them: "Bring breakfast down immediately!"
Tell Qaymaz when you reach the orchard's gates
    To bring the goose and cakes on silver plates!'
He then said, once he'd sent him on his way,
    'Wise friend, you are a jurist men obey,
But he claims he's a Sayyed for a pose—
    The things his mother did who really knows?
His mother's words will you count as sufficient,
    Trusting a woman—their brains are deficient.
Links with the Prophet and Ali he'll claim—   2200
    This world has many fools who say the same.'
Each person who was born through fornication
    Thinks saints are just the same despite their station:
When whirling gives a man a giddy head,
    He thinks the building is what spins instead.
What that vile gardener said is just the same—
    The Prophet's family are far from blame!
If he were not some sick apostate's child,
    The Prophet's kin he wouldn't have reviled.
The jurist soon agreed with this cruel plan;   2205
    He hurried then to kill the trusting man:
'Ass, to my orchard who invited you?
    Was stealing what the Prophet passed to you?
A lion's cub resembles him, but how
    Are you like the great Prophet—tell me now!'
This wretch who praised the Prophet's family
    Did what a Kharijite did to Ali;*
How long will monsters like Shemr and Yazid*
    Show hatred for his kin in word and deed?

He struck the Sayyed savagely, who said,   2210
   'Jurist, from dangerous waters I have fled.
You're now alone; stand firm; your time has come—
   Endure the body-blows now like a drum!
Even if I were not a Sayyed, still
   I'd be no worse than this beast who would kill.
To this cruel enemy you handed me—
   A dreadful recompense you're bound to see.'

The gardener killed the Sayyed, then returned:
   'What kind of jurist are you? Have you learned
That it should be your fatwa, amputee,*   2215
   To enter and not bother asking me?
Did you find proofs for this in the *Mohit*?
   Is it addressed at length in the *Vasit*?'*
He answered, 'Beat me! You know well the rule:
   Deserting friends earns this fate in our school.'

Resumption of the story of the sick man and the visit of the Prophet

Love's bond demands you visit friends who're ill,
   And it has more demands you must fulfil.
The Prophet soon decided to drop by,
   And saw his follower about to die.
If you stay far from God's elite, you are   2220
   From the Lord's presence also very far.
Parting from your companions brings distress,
   So how can parting from such kings cause less?
Seek the kings' shadows! Hurry up and run!
   Their shadows make you brighter than the sun.
If you should travel, leave with this intention;
   And if you stay home, give this full attention!

A shaikh tells Bayazid, 'I am the Kaaba, so circumambulate me!'

For Mecca Bayazid one day set out
   To make the pilgrimage of the devout.

At every town he passed along the way 2225
    He'd seek what local sages had to say:
He'd wander asking, 'Who here has the light?
    Who only leans on truth's supporting might?'
God said, 'When on your travels always seek
    The few who take from me each word they speak.'
Seek this real treasure, not mere worldly gain;
    This world is secondary; let me explain:
Wholesome wheat is the reason why we sow
    Their seeds, but straw as well from them will grow;
If you were to sow straw, no wheat would rise, 2230
    So seek a holy man—he's the true prize!
Head for the Kaaba when it's time to go
    And you'll see Mecca too, as all must know:
On the *me'raj*, God was the Prophet's aim;
    He saw the Throne and angels all the same.*

A story

A new disciple built a house one day.
    The master passed and saw it on his way,
Then questioned his disciple as a test,
    Knowing that his intentions were the best:
'Why did you put a window over here?' 2235
    'To let the light come in to make things clear.'
'That's secondary; it's not like breathing air—
    Your primary need's to hear the call to prayer!'

While travelling, Bayazid searched far and wide
    To find his epoch's Khezr, the perfect guide.
He came across a master very soon
    Who spoke like saints, though hunched like a new moon;
His heart received light, though his eyes were blind,
    Like elephants seeing India in their mind:
With eyes closed, you see things that cause delight, 2240
    But when they're opened none remain in sight.

While you're asleep the mysteries are all shown;
  Your heart's a window viewing the unknown.
The mystic even dreams while wide awake—
  Bow down and feel the ground beneath him shake!
So Bayazid then asked him, 'How are you?'
  This man was poor and had a family too.
'Well Bayazid, why did you take this road?
  Where is it that you're carrying that load?'
'Complete the Hajj* is what I aim to do.'   2245
  'When you move on what will you take with you?'
'Two hundred silver coins is all I've got;
  I've tied them to this garment with a knot.'
'Just walk around me seven times instead;
  That's better than the Hajj,' the old shaikh said.
'Then hand your coins to me, my generous friend—
  Complete your Hajj thus! Reach your journey's end!
You've run to Safa,* entered purity;
  You've done the Omra;* live eternally!
He judges me much loftier, I swear,   2250
  Than that mere house of His. Let us compare:
That Kaaba is the home of piety,
  But I contain His deepest mystery;
Inside the Kaaba no one's ever stepped
  And my pure heart none but God will accept;
When you have seen me, you have seen God too;
  You'll circle then the Kaaba that's most true.
To serve me is obeying God's decree,
  So don't suppose He's separate from me—
Open your inner eye, see if you can   2255
  Perceive the light of God inside a man!'
This mystic truth pierced into Bayazid
  Just like an earring, making him take heed,
For he had gained much wisdom from this friend,
  Enabling him to reach the journey's end.

How the Prophet perceived that the cause of that man's sickness
was arrogance in prayer

The Prophet saw the man was sick, and gave
   Kind care to his Companion in the Cave.*
On seeing him, that man recuperated,
   As if that moment he had been created.
'Sickness bestowed good fortune thus on me—   2260
   This sultan came to visit generously;
Well-being and good health came when this king
   Without attendants chose relief to bring!'
Thank God for sickness, fever, and distress,
   And for the agony of sleeplessness,
For in my dotage God has sent for me,
   Through His kind mercy, every malady!
Kind God has sent this backache too, so that
   At midnight I will wander like a bat—
So I don't sleep at night like buffaloes,   2265
   Through grace and mercy God such pain bestows!
God's mercy's stirred by my fragility
   And even hell has now stopped threatening me.'

Pain is a treasure—blessings lie within:
   The fruit's flesh shows once you have peeled the skin.
Dear brothers, living in the dark and cold,
   And bearing grief and pain as well, we're told
Is Life's Draught* and the pure intoxication,
   Since all ascents must rise from a low station:
In autumn, spring lies dormant till its turn,   2270
   And autumn does in spring too, you'll soon learn—
So stay with desolation, grief, and strife,
   And, in your own death, hope for a long life!
But when your self says it is rotten here,
   Since it opposes truth, choose not to hear!
Oppose it, as from prophets this instruction
   Has come down to us: fight your own destruction!

Consulting others is a must, my friend,
  So you will not be left shamed in the end:
Prophets knew stratagems that could confound   2275
  All men, and turn the hugest millstones round.
Your self seeks to destroy you, to mislead
  And dazzle simple men, so please take heed!
The people asked, 'Whose counsel do we need?'
  The Prophets said, 'The sages you should heed.'*
'Can a mere woman or a child lead too,'
  One asked, 'When they've no brain or point of view?'
'Still seek out their advice!' the Prophet said,
  'But do the total opposite instead!'*
Worse than a woman is your carnal soul,   2280
  For she is just a part, while it's the whole—
If you consult your carnal soul, then do
  The opposite of what it tells you to!
If it commands to fast and pray a lot,
  It is a trickster hatching a new plot!
Follow your carnal soul's advice this way:
  Do just the opposite! Do not obey!
You can't cope with its clever sophistry,
  And so you need to find good company.
Through other intellects, much strength we gain,   2285
  As sugar is perfected in the cane.
From the self's plots I've seen such shocking actions—
  Its magic steals one's vision through distractions.
It makes you promises from its rich store,
  Which it has broken many times before;
If for a century your life extends,
  Each day it will give new excuses, friends—
False promises it claims are really true;
  It ties up all the power left in you.

Come, Light of God Hosamoddin, I know   2290
  Without you plants in such weak soil won't grow!
From heaven's peak a curtain has been spread
  By curses from a lover whose heart bled.

It's fate alone that can transform this state;
   Brains are made giddy by the power of fate.
The snake can turn into a fiery serpent,
   But on this path it soon becomes subservient—
Serpents become mere sticks and snakes can too,
   The soul of Moses falls down drunk through you!*
'*Grasp it and do not fear!*'* the Lord has said,   2295
   So, in your hand, snakes turn to sticks instead.
King, please show us *your hand which has turned white!*
   Reveal a new dawn from the darkest night!
A hell has blazed forth—won't you breathe a spell,
   For that's more threatening than the sea to hell?
The self's so tricky it shows foam to you,
   Or hellfire to show it can warm things too;
Small to your eyes this foe likes to appear,
   So you might think it's weak and have no fear.
It's like an army which was large in size,   2300
   But still seemed tiny in the Prophet's eyes,
So, fearlessly, he launched a swift attack—
   If he'd known its true size he'd have held back.
That was God's favour—yours deservedly,
   Mohammad, so you'd not be cowardly.*
God made jihads of both kinds* seem so small
   To you and your companions who stand tall,
To make it simpler thus to live *with ease*
   And spare you *hardship** and anxieties.
Their seeming less brought victory that day,   2305
   For God was his friend, teaching him the way.
If you can't boast of God's support like that,
   Don't dare mistake a lion for a cat;
If you mistake a hundred foes for one,
   Deluded, you will fight instead of run.
*Zo'l-Faqar** too may look like a mere stick
   And rampant lions like meek cats; this trick
Will make the fool feel brave and join the brawl,
   This ploy will easily entrap them all—
The fools will journey fast on their own feet   2310
   Towards the fire, ignoring deadly heat.

He'll show what seems a blade of straw one day;
    You'll blow on it, to send it far away—
That blade has pulled up mountains, so beware,
    It makes the world weep while it has no care!
God made the river seem a shallow pool,
    So that the giant Og would drown, the fool!*
Blood flows, but looks like musk on His command;
    The deep sea too can look just like dry land:
Blind Pharaoh thought the sea was dry, and tried   2315
    To walk on it with arrogance and pride:
He stepped into the bottom of the sea,
    For Pharaoh's eyes could not see properly.
Encountering God brings vision to your eyes,
    But God won't meet with fools who fantasize:
Poison which kills looks tasty to this fool—
    He'll take the path which leads straight to the ghoul.

Heavens, you look down on our tribulation;
    Don't spin too quickly, treat well God's creation!
You're a sharp dagger pointing down at us;   2320
    Your murderous blade is long and poisonous.
Heavens, learn from God's mercy for our sakes!
    Don't hurt the harmless ants as well as snakes!
By the truth of that One who made you spin
    Above the realm that we are living in,
So you might change with mercy in your heart
    And choose then not to tear our roots apart!
You nurtured us, for light you would bestow,
    So that from soil and water we might grow.
By the truth of that Monarch who created   2325
    You pure, through whom you've been illuminated,
Who made you flourish and for long endure,
    So some claimed, 'They're eternal! We are sure!'
Prophets revealed your origins, and so
    We thank God they were sent to let us know:
A man knows that a house is really transient,
    But that poor spider hanging in it doesn't;

Gnats cannot know the garden's age: they fly,
 But, born in spring, by winter they will die;
The lowly tree worm has no clue at all   2330
 About how its tree looked when it was small;
If one should know, its essence then is known
 As intellect—a worm in form alone.
Intellect takes on many different guises;
 Distinct from them, it constantly suprises.
Born higher than the angels long ago,
 You're now a gnat descending far below;
Although your intellect could soar the skies,
 Blind imitation will not let you rise.
Knowledge through imitation is Man's bane, 2335
 A borrowed thing they've thought is theirs in vain.
Ignorant knowledge all of us must flee
 And then embrace complete insanity.
Flee now from profit to the furthest end!
 Drink poison not the Water of Life, friend!
View those who praise you as your enemies,
 Give up your wealth and other niceties!
Leave safety, head for danger fearlessly!
 Swap your good record now for infamy!
I've tried to think for too long with my head, 2340
 But now I'll make myself insane instead.

Dalqak excuses himself to the ruler who asked him why he had married a whore

The ruler asked Dalqak,* 'Did you propose
 In haste to that whore? Dalqak, heaven knows,
You should have told me what you planned to do,
 And we'd have found a good, veiled bride for you!'
He said, 'I've married nine like that before.
 All caused me grief, since each became a whore.
I chose this whore, who's not at all devout,
 Because I wondered how she might turn out.
So many times I tried to use my brain, 2345
 But now I'll seek the fruits of being insane!'

How an enquirer managed to trick a clever man
who had feigned madness into talking

A man once said, 'I seek a man who's wise
   To tell a problem, hoping he'll advise.'
'In our town,' he was told, 'your quest's in vain—
   There's only one sage here and he's insane:
He rides a cane as if it were a horse
   And runs with children, showing no remorse.
But he has wisdom which inspires—the sky
   Is not as vast, the twinkling stars as high.
Life to the Cherubim his glory gives;   2350
   Hidden in depths of madness this man lives.'
Don't think all madmen have worth mystically,
   Don't worship calves just like a Sameri!
A real saint has so clearly shown to you
   A million mysteries and secrets too,
But, lacking light, you've still not understood,
   Confusing filthy dung for aloes' wood.
Saints veil themselves with feigned insanity—
   How can the blind tell their identity?
Open the eye which makes things truly known—   2355
   A master you'll then see beneath each stone!
To such an eye, which can serve as a guide,
   Each cloak hides someone Moses-like inside.
It takes a saint to make a saint well-known;
   To whom he pleases he grants this alone;
You can't know who he is just by your brain,
   Because he makes himself appear insane.
When thieves steal something from a man who's blind,
   Can he detect it simply through his mind?
He can't know who they are if he can't see,   2360
   Even if they should taunt him spitefully.
If a dog bites a man with failing eyes,
   That rabid mongrel he can't recognize.

A dog attacks a blind beggar

A dog attacked a blind man down a lane
    Just like a lion no one can restrain;
Dogs like to bite the dervishes they hate,
    Though to such men the moon will sink prostrate.
The dog's barks made him feel so vulnerable;
    He told the dog it should be honourable:
He said, 'Brave lion of the hunt, of you   2365
    I beg don't hurt me, though you're able to!'
Once when obliged, a sage praised to the sky
    A donkey's tail with titles which rank high.
This blind man said, compelled, 'What will you win,
    Great lion, from a man like me, rake-thin?
Wild asses are what other dogs pursue,
    While you've trapped this blind man who's feeble too;
Your peers hunt the wild asses in the plain,
    While you've trapped me in this dark, narrow lane.'
The wise dogs hunt wild asses, you will find,   2370
    The worthless dogs alone attack the blind!
If dogs should learn the truth, false paths they'll flee,
    To hunt their prey in forests lawfully;
Clever dogs fight with cunning like a knave;
    One even joined the Sleepers in the Cave!*
Such dogs of the hunt's leader can catch sight—
    How do they see him, God? What is that light?
The blind don't recognize him from his glance,
    Not due to lack of sight, but ignorance;
They're not more sightless than the earth below,   2375
    And yet the earth, through God's grace, sees its foe—
It aided Moses, since it saw his light,
    But then it swallowed Korah in one bite!*
It quaked to blow apart each false pretender;
    To '*Swallow, earth!*'* it hurried to surrender.
Earth, water, wind, and fire are unaware
    Of us, yet of the Truth remain aware.

We humans easily recognize most things,
    But not God's warners and the truths each brings.
They *shrank from it*,* as their imagination   2380
    Was blurred too much by mixing with creation.
'We all detest this life!' wise men complained,
    'With animals alive, from God detained.'
You'll feel like orphans if you live apart
    From people, but God seeks this kind of heart.
When a thief steals from blind men, you will hear
    Each blind man start to wail in desperate fear
Until the thief tells them, 'I was the one
    Who stole from you; it was so easily done!'
How can the blind their own thieves recognize   2385
    When there is no light coming to their eyes?
When the thief speaks, grab him and hold him fast
    Until he tells you what he pinched at last.
The real jihad means grabbing the thief too
    And making him tell what he stole from you:
He stole the kohl through which your eyes gained light;
    Once you retrieve it, you'll reclaim your sight.
The wisdom which your heart used to contain
    From the heart's master you must now regain.
Despite your eyes and ears, if you are blind,   2390
    You can't trace thieves from marks they leave behind.
Seek from the man of heart, not marks instead—
    Next to him, other men are like the dead.

The man who sought advice approached his goal,
    And said, 'Advise me, master of my soul!'
He answered, 'We are closed, so go away!
    We're not revealing mysteries today;
If I could find the way to Placelessness,*
    I'd sit like shaikhs free from this world of stress!'

How a law-enforcer summoned to gaol a drunkard who was totally drunk

One night, a law-enforcer, standing tall,   2395
   Noticed a drunkard sleeping by a wall.
He shouted, 'Wretched drunk, what did you drink?'
   'What filled the jar,' he answered with a wink.
'But what was that? I want this clarified!'
   'That which I drank!' 'The truth don't try to hide!
What kind of drink? I'm sure it was forbidden.'
   'I drank what in the wine-jar was kept hidden.'
Like this they went on, reaching no conclusion;
   A donkey stuck in mud knows such confusion.
He told the drunk, 'Say: "Ah!" without ado!'   2400
   The drunk instead would shout aloud 'Hu! Hu!'*
'I said, "Say, 'Ah!'"' Why then shout "Hu!" at me?'
   'Because I'm glad while you're in misery:
An "Ah!" expresses suffering and distress,
   While drunkards' chants are howls of happiness.'
'Get up right now! I cannot comprehend.
   Your clever sophistry, drunk, has to end!'
'What is my state to you? Please go away!'
   'You're drunk! I'm taking you to gaol today.'
'Leave me alone! Your efforts are in vain: 2405
   Since I possess naught, what can you now gain?
I would have gone straight home if I could walk,
   Then we would not have met and had this talk—
If I had reason and ability,
   I'd sit like shaikhs on thrones of dignity!'

The enquirer once again draws that great one into conversation in order to learn about his state

That seeker asked, 'Great horseman on a cane,
   Ride your steed here a moment! I'll explain.'
'Speak quickly then!' he came to him and said,
   'My horse has a bad temper and wild head;

If you're too slow, it's bound to buck and kick— 2410
    Explain what you are seeking; make it quick!'
He felt this wasn't the right situation,
    And so he joked instead on this occasion:
'I seek a good wife from this neighbourhood—
    For my type do you know one who'd be good?'
'The types of women in the world are three:
    One treasure-trove, two which cause misery.
The first is yours completely when you wed;
    The second half-yours, half-apart instead;
The third's not yours at all, not for one day. 2415
    Now that you've heard this, I'll be on my way,
So that you won't be kicked at by my horse
    And fall flat on your face due to its force.'
The shaikh rode with the children, so this man
    Shouted to him then loudly as he ran:
'Come back and give a proper explanation!
    Please clarify your wife-classification!'
He said, 'The virgin is yours totally;
    Through her you'll be released from misery.
A childless widow is half-yours alone; 2420
    And one who's had a child you'll never own—
By her first husband she became a mother,
    And so her love and care is for another.
Get going now before my horse kicks you!
    It can cause much harm, if it chooses to.'

The shaikh went off and started soon to roar,
    Calling the children to himself once more.
The seeker shouted out to him again:
    'I have another question, pride of men!'
The shaikh went back and said, 'Speak, don't delay! 2425
    That darling boy I love now wants to play.'
He asked, 'When you are so refined and wise,
    Why act so strangely? What's this exercise?
True intellect could not have clarified
    The things you know—why now in madness hide?'

He said, 'From vulgar people I must flee,
    For as the city's judge they've chosen me.
When I refused, they stubbornly screamed, "No!
    There's no one who knows half the laws you know!
It would be wicked and unlawful too   2430
    For someone else to judge instead of you.
Islamic law does not give us permission
    To choose a man who has less erudition."
So I've become mad through necessity,
    Though inwardly I'm as I used to be.'

I am a ruin hiding a rare brain;
    Showing that treasure would make me insane.
Madmen are really those who've not gone mad—
    They don't flee, though the situation's bad.
My knowledge is the truth and absolute;   2435
    The vulgar, common folk it doesn't suit.
I am just like a field of sugar-cane—
    I eat it and it grows from me again.
Knowledge from reason or blind imitation
    Is ruined by the audience's negation;
Since it does not enlighten, it's mere bait,
    Like worldly knowledge, which one shouldn't rate.
Men will seek knowledge for so many goals,
    But not to find a way to free their souls:
They burrow at each angle like a mouse   2440
    Which has been driven too far from the house—
Though it can't find a way back to the light,
    It keeps on struggling in the dark all night.
If God sends wisdom's wings, this mouse will soar
    Like birds, and be a lowly mouse no more.
But if it doesn't seek wings, it will fall
    And have no hope of reaching stars at all.
Rational knowledge, which lacks soul inside,
    Loves just to see its audience satisfied;
During debates it boasts and brags a lot,   2445
    But if its customer leaves, it's worth naught.

My buyer's God; He drags me up above,
  For *God alone has bought us** through His love.
The beauty of the Lord meets my blood-price;
  It's lawful nourishment and will suffice—
So leave the penniless here, let them die!
  What can a piece of worthless clay now buy?
Never seek, buy, or eat clay; those who still
  Insist on eating clay will soon fall ill.
Consume your heart with love, stay young through grace!   2450
  Theophanies bring colour to your face.
Lord, Your bestowal we could not have earned;
  Your mercy's ways are hidden, as we've learned.
Take our hands! Buy us! Lift the veil in front,
  But please keep covered our embarrassment!
Buy us again from this vile self of dirt!
  Its knife has reached our bones and makes them hurt.
This solid chain who'll loosen and undo
  For helpless ones like us, Pure King, but You?
Apart from You, with Your grace like the sun,   2455
  Who'll open this strong lock, All-Knowing One?
Let's turn to You now from ourselves! You're dearer,
  Than our own selves; to us You're truly nearer.
You taught this prayer as well through Your kind grace—
  How else could roses grow in this vile place?
Except through Your supreme munificence,
  Flesh and blood can't convey intelligence;
And how could light rays give sight to each eye
  So that our vision should reach to the sky?
And how else could a simple flap of skin   2460
  Enable streams of wise words to begin
To flow to ears, which are no more than holes,
  And from these to the orchards of men's souls?
Such orchards are the realm of the divine;
  Ours are derived from them, which is a sign:
Those are the founts of joy which He'll bestow—
  Quickly recite: '*Beneath which rivers flow.*'*

Conclusion of the Prophet's advice to the sick man

The Prophet asked this question to discover
   His good friend's ailment, so he might recover:
'Did you pray in a way that's dangerous   2465
   Or, unaware, eat something poisonous?
Try to remember now the prayer you said
   When your self's plots consumed you with such dread!'
He said, 'I can't remember—help me, please,
   To bring back to my mind that prayer with ease!'
The Prophet's light-bestowing presence led
   His thoughts back to the last prayer that he'd said;
That window which links all hearts it passed through
   And flashed light which tells false apart from true.
He screamed, 'Dear Prophet, it's come back to me—   2470
   That prayer I said before so foolishly,
When I was overwhelmed by sin, the cause
   Of my attempts in vain to clutch at straws!
Your threat to sinners had filled me with dread
   About the heavy punishment ahead;
I felt so helpless, in a state of shock,
   Bound in strong chains with no key for the lock:
No point in patience, no route from this hell,
   No more repentance, no chance to rebel!
Like Harut and Marut,* I'd deeply sigh   2475
   With sorrow, "My Creator, tell me why!"
Harut and Marut chose from harm to flee
   To Babylon's pit, there immediately
To be chastised, instead of in the grave;
   And each of them was a most cunning knave.
By doing this they might have chosen well,
   Enduring smoke instead of flames in hell—
The trials in that world sound limitless,
   So suffering pain in this world seems much less.
Happy is he who fights a true jihad   2480
   Against his body, steers it from what's bad;

In order to flee what awaits him there,
   The yoke of worship here he'd rather bear.
My prayer was: "In this short life, please deal out
   The punishment that You have warned about,
So in the next world I might be exempt."
   Begging God like this I chose to attempt,
Then I was filled with suffering and alarm—
   Grief has deprived my soul of peace and calm;
I can no longer meditate or pray;   2485
   I've lost awareness of all things today.
If I'd not seen your face just now, O you
   With holy scent and pure all the way through,
In bondage like this, I'd have died alone,
   But, glorious king, kind sympathy you've shown!'

He said, 'Don't make again that supplication.
   Never uproot yourself from your foundation!
You feeble man, have you the strength now to
   Carry the mountain which He'll place on you?'
He said, 'My sultan, I repent! Hear me!   2490
   I'll never brag again so recklessly!'
This world's the wilderness Jews wandered in;
   You're Moses—we are stuck here due to sin;
Moses's people travelled constantly,
   But ended up at the start tragically:
For years we have been travelling like his nation,
   But we are also trapped at this first station.
If Moses had been with us satisfied,
   The proper path he would have clarified.
But if we'd made him feel despair and frown,   2495
   How could a feast from heaven have come down?
How then could fountains have gushed out from stone?
   How could we have survived out there alone?
Rather, fire would have come in the feast's place,
   Flames darting up towards each person's face.
Since Moses has been in two minds, we know
   He's sometimes like a friend, sometimes a foe:

His anger sets fire to what we possess,
  His mercy drags back arrows of distress.

To clemency how can such anger change?   2500
  From You, Great One, this kindness isn't strange.
To praise one when he's present will bring shame,
  So I instead use Moses's sweet name;
Otherwise, how should Moses still allow
  Mention of others while You're here right now?
A thousand times we broke our covenant,
  But Yours seems, like a mountain, permanent:
Our covenant's like straw in winds of change,
  Yours like a mountain—no, a massive range!
Commander of all changes, by Your power,   2505
  Have mercy on our changing every hour!
We've seen ourselves and realize our shame—
  King, don't put us on trial! We've tasted blame.
From further shame protect us from today,
  Most Generous God to Whom we humans pray!
You're limitless in beauty and perfection,
  While we're prone to distortion and defection!
Send down Your limitlessness, Generous Lord,
  To wipe out the corruption of this horde!
We were a patch, but now a thread is all   2510
  That's left: A ruined city now one wall.
Save what is left, Lord! Listen to our plea,
  So that vile devil won't dance joyfully!
Not for our sakes, but out of that same grace
  Through which You first helped men who'd lost their place:
You've shown Your power—please show mercy too!
  Our form is flesh and blood now due to You.
If this prayer makes Your wrath grow even more,
  Teach us the right prayer now, Lord, we implore!
Just as when, from Your garden, Adam fell;   2515
  You helped him flee from Satan and from hell.
Adam is not less than that evil cheat,
  So, in this fight, how could he taste defeat?

It led to Adam's gain eventually,
    But Satan was soon cursed with jealousy:
Being short-sighted, he sold all his gains
    To win one bout, but the real war remains.
He set fire to their fields, where seeds were sown,
    But winds blew that same fire back to his own.
Due to the curse, the devil could not see   2520
    And thought his tricks could harm his enemy,
But all his guile harmed his own soul instead,
    So Adam was his devil, whom he'd dread.
A curse is something which distorts your sight,
    Making you jealous, proud, and full of spite,
Hiding the fact: whoever does a wrong—
    It will come back to him before too long:
He'll see all masterstrokes, but back to front,
    So he'll be in check-mate and impotent.
But if he sees himself as naught, he'll view   2525
    His honour as destroyed and worthless too;
He will feel pain if he should look inside,
    And this pain will remove the veil of pride.
Until the mother's womb with pain feels torn
    There is no way her baby can be born.
The covenant is in your pregnant soul;
    Enlightened counsel plays the midwife's role:
'There is no pain,' the midwife has to say,
    But there must be some pain to pave the way.
The one without pain is a thick-skinned thief;   2530
    He'll say, 'I am God,' and still feel no grief—
To say 'I' in this way is a disgrace,
    But, when it's true, to say 'I' has a place:
Mansur's 'I' was a blessing certainly,
    Pharaoh's 'I' was a curse eternally.*

Cocks crowing at the wrong time lose their head,
    A warning that one mustn't be misled!
Slaying the self is true decapitation
    In holy war, and pure renunciation;

It's like removing scorpions' stings—then who   2535
    Would need to kill them for harm they might do?
Or pulling out a poisonous snake's fangs, so
    It might be spared the rocks that men would throw.
The self's slain by the master's shade alone—
    Hold tightly his cloak's hem! Your self disown!
It's through God's aid that you perform this action:
    The strength you find comes from His own attraction.
Heed well: '*You didn't throw that time you threw!*'*
    Whatever your soul gains comes from Him too.
He'll take your hand, your burdens He will bear—   2540
    Long for a breath from Him! Do not despair!
Don't lose hope, though you've stayed away for long!
    You've heard He holds on and His grasp is strong:
For long His grace has held you in embrace;
    Not for one breath is He not where you face.
If you still need proof and an explanation,
    Choose '*By the morning*'* as your recitation!
Since bad things too come from Him, you feel doubt—
    His grace can have no flaws; it's pure throughout:
Giving bad things is part of His perfection—   2545
    Just listen to this tale which aids reflection:
A painter painted two works on a wall,
    One stunning and one with no worth at all:
He painted houris and fair Joseph's face,
    Then demons' heads in the remaining space.
Both types of forms show His intelligence;
    It's not His ugliness, but eminence:
He makes the vile as ugly as can be—
    All ugliness surrounds them totally—
To manifest His knowledge's perfection;   2550
    Deniers of this fact must face rejection.
Don't claim he can't make ugliness as well!
    He makes the faithful and the infidel;
Belief and unbelief both testify
    That He is God—the pair prostrate will lie:
Believers fall prostrate, obedient,
    Hoping that He will be with them content;

The infidel bows, but against his will—
 His worship's goal is something different still;
The king's fort he must keep in good repair, 2555
 But he claims he commands, though it's hot air:
This rebel claims the whole fort he now owns,
 Although the king will take back what he loans.
Believers conquer just for their King's sake;
 For them no personal profit is at stake.
The ugly tell God, 'You made our forms too—
 Since you make fair and ugly, we blame you!'
'Great King of Beauty,' beautiful men say,
 'You've made me free from flaws—to You I pray.'

How the Prophet gave advice to that sick man and taught him a supplicatory prayer

The Prophet told that sick man, 'Pray each night: 2560
 "O You who makes what's difficult seem light,
In this world give us good things, this I pray,
 And also *give good things on Judgment Day!*
Make our path like a garden in the spring;
 You are our destination, Noble King!"'
Believers at The Gathering* will say:
 'Dear angel, isn't hell along the way
Which infidel and faithful men pass by?
 But we did not see flames and wonder why?
Here is the paradise and court of grace, 2565
 So where precisely was that wretched place?'
The angel will reply: 'That greenery
 Which at a certain point you all could see—
That was hell, where men face horrific trials;
 To you it was an orchard raising smiles.
Since you waged war against that vile deceiver,
 Your firebrand self, which is an unbeliever,
To make your soul become completely pure,
 And quenched its fire for God's sake, you're secure:
The fire of lust with flames that steal men's sight 2570
 Has changed into true guidance's soft light;

Anger's fire turned to gentleness through you,
    And ignorance you've changed to knowledge too;
Greed's fire is now unselfishness instead,
    That thorn-like envy now a flower bed.
Since you have put these flames out on your own,
    Ahead of time and for God's sake alone,
And turned to orchards fiery selfishness,
    And sown in them the seeds of faithfulness
(So now the nightingales of chant and prayer   2575
    Sing sweetly by their streams without a care),
And answered God's call to attract down here
    Water to make your self's flames disappear,
Our hell seems a rich pasture now to you—
    It's rich with rosebuds from your privileged view.'

What's the reward for acting well, my friend?
    Kindness and goodness with a pleasing end.
'We are self-sacrificing,' you would say;
    'Before His attributes we pass away.'
Whether insane or a sharp, cunning knave,   2580
    The Saqi made us drunk with wine he gave.
We lay our heads down to the Lord's commands,
    Gambling our lives, which we place in His hands.
While in our hearts is the Beloved's portrait,
    Our work's to serve, and our own souls to forfeit—
Wherever suffering's candle has been lit
    A million loving souls are burned in it;
The lovers who are found inside this space
    Are moths around the candle of His face.*
Head to where they are straight with you, dear heart,   2585
    Where coats of mail from harm keep you apart,
Where, when you're victimized, they'll comfort you
    And make room for you in their own hearts too;
Inside their hearts they'll make for you a place,
    Then fill you like a cup with wine of grace.
Settle among their souls and do it soon!
    Make your home in the heavens, radiant moon!

They'll open the heart's book like Mercury,*
    To thus reveal to you each mystery.
Stay with your kin, don't roam like a lost foal! 2590
    A stray piece of the moon must seek the whole:
Why should a part stray far from its own source?
    Why mix with those who'll block the path by force?
Watch how one type transforms into another,
    How hidden things are brought to view, my brother!
Like fickle women you love flattery—
    From such vain falsehoods when will you break free?
Sweet words and flattery you choose to buy,
    And like vain women you don't question why.
Reproachful slaps from mystic kings help more 2595
    Than praise from those who've strayed far from His door—
Take these kings' slaps, shun honey from the base!
    Become a real man through the saints' pure grace!
Bestowing robes of honour is their role;
    Through spirit, body can be changed to soul.
If you should see a destitute man here,
    That he has left his teacher will be clear;
His heart's own fancy he preferred to find—
    His efforts failed, though, since his heart is blind;
His teacher's wish for him if he'd achieved, 2600
    High rank and honour he'd then have received—
The one who for the world's sake flees his master
    Is fleeing from good fortune even faster.

You've learnt skills, so material wealth you'll earn—
    Now a new mystic skill you need to learn.
In this world you've become rich and well-dressed,
    But in the next how will you pass the test?
Learn mystic skills, so in the next world too
    You'll profit from the mercy shown to you.
That world's a city bustling with much trade— 2605
    Don't feel content with worldly gains you've made:
The earnings in this world, God has declared,
    Are toys when with the next world's they're compared.

You're children wriggling on each other to
   Imagine having sex as adults do.
Children act like greengrocers when they play
   Their pointless game to pass the time away;
The 'grocer' goes home hungry with no gain;
   When 'shoppers' leave, alone he must remain:
This world's a playground and the night is death—   2610
   You go home empty-handed, out of breath.
Mystical gain means inner zeal and love,
   Capacity to catch light from above.
Your vile, base self wants just material gain;
   For worthless profit you'll endure much pain,
But if your self seeks noble gain from you,
   This is a plot—be careful what you do!

Satan wakes up Mo'aviya, saying 'Get up, it's time for prayer!'

Mo'aviya* was fast asleep one day
   Inside his palace, while the rest would pray.
He had locked up the palace from within,   2615
   Tired of his subjects' visits and their din—
Someone shook him, but when he looked around
   Whoever it had been could not be found.
'None has the right to enter!' he declared,
   'To show such brazen arrogance who's dared?'
He searched for him, so he could have him banished,
   But found no trace at all, for he had vanished.
Behind the curtains then Mo'aviya tried
   And found the culprit had gone there to hide;
He shouted, 'What's your name, wretch? Answer me!'   2620
   He said, 'I am cursed Satan; can't you see?'
'You came to wake me up just now, but why?
   Answer me truthfully and don't dare lie!'

How Satan tried to fool Mo'aviya with pretence and how Mo'aviya answered him

He said, 'The dawn prayer's period nears its end—
   You must run quickly to the mosque, my friend!
"Rush to good deeds before they disappear!"
   The prophet shared this pearl which is so clear.'
Mo'aviya said, 'It's not your intention
   To guide me to good deeds with what you mention,
For if a burglar in my house should say: 2625
   "I'm guarding it for you, my friend, today,"
Should I then trust that thief? How can thieves know
   About good deeds and what God will bestow?'

Again Satan answers Mo'aviya

He said, 'I was an angel at the start,
   Travelling the path of God with all my heart.*
Mystical travellers, as good friends, I've known,
   Including those who now sit near God's throne.
You can't forget skills you learnt long before,
   Just as your first love lasts for evermore;
Although while travelling stunning sights you'll see,   2630
   Love of your home still lasts eternally.
I've also got drunk from the wine He poured,
   When I was a famed lover of the Lord.
My cord was cut for love of Him alone,
   And in my heart seeds of His love were sown.
From fate I've seen good days which made me sing;
   Water of mercy I've drunk in the spring—
Wasn't I planted by His mercy's hand,
   Raised thus from non-existence to this land?
He showed such kindness that still can't be told—   2635
   In His approval's rose-garden I've strolled;
His hands of mercy on my head He'd place
   And open for me fountains of His grace.

In my first days who found the milk for me?
    Who rocked my tiny cradle lovingly?
From whom did I receive my milk, from whom?
    None but the One who fed me in the womb.
That nature which with milk comes into men—
    How can that nature be drained out again?
The Sea of Grace reproach to us might roar,   2640
    But grace and mercy never close their door.
The substance of His coin is loving grace,
    While wrath, to Him, is like an alloy's trace.
He made the world, so kindness we would meet;
    His sun caressed all atoms with its heat.
His separation's pregnant with His wrath
    Only so we'll seek union like a moth;
This separation's meant to make souls burn,
    So union's value they can truly learn.
The Prophet said once, it has been related: 2645
    "God said, 'For doing good deeds I created:
I made the creatures, so they'll gain from me,
    So that my honey they'll eat joyfully,
Not so I would myself make any gain—
    I don't snatch coats from paupers in the rain!'"
He barred me from His presence a few days,
    But on His face I kept my constant gaze—
"Amazing! Wrath from such a face!" I sighed.
    With lesser things the rest are occupied.
I don't look at effects—they've little worth;   2650
    Mere transient things to transient things give birth.
I look at grace, from which the rest all start;
    Subsequent transient things I tear apart!
I spurned prostration as I was possessive:
    It was through love; my act was not dismissive.*
All jealousies we feel arise from love,
    The wish to sit with none but Him above;
Love's natural outcomes are such jealousies,
    Like saying "Bless you!" after people sneeze.
There was no other space left on the board   2655
    When "Make your move!" I was told by the Lord;

I made the one move open, lost the game,
   And threw myself into the trial of blame.
In agony I taste deep pleasure still:
   I've been check-mated by Him—that's His will.
Good man, how can we ever find release
   When we're trapped here like a backgammon piece?
From the Whole One how can its part escape,
   Even one given such an ugly shape?
Whoever's in this realm lives in the flames,   2660
   But God can help us reach the loftier aims.
Both faith and unbelief are equally
   His own work, part of His rich tapestry.'

Again Mo'aviya exposes the deceitfulness of Satan

Mo'aviya said, 'This may be correct,
   But your role here I totally reject:
You've pounced and robbed so many men like me,
   Digging holes, sneaking in the treasury.
You're fire, and you'll burn me, I understand—
   Whose clothes have not been ripped by your base hand?
Bonfire, since it's your nature thus to burn,   2665
   You've no choice, no direction left to turn.
That He makes you burn things is your own curse,
   And you rule all the thieves and make them worse.
You spoke with God directly long ago—
   Who am I to face up to such a foe!
Like hunters' whistles is your sophistry,
   Attracting birds to traps deceitfully:
A hundred thousand birds we have seen falling,
   Thinking your sound's a true friend who is calling;
Each hears from far above your whistle's sound   2670
   And then swoops down to get trapped on the ground.
Your trickery made Noah's people mourn—
   Their hearts were roasted and they felt forlorn.*
You helped destroy the Aad community,
   Throwing them into fits of agony.*

You had a part in stoning Lot's vile nation;
  They drowned in filth for their abomination.*
You shredded into long strips Nimrod's brain—
  You've caused so many troubles and much pain!*
Like a philosopher's was Pharaoh's mind;   2675
  His cleverness was false—you made him blind.
Bu Lahab you led into flames to burn;
  Bu'l-Hakam to Bu Jahl you helped to turn.
On this world's chessboard of extreme disasters
  You have check-mated millions of grand masters.
Your challenging game-plan when you attack
  Has burned our hearts while yours has turned pitch black.
Ocean of plots, our guile is just one drop;
  Mountain, we're simple atoms, so please stop!
Who is spared plotting for which you're renowned?   2680
  Except those God protects, the rest get drowned.
The brightest stars you have made disappear,
  And you have weakened armies most would fear.'

Satan again responds to Mo'aviya

Satan told him, 'Untie the knot, behold!
  I am the touchstone which detects real gold.
I give God's test to dogs and lions too,
  Like gold and counterfeit—I see what's true.
How can I ever blacken gold that's real;
  Like money-changers I can only deal:
I guide to goodness every passer-by,   2685
  And break off only branches which are dry.
Why is it that I place the fodder here?
  So that the beast's identity is clear:
If to a deer a wolf should bear a child
  And you're unsure if it is tame or wild,
Drop grass and bones before it to discern
  From the direction it should choose to turn:
If it moves to the bones, then it is clear
  That it's a wolf; if to the grass a deer.

Forces of wrath and mercy were once mated—   2690
   The world of good and evil they created.
Put bones and grass before men in their bowls,
   Food for their selves and food good for their souls—
If one devours the self's food, he is base;
   If the soul's food, a credit to his race.
If you should serve the body, you're a fool;
   If you dive in the soul, you'll find the jewel.
Though good and evil are two separate things,
   They both do one job for the King of Kings.
The prophets all do good deeds and obey;   2695
   Their foes serve lust and they live in its sway.
I can't make good men bad—I'm not their Maker!
   I call to God's path—I'm not their Creator!
I can't make fair men ugly suddenly;
   I'm just a mirror for each kind, you see!
An Indian burnt his mirror when in pain,
   "This makes men's faces look black!" he'd complain,*
"It's not my fault!" the blameless mirror said,
   "Blame the one who has polished me instead!
He made me tell the truth and never lie,   2700
   The fair from ugly to identify."
I am a witness—gaol is not for me;
   I don't belong there. God will make you see!
When I see a fresh sapling taking root
   I nurture it until it bears some fruit,
But when I see a dry and bitter tree
   I chop it down, so musk from dung can flee.
The dry tree asks the gardener, "With such force
   You chop my head off—don't you feel remorse?"
"Shut up you ugly thing," this man will yell,   2705
   "Your dryness is your own fault—go to hell!"
"I'm straight not crooked!" then the tree will say,
   "How can you chop remorselessly away?"
"If you were blest and lucky," he'll reply,
   "Even if crooked, you'd be moist not dry:
Water of Life you would have then been shown
   And thus become drenched, not dry as a bone.

Your seed and root were bad initially,
    And you're not grafted to a healthy tree!"
If one grafts bitter branches with the sweet,   2710
    Those sweet ones soon a sorry death will meet.'

Mo'aviya is severe with Satan

Mo'aviya said, 'You must stop your lying!
    You can't convince me, so don't bother trying!
I am a foreign trader, you're a con—
    I won't buy clothes from you or put them on.
Don't stare at my belongings, infidel!
    No faithful man to you his goods would sell!
You're not a customer whom I would choose;
    You act like one but it is just a ruse.
What does he now have hidden up his sleeve?   2715
    God save us from this foe who can deceive!
If he says one more clever thing to me,
    He'll rob me of my wits then totally!'

Mo'aviya complains to God about Satan and asks for His help

'O God, this talk of his is just like smoke—
    Please help or it will blacken my new cloak!
I can't beat Satan in debating bouts,
    For in both base and great men he sows doubts:
Adam, *to whom He taught the names,** can't race
    This wretched cur who moves at lightning pace.
From paradise he forced him out as well;   2720
    Just like a fish in Satan's net he fell:
*'We've wronged ourselves!'** he cried out in distress.
    His cunningness and guile is limitless!
For every word he speaks, harm lurks behind;
    A thousand evil tricks are in his mind.
Men's honour he'll tie up and cause to dwindle,
    While men's and women's lusts this foe will kindle—

Satan, man-burner, trouble-stirrer, why
   Did you awake me? Tell the truth, don't lie!'

Satan again exhibits his deceit

'Whoever has bad thoughts,' then Satan stated,   2725
   'Can't hear the truth though often it's related,
For everyone who nurses doubts soon finds
   Doubts grow when reason enters in their minds.
Words enter minds and make those people sick:
   A knight's sword changes thus to a thief's stick.
Silence is the correct form of reply;
   Talking with fools is madness—don't you try!
So why complain to God about my role?
   Complain instead about your carnal soul!
Too many sweets will cause spots in the end   2730
   And fevers which destroy your health, my friend.
You swore at blameless Satan, but denied
   That this deception comes from deep inside;
It's not from Satan, but from fickle you.
   Like foxes you are chasing sheep's tails too:
If a sheep's back-side should attract your eyes
   It is a trap, but you don't realize,
Because that back-side now controls your brain—
   Hot lust is something you fail to restrain.
The Prophet said, "*Love for things makes you blind*   2735
   And deaf; by your own soul you're undermined."
Don't see things upside down, and don't blame me.
   Since from greed, spite, and evil I am free!
I did a bad thing but am now contrite;
   I wait for day to end my mournful night.
People accuse me of their own vile sins:
   The blame for sins on me each person pins;
Although the helpless wolf is hungry, still
   They claim it's spoilt and always eats its fill;
When it's so weak it can't move, all the same,   2740
   "It's overeaten—look!" such people claim.'

Mo'aviya again stands firm before Satan

Mo'aviya said, 'Truth will set you free;
   Justice demands you speak the truth to me,
So tell the truth to flee a grasp so tight—
   Your trickery won't make me stop this fight!'
Satan said, 'Truth from lies how can you tell
   When futile fancies hold you in their spell?'
'The Prophet gave a sign which makes me bold,
   The touchstone which tells false gold from real gold:
He said, "*Lies give your hearts uneasiness,*   2745
   While honesty brings joy and peacefulness."
Lies cannot calm one's heart; try as you might,
   Water and oil won't mix to give out light.
True speech is comfort for the heart when shared—
   Truth is the bait with which the heart is snared.
The heart falls ill if it fails to discern
   The taste of different things—it needs to learn.
From sickness when a healthy heart recovers,
   The taste of truth and lies it then discovers.
When Prophet Adam's greed for wheat increased,*   2750
   It harmed his health—strength in his heart decreased;
He listened then to your lies and seduction
   And drank the poisonous drink of self-destruction.
He couldn't tell a scorpion from wheat grains:
   When drunk with lust discernment leaves men's brains.
People are drunk with passion and with lust—
   That's why in your false tales they place their trust.
From passions if a man has separated,
   With mysteries he'll be illuminated.'

A judge complains about the trial of holding his office, and his deputy responds to him

A new judge was once seen begin to cry;   2755
   The deputy asked, 'Judge, please tell me why!

It's not the time for tears and lamentation;
    It's time for joy and much congratulation.'
He said, 'Can someone who's unsure give judgment
    On those who know what happened while he doesn't?
Those two foes know the truth about their case,
    So, when the judge does not, where is his place?
He's ignorant of facts and their conditions,
    So with their lives how can he make decisions?'
'These two foes should remember what is right,   2760
    But they're unsound, while you shine out God's light,
For you're not biased and won't compromise;
    Immune to flaws, you give light to our eyes.
Lust blinds those two and makes their thoughts unsound,
    Burying all their knowledge in the ground.
Flawlessness can make ignorance transform
    To knowledge, while unsoundness will deform.
So long as you don't take bribes, you will see;
    If greed rules you, you'll lose sight totally.'
I've kept my nature free from greed's thick rust,   2765
    By eating fewer morsels of vile lust;
My heart has grown as radiant as the sky
    For it can tell what's true and what's a lie.

Mo'aviya makes Satan confess

Mo'aviya demanded, 'Why wake me
    When you are wakefulness's enemy?
Like opium you put everyone to sleep,
    Like wine all wisdom from our minds you sweep.
Confess the truth to me now, I implore!
    I know what's right, so don't cheat any more!
From others all I hope is that they'll show   2770
    What their true nature is, so I will know.
I don't seek sweetness out in vinegar,
    Nor take a weak man as a warrior;
Unlike the infidels, I do not yearn
    For idols as gods to whom I can turn;

From dung I don't expect to breathe musk's smell,
    Nor seek dry bricks from rivers or a well—
I don't expect from Satan this convention:
    That he should wake me with a good intention.'
Satan spoke many words of trickery,   2775
    But he resisted them all critically.

Satan says truthfully to Mo'aviya what was on his mind

Reluctantly then Satan chose to tell:
    'It was for this I woke you, so heed well:
So you would join the others for the prayer,
    Follow the Prophet thus by reaching there,*
For if the prayer's time passed while you were sleeping,
    In deep despair you would have started weeping;
In shame and pain, tears would have filled your eyes
    And flowed as if from flasks or heavy skies.'
From acts of worship all gain a sweet taste,   2780
    So missing out seems such a tragic waste—
Than this deep pain a hundred prayers earn less;
    What's prayer next to light gained through neediness!

The excellence of the remorse felt by that pious one for having missed congregational prayer

A man approached the mosque to join the prayer,
    But saw men coming out as he reached there.
He asked, 'What's happening to all these men?
    Why are they exiting the mosque again?'
'The Prophet has already prayed,' one said,
    'The congregation's prayers the Prophet led—
Why have you come so late? Do you not care   2785
    The Prophet has already led the prayer?'
He breathed such a deep sigh it gave off smoke
    And spread his heart's blood's scent, which made men choke!

The man who'd prayed said, 'Give me that deep sigh
　　And take my prayer's rewards, which it can buy.'
He said, 'I'll give my sigh and take your prayer.'
　　The other grabbed that sigh which seemed so rare
And in a dream that very night was told:
　　'Water of Life now and the cure you hold.
In honour of the wise way you've selected,　　　　　　2790
　　The congregation's prayers are all accepted.'

Conclusion of Satan's confession of his deceit to Mo'aviya

Satan then said, 'Majestic prince, now I
　　Must clarify the reason for my lie:
If you had missed the morning prayer today,
　　You would have sighed and moaned in deep dismay—
That aching neediness and lamentation
　　Would have earned more than prayers and meditation.
I woke you up for fear that such deep sighs
　　Would burn away the veil before your eyes,
So such sighs wouldn't come to your possession,　　　2795
　　So you'd not learn to sigh with desperate passion.
Envious, I did it out of jealousy;
　　Lying through spite, I am the enemy.'
Mo'aviya said, 'Now the truth you tell.
　　Deceit comes from you and you suit it well!
You are a spider: your prey is the fly;
　　I'm not a fly; my rank is much too high!
I'm a white falcon prized by royalty—
　　How can a spider weave webs to catch me?
While you still can, go out and catch some flies!　　2800
　　Call all of them to your trap with your lies!
If you call them to honey that is pure,
　　They will instead find yoghurt or manure.
You woke me, but to deep sleep actually;
　　You showed a boat, but then tried drowning me.
You called me to good purpose on this day,
　　From better things to drive me far away.'

How a burglar escaped when someone called the owner of the house who had already almost caught him

A burglar was seen in a house one day
  And by the owner he was chased away;
The owner chased him for a mile or more   2805
  And quickly tired as sweat began to pour.
When he had almost caught up with the wretch
  And could have grabbed his collar at a stretch,
Someone inside his house screamed, 'Come and see
  These indications of calamity!
Hurry up! Come at once! Please turn around,
  So you can see the tragic things I've found!'
The owner thought, 'Another burglar might
  Be there, and that could be a much worse plight!
To my sweet wife and children he'll creep near—   2810
  How will it help to tie up this thief here?
A good man's helping me now with his call;
  If I don't head back, I'll regret it all!'
Hoping for kind help from that man, he then
  Let the thief go, to head back home again.
'Good friend, what's happening?' he then yelled out,
  'What are these screams and moaning all about?'
'A burglar's footprints—look, they are so clear!
  That bastard burglar must have walked through here.
Look at the footprints! You'll soon apprehend   2815
  The scoundrel, if you follow them, my friend.'
'Is that all, idiot?' the owner said,
  'I'd almost caught him, but turned round instead:
Because I heard you shout, I let him go;
  That you're a stupid ass I didn't know!
What gibberish and nonsense comes from you!
  I'd found the truth—what good now is a clue?'
He said, 'A vital clue I chose to show,
  Though the entire facts I already know.'
'You're stupid or pretending that you care;   2820
  No, you're a thief—that's how you are aware!

I'd nearly grabbed and tied my enemy,
  But you screamed, "Here's a clue!" and set him free.
You talk of signs, but I'm beyond that station:
  Signposts have no use at the destination.'
If veiled from attributes, watch His creations;
  God's attributes are seen from higher stations;
But in God's essence if annihilated,
  His attributes then can't be contemplated:
When you are swimming in the deepest river,   2825
  Why wonder then 'What is the water's colour?'?
To check the colour if you should swim back,
  You're swapping silk for a moth-bitten sack!
The common man's good deed is the saint's sin;*
  To saints, their 'unions' are veiled states they're in:
For if a king should make his own vizier
  A law-enforcer, this would be severe—
A big sin that vizier must have committed,
  For not without a cause is this permitted.
However, if he'd been one from the start,   2830
  He might have loved this job with all his heart.
All good viziers would feel most disappointed,
  If as a law-enforcer they're appointed:
If from the threshold he has summoned you,
  Then driven you away, this is a clue
That you've done something inappropriate
  And ignorance has brought this twist of fate.
You might claim that this was your destiny—
  Was it just luck before then? Answer me!
Ignorance has deprived you of your lot;   2835
  Worthy men make their portion grow, not rot.

The story of the hypocrites and their building of the Mosque of Opposition

A similar parable I offer next;
  You would have read it in the Holy Text:*

The hypocrites played such a crooked game
    When to Medina first the Prophet came:
'For the sake of Mohammad's faith,' they said,
    'We'll build a mosque!' But they sought sin instead.
They cheated in the game that they'd selected:
    A new and separate mosque these men erected,
With floor and dome so finely decorated,   2840
    Hoping that Muslims would be separated.
They then approached the Prophet in petition,
    Kneeling the way that camels take position,
And pleaded, 'Would you trouble your pure feet
    To come and see our mosque across the street,
So, through your footsteps, this most humble place
    Might benefit—may yours be lasting grace!
This is a mosque for dark and cloudy days,
    For poor folk suffering a needy phase,
A strangers' shelter offering charity.   2845
    This place of service might grow rapidly,
And our religion's rites more men might learn—
    With friends' help, bitter things to sweet can turn.
Please grace us with your presence for one hour,
    Purify us! On us your praises shower!
Please bless this mosque and us; we are the night
    While you're the moon; with us one hour unite,
So, through your beauty, night will seem like day—
    You send each soul-illuminating ray!'
If only they had meant what they had said,   2850
    Their wish might then have been fulfilled instead.
Soundest proofs on a tongue that's insincere
    Are like grass placed on ash-heaps, so keep clear!
Observe them from a distance and then run!
    They are not fit to swallow down, my son.
Don't let talk from the insincere tempt you,
    For it's an old, weak bridge which looks like new:
If a fool steps on it, the bridge will break
    And his feet will be crushed by this mistake.
Whenever a large army tastes defeat   2855
    It's due to weaklings who are too effete:

One joins with arms as if he's really brave
    And men say, 'He's a comrade in the cave!'*
But he will scamper if their foes attack
    And his escape will break his army's back.
These issues are vast, and expand as well—
    Explaining would delay what we must tell.

The hypocrites tried to deceive the Prophet, so they might take him to the Mosque of Opposition

They chanted to God's Prophet spells like these;
    Riding the steed of cunning, they'd beg: 'Please!'
That generous Messenger whom God had sent   2860
    Answered with naught but smiles and kind assent:
He thanked them generously, as they soared high
    With joy on hearing his polite reply.
Like hair which floats on milk he then could see
    Each single aspect of their trickery,
But spoke as if it were invisible;
    Thus to such milk he screamed: 'How wonderful!'
A hundred hairs of trickery were there
    And yet he lowered his eyes, and would not stare!
That ocean of pure kindness made it clear: 2865
    'I'm kinder to you than yourselves—don't fear!
I sit next to a fire that's devastating;
    Its flames are deadly and for you they're waiting,
And just like moths you rush there, come what may—
    My hands, like swatters, must swipe you away.'
The Prophet thus agreed there to be led,
    But then 'Don't listen to the ghoul!' God said,
'They've plotted trickery, so you must know
    The truth's the opposite of what they show:
Their aim is only to bring shame to you;   2870
    Don't seek concern for your faith from their Jew!
They've built a mosque upon the edge of hell
    And played the game of cheat with God as well;
The Muslims they would split up and displace—
    How can such meddlers recognize God's grace?

From Syria, they want to bring that Jew*
  Whose sermons give them hope they'll challenge you.'
The Prophet said, 'I will, but not today;
  To our next battle we are on our way.
When I return from my next distant raid   2875
  I'll come and see this mosque which you have made.'
Before he went, he sent them home again,
  Thus played tricks with the trickiest of men!
On his return, the tricksters came once more
  To seek what he'd agreed to do before.
God then said, 'Prophet, show their treachery!
  And if a war should break out, let it be!'
He said, 'Be silent, liars! Don't go on
  Or I'll reveal the truth to everyone!'
He then revealed some clues about their ruse   2880
  And they grew scared of what they had to lose.
Their leader then returned to him, to say:
  'Allah forbid that we should act this way!'
Holding Qur'ans, each hypocrite then came;
  To trick the Prophet was their only aim.
They took oaths as a shield for self-protection;
  Taking oaths is the crooked man's convention—
Because to the religion he's not true,
  Each moment he will break his oath to you.
The truthful don't need oaths; they can sense lies   2885
  Because they see the truth with their own eyes.
Breaking a covenant is so disgraceful;
  Keeping one's word reveals that someone's faithful.

'Should I accept your oaths?' the Prophet said,
  'Or is the word of God the truth instead?'
They took some more oaths, holding the Qur'an,
  Each one as though he were a righteous man,
Saying, 'On the Qur'an, this oath I take:
  Building the mosque was solely for God's sake.
No falsehood or deceit is found in there,   2890
  Just space for meditation and for prayer.'

The Prophet said, 'God's voice to me is clear,
  Just like an echo sounding in each ear,
But God has sealed your ears due to your choice,
  And so they'll never get to hear His voice.
God's voice comes to me as a revelation,
  And it is free from all contamination.'
Moses once from a bush heard God's voice say:
  'You lucky, fortunate one!' and knelt to pray;
Also, '*Lo, I am God!*' from it he heard,*   2895
  With lights accompanying every word.
Once startled by God's revelation's light,
  Those false men took more oaths in utter fright.
God called oaths 'shields', and nobody will see
  An enemy drop his shield willingly.
The Prophet called them 'liars' once again;
  He said, '*You lied!*'* to these deceitful men.

One of the Companions went away, asking himself: 'Why doesn't the Prophet throw a veil of discretion over their situation?'

One of the Prophet's followers that day
  Disliked the Prophet acting in this way.
He thought, 'Such virtuous, pure, and pious men   2900
  The Prophet is embarrassing again.
To hide their faults is generosity—
  The Prophet should not let the others see.'
But then he begged forgiveness with much haste,
  Since faulting him will leave a man disgraced.
The hypocrites will bring bad luck to you;
  If you befriend them, you'll turn ugly too.
He begged, 'You who know my deep secrets well,
  Don't let me think still like an infidel!
I don't control my heart like my two eyes—   2905
  I'd burn it now in anger otherwise!'
He then lay down, so he could sleep a bit,
  And dreamt these people's mosque was made of shit:
Its bricks were laid in filthy shit throughout
  And from those bricks a foul black smoke blew out.

Smoke filled his throat and made it sore and red,
   Due to its bitter stench—he leapt from bed,
Then fell prostrate and wept in fits at once:
   'It's due to my denial and arrogance!
In this case, treating them like foes is right;   2910
   Kindness risks stealing from my heart faith's light.'
Form-worshippers' deeds if you should compare,
   You'll see they stink like onions, layer by layer,
Each one more empty than the one before,
   While, for good men, each new deed is worth more.
Around their cloaks a hundred belts they've bound,
   The Mosque of Qoba* to raze to the ground,
Like those who with an elephant once came,
   Whose house of worship God had set aflame:
They tried to crush the Kaaba in return;   2915
   About what happened to them you should learn.*
Disgraced men like this group do not have tools
   Apart from plots which trap the weakest fools.

All the Companions* then could clearly see
   That vile mosque's nature in reality.
If these men's inner states I should spell out,
   All doubters would see they were pure throughout;
The truth about their states I dare not share—
   One has to treat such men with extra care;
They know God's laws without blind imitation,   2920
   Gold coins without a touchstone—that's their station!
Qur'anic wisdom's the believer's stray;
   Each knows his own stray camel straight away.*

*The story about a man who was looking for his
stray camel and asking after it*

You've lost a camel—now you seek it out;
   On finding it, that it's yours you won't doubt.
You've lost the camel you are used to riding;
   It has escaped your hold and now is hiding.

The caravan is ready to move on;
   They have all packed up, but your camel's gone—
With parched lips you are searching left and right;   2925
   The caravan sets off, and soon it's night.
Your things have just been left there on the ground,
   While in your search you have been wandering round,
Asking: 'Who's seen a camel come this way?
   It fled its stable earlier today.
About my camel pass me information
   And I'll give you a generous compensation.'
You seek a clue like this from everyone,
   So all the scoundrels see you and poke fun,
Jesting: 'We saw a camel head that way,   2930
   A reddish camel, searching for some hay.'
One asks, 'Was it crop-eared and quite perplexed?'
   'Its saddle was embroidered,' claims the next.
Another asks, 'Did it have just one eye?'
   The next, 'Was it sick and about to die?'
Each wretch in hope of a reward from you
   Presents to you his fabricated clue.

On becoming perplexed due to different schools of thought, and how to find escape and deliverance

All men try to describe the mystery
   Of truth, each one of them so differently:
Philosophers describe it in one way,   2935
   While theologians counter what they say;
Another one refutes them both, and he
   Whose soul is blind tries to refute all three.
About the true path each informs a bit,
   Such that you might think they belong to it.
They are not all correct in what they say
   And neither are they totally astray.
Without the real one there would be no fake:
   False gold for real gold simple men mistake.
If in this world there weren't authentic gold,   2940
   How could a counterfeit of it be sold?

Without the truth, how can there be a lie?
  All falsehoods on the true facts must rely.
Men buy a bent thing, thinking that it's straight:
  Poison appeared like sugar, so they ate.
Were there no wheat which men prefer to eat,
  None would then pass mere barley off as wheat.
Don't say all talk is wholly counterfeit!
  False talk attracts since some see truth in it;
It's all mere fantasy you might insist—   2945
  Without truth, fantasy would not exist:
Truth's like the Night of Power,* which makes your soul
  Check each night to tell which fulfils this role—
Not all nights are the Night of Power, just one,
  Neither are they all void of power, my son.
Among those who wear dervish garb today
  Just one is true—find him without delay!
Where's the *discriminating, faithful sage**
  To tell the base from great men in this age?
If nothing flawed or counterfeit were made,   2950
  Simple men too would try their hand at trade;
Choosing the best goods would be easy then,
  So who'd know competent from useless men?
Knowledge won't help if everything's flawed too—
  Why bother then perfection to pursue?
The stupid man says everything is true;
  A man who says all's false is foolish too.
Those who trade with the prophets gain in kind,
  While those who seek material things turn blind.
In eyes which seek wealth, snakes will soon appear—   2955
  Rub well your eyes so this will be made clear!
If you think profits will bring happiness,
  Remember Pharaoh's and Thamud's* distress!
Keep looking at the sky above your head,
  For '*Turn your gaze back there!*' God clearly said.

On testing everything until its good and bad traits become apparent

Take more than one glance at the dome of light—
    Look often! *Are there any flaws in sight?**
He has told you to look up frequently
    Like someone seeking flaws, not leniently;
Like when we must inspect dark earth in full,   2960
    To make sure that it is approvable.
A huge amount our intellects endure
    So as to tell the dregs from men who're pure.
The trials faced in winter and in fall,
    The summer's warmth, spring's gift of life to all,
Winds, clouds, and lightning—all from God come here,
    So that all differences can be made clear,
So that dust-coloured earth will then make known
    What it contains: a ruby or mere stone?
So many things dark earth grabs stealthily   2965
    From Bounty's Ocean and God's treasury.
God's viceroy, providence, says, 'Earth, admit
    What you have pilfered! Every bit of it!'
That robber, earth, claims, 'Not a thing, I swear!'
    The viceroy grabs and wrings it like a bear.
This viceroy may speak like a sweet, kind man,
    Then later speak as harshly as one can,
So that all hidden things, through wrath and grace—
    Fear and hope's flames—reveal to us their face.
Spring sends God's kindness, but, lest men forget,   2970
    Autumn shows them God's terror and His threat;
The winter is the inner crucifixion,
    When, hidden thief, truth is made clear from fiction.

At times the holy warrior feels expansion,
    At other times pain, torment, and contraction.
Our earthly bodies try with all their might
    Denying and then stealing our soul's light.

God places grief and pain, hot things and cold,
   Upon our bodies, so you must be bold!
Poverty, hunger, handicaps, and fear   2975
   Are sent so the soul's nature is made clear.
He has made promises and threats of terror,
   Due to the good and bad He's mixed together;
The truth and falsehood have been muddled up,
   Like putting real and false gold in one cup.
A mystic touchstone therefore is required,
   One who has seen trials and has been inspired,
In order to discern all falsehoods, and
   To organize things just as they were planned.
'Mother of Moses, give him milk!' we scream.   2980
   'Don't worry when you place him on the stream!
All who have drunk milk at *Alast* can test,
   To find out which milk's from their mother's breast;
If you would like your child to learn this skill,
   *Suckle him,** mother of Moses, so he will
Know how his mother's milk tastes; stop his head
   From reaching evil nurses' breasts instead!'

*Explanation of the moral of the story about that
person searching for his camel*

You've lost a camel that belongs to you
   And everyone is offering you a clue;
You don't know where that camel chose to go,   2985
   But that their clues are false you clearly know.
A man who hasn't lost a camel now
   Competes with you in searching anyhow;
He'll claim, 'I've lost a camel, everyone!
   I'll give a big reward for her return.'
To share your camel is this mimic's aim;
   Because he covets yours, he plays this game.
From false clues he can't tell a truthful clue,
   But, for this mimic, your words serve as cue:
If you declare, 'That clue's false!' you will see   2990
   Him do the same, but it's just mimicry.

And if a man gives clues you think are true,
   Sureness *which leaves no doubt** then comes to you:
Such clues heal your sick soul of all its pain;
   Your health, strength, and complexion you regain,
Your eyes light up, your feet feel quick anew,
   Body like soul, and soul like spirit too!
'You were right, truthful friend!' you then will say,
   'These clues are *messages as clear as day*
*In which are signs of truthful information.**   2995
   You have truth's license and you've earned salvation!'
When someone's given such a clue, you'll say:
   'It's time for action, so please lead the way!
Truth-teller, I will follow from behind;
   With this clue my lost camel you will find.'
To that man who did not before possess
   That camel, but who seeks it none the less,
More certainty will not come from this clue
   Unless it's through a man whose search is true:
He'll see from your zeal that the clue is serious,   3000
   And that your screams of joy are not delirious.

That liar has no claim, but still I say
   He'd also lost a camel in a way;
Desire for someone else's veils his mind,
   So he's forgotten what he'd left behind.
The owner runs to search; he follows there;
   Through greed, the owner's pain he starts to share:
A liar in the truthful's company
   Will find his lies become truths suddenly.
Where your stray camel is when you've been brought,   3005
   This mimic finds his stray, which he'd not sought;
He first recalls her when he sees her, then
   He covets no more those of other men.
That mimic's search first starts thus when his eyes
   Notice his own lost camel by surprise:
He only seeks to find his camel when
   By chance he sees her; he'd not searched till then.

From that point he learns to move on alone,
  Now having opened his eyes to his own.
The truthful man asks, 'Have you left at last?   3010
  Is your concern about me in the past?'
He says, 'Till now I simply would pretend;
  Desire made me your sycophantic friend,
But now I sympathize deep in my heart,
  Though, through this search, we have been led apart.
I stole descriptions of her straight from you;
  My soul was stunned, though, when mine came to view.
I wasn't seeking her, if truth be told—
  Copper has now been overwhelmed by gold:
My evil deeds were righteous deeds somehow—   3015
  Folly has left and seriousness rules now!
My sins became the means to reach the Lord—
  Don't criticize them any more, applaud!
Sincerity made you a seeker, while
  My search led me to it, and so I smile:
Your search was due to your sincerity;
  Sincerity, through seeking, came to me!
I sowed my fortune's seed in fertile soil,
  Although I'd thought it would be fruitless toil.
It wasn't unpaid work to my surprise: 3020
  I sowed one seed and saw a hundred rise.
A thief had sneaked into a house at night—
  He saw it was his own house in the light.'

Be warm, cold one, so more heat reaches you;
  Accept the rough, so smoothness finds you too!
There was one camel in reality;
  Words can't contain the depths of meaning's sea:
Expression can't reach meaning's depth; instead
  '*His tongue will falter,*' our great Prophet said.
Speech is just like an astrolabe, my friend—   3025
  The mystic sky how can it comprehend?
That sky next to which heaven seems so small,
  Next to whose sun your sun's a tiny ball.

Explanation of how in every soul there is the Mosque of Opposition

When it was clear this mosque was just a ruse,
    A wicked trap of lies set by the Jews,
The Prophet ordered that it be knocked down
    And serve as rubbish heap for all the town.
The owner, like the mosque he had erected,
    Was false: this bait he'd carefully selected.
The bait which draws the fish and makes it bite   3030
    Is not the kind gift it seems at first sight.
The Mosque of Qoba was inanimate—
    To stand near it that mosque was still unfit.*
Inanimates before had not earned shame
    Like this—the Prophet set that mosque aflame.

Lofty things, such as human essences
    Among them too possess such differences,
For one man's life is never like another's
    Nor will his own death be just like his brother's,
Nor will the graves where they will finally lie;   3035
    On high, such differences will multiply.
Check your work with a touchstone, to make sure
    You won't build mosques like theirs, which was impure!
Though you've mocked builders of that mosque with glee,
    You're just like them if you look carefully!

Story about the Indian who fought with a friend about something and was not aware that he too was afflicted by it

Four Indian friends went to a mosque one day,
    To worship at the proper time to pray;
They started by declaring their intention,
    And humbly followed each approved convention.*

When the muezzin entered in the hall,   3040
    While praying one asked, 'Did you make the call?'*
These words escaped his lips; another there
    Said, 'Brother, you have nullified your prayer!'
The third one said then to the second one:
    'Why bother him? Look at what you have done!'
The fourth one said, 'God has protected me
    From falling in the same pit as those three!'
The prayers of all four men were spoilt this way;*
    These four fault-finders thus went more astray.
Blessed are those who their own flaws can see,   3045
    And will accept responsibility.
Half of each human is by nature flawed,
    The other half, though, is linked to the Lord.
Since you have ten wounds on your head and need
    To treat them, so the pain might then recede,
To find faults with yourself is your best cure—
    '*Have pity!*'* needs humility that's pure.
Even if you don't have the same flawed trait,
    It may come to you at a later date.
Since you've not heard from God His '*Don't you fear!*'*   3050
    You can't assume that you're in safety here.
Satan for years could boast much-envied fame,
    But was disgraced—now look at his deep shame!
Once in the world he had a lofty station,
    But now he's cursed—witness his degradation!
Don't seek fame till you have security.
    Wash fear from your face, then let others see.
Until your own beard grows, good man, don't dare
    To mock one whose chin lacks a single hair!
The devil faced a trial, and then he fell,   3055
    To serve as your own special warning-bell—
Don't fall in and thus warn that beast instead!
    Poison he drank—God's sugar you'll be fed.

The Ghuzz Turks* strove to kill one man, so another might be frightened by this

One day blood-spilling Ghuzz Turk warriors came
    Upon a village, plunder their sole aim.
They found two local men along the way
    And tried to kill one of them straight away;
They bound his hands to kill him, but he said:
    'Great noble men, by whom vast tribes are led,
Before you murder me please tell me why   3060
    You thirst for my cheap blood—why must I die?
What is the point of killing one like me?
    I'm poor, and naked too, as all can see.'
One said, 'Your friend we aim to terrify
    So much he'll tell us where the treasures lie.'
'But he's much poorer!' then this man implored.
    'He's just pretending he knows where it's stored!
We're both the same in your imagination,
    In guesswork's dubious and rough calculation,
So kill him first, not me, as I'm not bold,   3065
    And I will show you where to find the gold.'
Witness God's kindness to us, my good friend,
    That we've come later, closer to the end:
Our cycle's better than those of the past—
    The Prophet said: '*The best ones are the last.*'
The sorry fates of Noah's and Hud's* nations
    Reveal His mercy to our generations:
He killed them, wishing we'd be fearful men;
    If he had done the opposite, what then!

Explaining the state of the self-conceited and those ungrateful for the blessing of the existence of prophets and saints

When good men warn of major faults and sin   3070
    And stony hearts and blackened souls within,

And taking very lightly God's command,
 And not expressing fear of what He's planned,
And being weak like women who feel lust,
 And loving this base world made of mere dust,
And fleeing from our counsellors' advice
 (Avoiding meeting them at any price),
And straying from our own hearts and from gnostics,
 And being sly and false to noble mystics,
You call them beggars so disdainfully,   3075
 And jealously think them the enemy.
You'll call each 'beggar' if he should receive
 Your gift; if not 'He just wants to deceive!'
Should he approach, you'll claim, 'He's covetous!'
 If not, 'His arrogance is nauseous!'
Or, like a hypocrite, you'll try the plea:
 'My time's spent working for my family;
I don't have time to even scratch my head
 Let alone think about my faith instead.
Remember me in your deep states, my friend,   3080
 So I'll become a great saint in the end.'
Your type don't ever speak through inner pain,
 But mumble sounds then fall asleep again.
You'll claim, 'I'm poor; I've no alternative—
 I must work hard for lawful means to live.'
Your blood's the only lawful thing I see;
 You're now as far astray as one can be,
Forsaking God but holding on to bread,
 Abandoning faith to follow fools instead.
You feel that you can't ever live without   3085
 This world, but not *the Lord who spread it out.**
You cling to comforts, niceties you hoard,
 But how can you go on without the Lord?
You can't bear life without created things,
 Yet you would live without the King of Kings.
Abraham left the cave and screamed, elated:
 '*This one's my lord!** Its form, though, who created?'
I'll look through both the worlds until I find
 The one by whom all objects were designed;

If I don't see God's attributes, my food   3090
   Will stick inside my throat and spoil my mood:
How can I swallow while I can't observe
   The rose-garden of God, the lord I serve?
Save in the hope for God, how can one drink
   Unless one is a beast who cannot think?
They are *like cattle, only more astray*:*
   They're devious, smelly, and will not obey.
Their tricks rebound on their own souls, my friend,
   And what remains of their lives will soon end.
Like senile men, their brains become too slow,   3095
   And when their lives end, nothing's left to show.
Each one will claim, 'I'm thinking of that day,'
   But that's a tale his ego loves to say.
'*He is forgiving*,'* each of them will cry,
   But that's their ego's way to cheat and lie;
Through lack of food you grieve as if half-dead—
   If He's forgiving, why do you feel dread?

An old man complains to a physician of his ailments and the physician answers him

An old man told his doctor, 'I'm in pain:
   I'm suffering due to problems with my brain!'
'Old age is where the cause of this pain lies.'   3100
   He then said, 'There are dark spots on my eyes!'
The doctor answered, 'That's old age as well.'
   And next he said, 'My back now hurts like hell!'
'Old age has caused that too, I must conclude.'
   'I also can't digest at all my food.'
'Weak stomachs come with old age too, my friend.'
   'Breathing is hard for me—when will it end?'
'Shortness of breath is common as are wheezes;
   Old age will bring a myriad of diseases.'
'Can you say nothing more?' the old man said,   3105
   'On medicine is this all that you've read?

Does this mean that your knowledge is so poor
   You don't know for each pain God's made a cure?
You are a stupid man of little worth;
   You're base—that's why you're trapped upon this earth.'
And so the doctor said, 'Old man, this rage
   And temper is as well due to old age.
Your body parts are weak; you'll now begin
   To witness that your patience has grown thin.'
Old men can't tolerate two words without   3110
   A screamed retort: they drink then spew it out,
Except wise elders who're intoxicated
   With God—*the blissful life** they've demonstrated.
Each one just looks old, but is young inside—
   Like this why do the saints and prophets hide?
What are they if by most they can't be seen?
   Why do they turn base men through envy green?
If they can't see God's saints with certainty,
   Why do their foes hatch plots with enmity?
And if unsure of Judgment Day's rewards,   3115
   Why do they throw themselves against their swords?
One smiles at you—don't look back with a grin!
   Great resurrections he contains within:
Heaven and hell are parts of this man, who
   Transcends whatever is conceived by you.
Whatever you conceive dies in the end,
   For only God can't be conceived, my friend.
Why, at the saint's door, are some puffed with pride?
   Don't they know who it is that lives inside?
The mosques are what the stupid venerate,   3120
   While they attack the mystics with sick hate—
Donkeys, your mosques are only transient things!
   The real mosques are the hearts of mystic kings;
The saint's heart is the greatest mosque around
   Because that is the place where God is found.*
When a saint was attacked, and only then,
   Did God first choose to put to shame some men:
They fought the prophets,* who looked just the same
   To them; they only saw their human frame.

If you have your forefathers' bad traits too,   3125
    Are you not scared the same fate waits for you?
Those traits can be seen in you easily,
    For you are one of them—where will you flee?

The story of Johi * and the child who lamented
at his father's funeral

Before his father's coffin, once a child
    Would weep and beat his head like someone wild.
'Where are they taking you?' the child would say,
    'That they are lowering you down this way?
Is it a narrow house of pain down there
    Without a carpet, like a house that's bare,
No lamp at night and no meals there by day,   3130
    Where even whiffs of food won't waft your way,
No roof, nor doors that open properly,
    No neighbour who might offer sanctuary?
Your eyes which were admired by all around
    Surely to such a bleak, dark place aren't bound,
A cramped and gloomy place that's unprotected,
    In which no sign of life can be detected!'
He listed features of this awful place,
    Wept tears of blood which trickled down his face.
To his own father Johi turned to say,   3135
    'They're taking that man to our house today.'
His father scoffed, 'Don't be an idiot!'
    He said, 'But all the signs are accurate:
He has described each one of them in turn
    And they match our own house, if you discern:
No rug, nor lamp, nor food is found inside,
    Nor roof, nor doors through which to reach outside!'

The vile display a hundred signs like these
    But, though they're clear to us, none of them sees.

The heart's house starved of radiance totally   3140
    Lacks rays from the sun of divinity;
Like a denier's soul—a cramped, dark waste—
    Of love's king it has never had a taste;
Neither in that heart does the sunlight fall,
    Nor does it feel expansion's joy at all.
The grave is better than this wretched heart—
    Ascend from your own heart's grave and depart!
You who're alive and seem so animated
    Must feel in this cramped tomb so suffocated!
The Joseph of your age, the sun of grace,   3145
    Escape this well and gaol, then show your face!*
You're Jonah, who inside a whale spent days,
    But managed to escape it through God's praise;
The belly of the whale would otherwise
    Have been his cell till that day *all must rise*—
Through praising God, Jonah escaped at last;
    Praise is a sign which points back to *Alast*.
If you've forgotten now the inner praise,
    Listen to mystic fish and learn their ways.
Those who see God become divine, my friend;   3150
    Those who swim seas become fish in the end.
The body is a whale, the world an ocean;
    Spirit is Jonah, blocked from light and motion;
If it starts praising God, it then breaks free,
    If not then it's consumed there instantly.
The ocean has fish of a mystic kind,
    But you can't see them, fool, because you're blind.
Those fish for fun now bounce themselves off you—
    Open your eyes to verify it's true!
Though your eyes cannot see them, my dear friend,   3155
    Your ears will hear God's praises which they send.

To practise patience is the best of ways—
    Be patient, for that's the best form of praise!
No praise is to a similar degree—
    Be patient! *For relief it is the key.*

Patience is heaven's bridge which must cross hell;*
  Beauties wait there, their ugly slaves as well—
If you flee from her slave, you'll be denied
  Her presence, for that slave won't leave her side.
Patience is still unknown to your weak heart,   3160
  Since from a beauty you're not kept apart.
Real men seek glory through love's inner fights;
  The penis is what's loved by sodomites:
They've left faith due to penis adoration;
  Their thoughts have caused their shameful degradation!
Don't fear them even if they fly above,
  For all they've gained is vile, debasing love.
Each leads his horse down a most steep descent,
  Although he claims his aim is an ascent.
Why fear the banners beggars wave ahead?   3165
  Those banners are just means of gaining bread.

A child is frightened by a huge man, who says, 'Don't be scared, child, for I am not a man'

A huge man found a child alone one night.
  What did he want? The child grew pale with fright.
'Now rest assured, my handsome boy,' he said,
  'That you will mount on top of me instead.
View me as impotent, though I am strong;
  Ride me as if a camel—come along!'
In form a man, but twisted actually,
  Outwardly human, devilish inwardly.
Fat like the Aad,* he seemed a drum in form   3170
  On which the wind strikes branches in a storm.
A fox released its prey, and then turned back,
  Attracted by a drum-like empty sack.
On finding its 'drum' empty, it complained:
  'A pig is better than what has remained!'*
Foxes fear drum beats, which make them act meek—
  The wise beat their drums hard to say '*Don't speak!*'

The story about an archer's fear of a horseman who was riding in the forest

An armed and frightening horseman rode ahead
    Into a forest on a thoroughbred.
An archer standing there saw him and drew   3175
    His bow in fear, not knowing what to do.
He aimed to shoot; the rider shouted out:
    'I'm weak—don't let my huge frame make you doubt!
Please listen! Don't just judge me by my size!
    I'm weaker than a crone who sits and cries.'
The archer said, 'Please pass; your words ring true.
    If you'd not spoken I'd have shot at you.'
Weapons kill those who hold them frequently,
    When they lack the required maturity:
If you hold Rostam's weapons and feel fear,   3180
    Not man enough, your soul will disappear.
So make your soul a shield and drop your sword—
    The headless will gain new heads from the Lord.
Your weapons are your trickery and plots—
    They've wounded your own soul by taking shots.
Since from your tricks you've gained naught in the end,
    Abandon them, so God good luck might send!
Since from men's arts you've seen no actual gain,
    Seek *Bounty's Lord* and from such arts abstain!
Men's sciences are not the fortunate kind,   3185
    So be a dunce and leave bad luck behind;
Then, like the angels, say, '*God, we know naught*
    Except the knowledge which You've kindly taught.'*

The story about the Bedouin who put sand in a sack and was criticized for this by a philosopher

A Bedouin made his poor camel strain
    By loading two big sacks—one full of grain.

He sat on them when he began to ride;
  A scholar questioned him, one puffed with pride.
This scholar started thus a conversation,
  Which was an eloquent interrogation:
He asked, 'What do those two big sacks contain?   3190
  Tell me with what they're filled and what you'll gain!'
He said, 'One of those sacks is filled with wheat,
  The other sand not fit for men to eat.'
'Why bring a sack of sand with you today?'
  'The other might feel lonely on the way.'
'Pour half the wheat which fills that sack instead
  Into the other sack!' the scholar said,
'Lighten your camel's load, while you still can.'
  The Bedouin screamed, 'Bravo, learned man!
You have a subtle mind, your judgement's sound—   3195
  Naked and tired why must you walk around?'
He pitied the poor scholar, so his plan
  Was to seat on his camel this wise man.
He asked him next, 'Well-spoken sage, please share
  With me a bit about your own affair;
With such intelligence and talent too,
  A minister or king—which one are you?'
'I'm just an ordinary man, my friend—
  Look at the way I dress and comprehend!'
'How many camels then do you possess?'   3200
  'None. Please don't ask what causes me distress!'
'What kind of goods do you sell at your store?'
  'I have no store—don't press me any more!'
'Well, please inform me how much gold you own,
  Peerless sage, whose good counsel is well known;
You can transform this world with alchemy,
  And you boast precious and rare sophistry.'
He answered, 'All the wealth that I possess
  Can't buy food for tonight—it is much less!
Barefoot and naked I must run around,   3205
  Heading wherever free food can be found.
From all this art and wisdom all I gain
  Is headaches and vain fancies in my brain!'

The Bedouin then said, 'Get far away,
  So that your bad luck won't descend my way!
Take your ill-fortuned wisdom far from me!
  It brings bad luck to our community.
You go that way, I'll go this way instead;
  Or I'll walk backwards if you walk ahead.
Mere sacks of wheat and sand are in my eyes   3210
  Worth more than being uselessly so wise!
My idiocy's a blessing I've no doubt,
  Because my heart's content, my soul devout.
If you want to reduce your misery,
  Rid yourself of your wisdom—be like me!'
He meant the wisdom in one's outward nature,
  Not that sort which is light from the Creator;
With worldly wisdom doubts will multiply,
  While mystic wisdom makes your soul soar high.
These days the vile, depraved men who are clever   3215
  Claim higher ranks than any mystic ever.
Students of trickery themselves have burnt;
  Pretence and plotting is all they have learnt.
Patience, self-sacrifice, and chivalry,
  Which are real gains, they've thrown out heedlessly.
Real thought is that which opens paths inside;
  The path is that on which the true kings ride.
The proper king is king in his own right,
  Not through his treasures or his army's might,
And so he always will hold this position,   3220
  Just like the glory of Mohammad's mission.

The miracles of Ebrahim-e Adham* on the ocean's shore

About Ebrahim-e Adham they say
  That he stopped on the ocean's shore one day,
And sewed his cloak while resting briefly there.
  A prince arrived and soon began to stare;
As a disciple of this shaikh, he knew
  Just who he was, and bowed as he should do.

He was astonished at the garb he wore,
  For he'd transformed from what he was before:
A comfortable life of prosperity   3225
  He'd given up to live in poverty.
He thought, 'He has renounced enormous riches.
  Now, like a beggar, woollen cloaks he stitches!'
The shaikh could read this person's thoughts with ease—
  Hearts are the jungles which this lion sees:
He enters in their hearts like hope and fear;
  The secrets of the world to him are clear,
So guard your hearts, you useless slaves of greed,
  When near the masters of your hearts—take heed!
For worldly men, respect is shown outside,   3230
  Since God the unseen realm from them will hide;
For mystics though, respect's shown inwardly,
  Because their hearts see every mystery—
You do the opposite: for a position
  You'll kneel before the blind men in petition!
You don't behave near mystics as you should,
  And so in fires of lust you'll burn like wood;
Since you lack true perception of God's light,
  You put on make-up for men lacking sight;
And for the mystics you rub on your face   3235
  Manure, then pose imagining you've grace!

The shaikh then tossed a needle in the sea
  And called for its return immediately.
Myriads of divine fish came to sight,
  Gold needles in their lips, which were pressed tight—
They raised their heads thus from God's ocean and
  Said, 'Take God's needles, shaikh, with your pure hand!'
He turned his face toward the prince and said,
  'The heart's wealth or the wretched kind instead?'
This is the outer sign, and nothing more—   3240
  Wait till you see within what lies in store!
Just one branch from the garden men bring down—
  They can't bring the whole garden to your town;

When heaven's just one leaf of it—heed well,
    That it's the kernel while this is the shell.

If you're not rushing to the garden, friend,
    Seek more scent to make your congestion end,
And then the scent will give your soul delight,
    Attracting you like light which gives eyes sight.
Jacob's son Joseph, due to that scent's trace,   3245
    Instructed, '*Throw it on my father's face!*'*
The Prophet often said for that scent's sake:
    '*In ritual prayer the most delight I take!*'*
Our senses are connected, as we've shown,
    Since from the same root each of them has grown;
Strengthen one and it will make strong the others—
    Each one becomes the Saqi for its brothers.
Seeing makes love grow and intensify,
    And love gives truthful vision to each eye;
Such true perception wakes your other senses   3250
    To deeper and direct experiences.

*How the mystic's illumination begins with the light which
sees the hidden world*

When from its bonds one sense should be set free,
    The rest transform as well accordingly.
If one sense sees what is invisible,
    Then for all senses that's perceptible:
When one sheep jumps across the stream, each one
    Will copy then what that first sheep has done.
Drive on your senses' sheep, so there they'll graze:
    '*He brings forth pastures,*'* God's divine book says,
Where they can savour flowers, herbs, and trees,   3255
    And find the rosebud of realities.
Each sense will be a prophet for the others,
    So all of them reach paradise like brothers.

Your senses of the secrets they'll inform
  Without tongues, without meaning, without form,
For meaning's open to interpretations,
  And idle whims spring from loose estimations;
But inner truths which are made manifest
  Can't be interpreted, unlike the rest.
When each sense is the slave of that first sense   3260
  The heavens too will show obedience:
If there's an argument about the shell,
  The kernel's owner owns that shell as well;
And if a quarrel starts about some straw,
  Find out who owned the seeds—this is the law!
The sky's the shell, the spirit's light the kernel,
  One manifest, one hidden and eternal.
Bodies are seen; spirits are what they hide:
  Bodies are sleeves; spirits the arms inside.
Intellect is more hidden than that spirit   3265
  Which gives us life, for senses can't perceive it:
You know a man's alive if he should move,
  But that he has a brain you still can't prove
Until he starts to move deliberately,
  And changes movements thus with alchemy:
Through the appropriate manner his hands move
  Intellect's presence you can easily prove.
But revelation's spirit's more concealed—
  It's from beyond and seldom is revealed:
The Prophet's intellect was clear to view,   3270
  His spirit, though, could be perceived by few.*
The spirit has clear movements of its own,
  But through the intellect they can't be known;
Sometimes it thinks it mad, sometimes undone,
  Since it is veiled until they join as one:
Like Khezr's each divinely guided action—
  Moses's brain grew troubled in reaction;
His actions seemed so inappropriate—
  To understand them Moses was unfit.
Unseen truths Moses couldn't comprehend,   3275
  So what can a mere mouse perceive, my friend?*

*

Knowledge that's rote-learnt is what's usually sold,
  Its source of joy a buyer who brings gold.
Experiential knowledge God will buy;
  His market's profit is forever high.
Lips sealed, drunk on the rapid rate of business,
  Since *God has bought them*,* shoppers here are countless.
Angels will buy what Adam has to teach,
  But for the demons this is out of reach.
Adam, *to whom We taught the names*,* please share   3280
  With us God's secrets, every detail there!
A man who suffers from shortsightedness
  Will be unstable and lack steadfastness;
Since this man lives on earth I call him 'mouse';
  In soil is where you find the mouse's house;
He knows some paths, but they're all underground;
  He's penetrated mud-piles all around.
The mouse-soul is a nibbler ruled by greed;
  Its brain is in proportion to its need,
Since God does not give anything for free   3285
  Without there being a necessity.
If this world gave us no real benefit
  The Lord then wouldn't have created it;
If shaky earth did not need to keep still,
  It wouldn't be pinned down by every hill;
If there were really no need for the skies,
  He wouldn't have displayed them to our eyes;
The sun, the moon, and stars that sparkle too—
  Except through need, how were they brought to view?
Thus, need is the lasso which you must throw;   3290
  According to your needs He will bestow:
Increase your neediness now rapidly—
  His sea will surge with generosity.
Beggars and handicapped men fill the street
  To show their neediness to those they meet:
Their blindness, their paralysis and pain
  They show, so they might from men's kindness gain.
Does anyone say, 'People, please feed me
  Because I have food, wealth, and property?'

God hasn't given eyes to moles, since they   3295
   Don't need them to trap food in their own way;
They can survive without sight, but not blood:
   They don't need eyes to live in dark, damp mud.
They won't come out, unless they start to long
   For God to free them, cleanse them of all wrong,
So they might gain wings, each fly like a dove
   Or angel, circling in the sky above;
Then in thanksgiving's rosebush constantly
   They'd sing like nightingales in ecstasy:
'You freed us from all ugliness and vice,   3300
   And hellfire You transformed to paradise;
To lumps of fat called "eyeballs" You give sight,
   And hearing to mere bones—You have such might!'

The spirit and the body's link's the same
   As that between our knowledge and its name:
Names are nests, knowledge birds that live therein;
   Bodies are ditches, spirits streams within.
The streams flow, though they seem so motionless;
   The waves pass by, though one would never guess.
If you, in truth, can't see the water flow,   3305
   What do the passing twigs on it then show?
Your twigs are forms which in your mind you see;
   These virgin forms arrive continually;
They're carried on the flowing stream of thought;
   Some of them are delightful, some are not.
The husks on flowing water all have been
   Brought from the garden of the Deep Unseen—
Seek out the kernels; it's not a vain dream,
   Since from the Garden to us flows this stream.
If you can't see the Water of Life flow,   3310
   Look at the stream—watch straws slide to and fro!
When water flows in greater quantity,
   The husks of forms too move more rapidly;
And when the stream's flow is extremely fast,
   The mystic's conscience is stress-free at last,

For when its flow is rapid, full, and strong,
    Then nothing else but water flows along.

A stranger reviles a shaikh and the shaikh's disciple answers him

A man pinned on a Sufi shaikh much blame:
    'He's wicked and depraved, and he lacks shame!
He drinks wine; he's a fraud—he's so astray!   3315
    How can he lead disciples on the way?'
That shaikh's disciple said, 'Observe respect!
    It's serious such great masters to suspect!
For someone like him with such sanctity,
    A deluge can't reduce his purity.
Don't make against such saints false accusations!
    Turn over a new leaf—stop fabrications!
They're false, but even if your words were true,
    What harm to a huge sea can one corpse do?
He's more than *the two jarfuls and small pool**   3320
    That one small drop could ruin him, you fool!'
Abraham's fire was not reduced one bit—
    So warn the Nimrods: 'Be afraid of it!'
The self is Nimrod; spirit is God's Friend:*
    The self needs signs; spirits can view the end.
Signposts serve those still travelling, since they
    Inside the desert often lose their way.
The eyes of those who've reached the destination
    Don't care for signposts to another station;
If such a man refers to signs, it's so   3325
    The scholars too can have a chance to know:
A father for his child makes baby sounds,
    Even if his own knowledge knows no bounds;
The teacher may have great ability,
    But still she'll start her class with ABC.
To teach a toddler who can hardly stand
    One must use words that he can understand;
You must use the same words as children do,
    So they can learn new knowledge then from you—

We are like children lagging far behind;   3330
   While teaching us, shaikhs keep this fact in mind.

The shaikh's disciple carried on this way,
   Regarding him so dangerously astray:
'Don't slash now at yourself with a sharp sword!
   Don't start a fight now with this wondrous lord!
A pool next to an ocean in an instant
   Removes itself, becoming non-existent.
He is an ocean which is limitless—
   Your corpse can't make its value any less.
There are constraints to infidelity—   3335
   His light has no constraint or boundary.
All transient things are worthless entities:
   *"All but God's face must perish,"** He decrees.
Near him no faith nor unbelief can dwell,
   Since He's the kernel, while they are the shell.
We cover up his face like veils outside;
   The lamp beneath a bowl we temporals hide.
Your physical head veils another head;
   An infidel veils one divinely led.
Infidels doubt the shaikh's fidelity;   3340
   Corpses can't see the shaikh's vitality.
In life's test, knowledge is the thing that counts:
   If you have more, your life to more amounts.
Animal souls to our souls are inferior,
   Because in knowledge ours are far superior;
But angels' souls are higher than ours, friend,
   Because the physical realm they transcend;
But higher still are souls of mystic greats—
   Cease the bewilderment this fact creates!
At Adam's feet who was then the prostrator?*   3345
   His soul was therefore obviously the greater:
For a superior being to prostrate
   To those worth less is inappropriate—
The Lord's kind justice, which we count upon,
   Won't let our rose bow down before a thorn.

When the pure soul grows, passing every limit,
    The souls of other things must all obey it;
Birds, fish, and every other animal,
    And even men—it's incomparable!
The fish make needles for his sufi cloak;   3350
    Threads follow needles just like trails of smoke:

Remainder of the story about Ebrahim Ebn-e Adham on the shore

Once the prince saw the shaikh's command fulfilled,
    He felt ecstatic and extremely thrilled:
'Mere fish of mystic masters are aware—
    We're cursed if we're unable to reach there!
The fish can recognize, while we're unsure;
    Though we're the ones with wealth, we're much more poor!'
After prostrating, he felt love's deep pain;
    Through yearning for *the gates,** he went insane.

Disgraced wretch, what is your concern and aim?   3355
    Through envy whom do you now fight and blame?
You're playing with the lion's tail—stand back!
    The angels why do you wish to attack?
Why speak ill of pure goodness? You have lied;
    You even say humility is pride.
What's evil like then? Cheap, deficient copper.
    And shaikhs? The alchemy which lasts forever.
Copper which won't respond to alchemy
    Can't harm it with its own deficiency.
What's evil like then? Rebels filled with fire.   3360
    Who is the shaikh? The sea which won't expire.
Fire always fears the water, but why should
    Water fear being burnt like planks of wood?
You're picking faults with the moon's radiant face—
    In paradise you seek thorns, vile disgrace!
Thorn-picker, if you go to heaven too,
    You won't find any thorn apart from you.

You're covering the sun with mud, buffoon!
   You want to find chinks in a bright, full moon!
How can a sun which shines so brilliantly   3365
   Be hidden for a bat's sake? Answer me!
Dislike by masters will make things defective;
   Secrets are kept when masters feel protective.
If you are far, through service cut the distance!
   Be fast and be efficient in repentance,
So that you might be sent from them a breeze!
   Why block His mercy's flow through jealousies?
If you're far from them, wag your tail and sway!
   *Wherever you are, turn your face His way.**
When an ass falls in mud, then you will see   3370
   It try to get up, struggling constantly—
It knows the mud is not appropriate,
   That it is not the proper home for it.
Are you less than an ass? Has your heart blood?
   Why won't you jump away now from the mud?
In mud you deem it worthy now to stay,
   As you don't want to pull your heart away:
'Since I'm compelled, it is allowed for me—
   God wouldn't punish helpless men, would he?'
He's punished you already, but you're blind,   3375
   More hoodwinked than a blind hyena's mind:
The hunters shout, 'Hyenas aren't inside
   This cave; none hide in there—let's search outside!'
They say this just to trap one and creep near,
   And that hyena thinks, 'I'm safe in here.
If these foes know my hiding-place, then why
   Would they shout, "Where is it?" at passers-by?'

*Someone claims, 'God will not punish me for sin,'
and Sho'ayb* answers him*

In the time of Sho'ayb, a man once claimed:
   'God sees my faults, for which I should be blamed;
He's seen so many sins of mine, yet He,   3380
   Out of sheer kindness, will not punish me!'

God whispered in Sho'ayb's ear from on high
   So clearly that this would be His reply:
'You have just said, "I've sinned so many times;
   God has not punished me though for my crimes"—
The truth's the opposite of what you say,
   You who have left the path and gone astray:
Often I punish you, but you don't know,
   And you are trapped in chains from head to toe!'
Black pot, the layers of rust on you now cover   3385
   And spoil your inner face, as you'll discover:
Rust has spread to your heart like a disease,
   Making it blind to lofty mysteries.
If we should put a clean pot in your place,
   Heat from the flames would leave an obvious trace,
Because through opposites all things are known:
   On something white, black markings will be shown.
But once the pot's turned black, the fire's effect
   No eyes will still be able to detect.
And if the blacksmith is of the black race,   3390
   The smoke will match the colour of his face;
But if the blacksmith is a pale-faced Greek,
   The smoke will leave black patches on his cheek,
So he will quickly learn the price of sin,
   And then to beg forgiveness he'll begin.
If you persist with sins of degradation,
   You'll throw dust in the eye of contemplation—
You won't repent at all; your heart will swell
   With love for sins, just like an infidel,
And so you won't perform remorseful prayers;   3395
   Rust will form on your mirror many layers;
Rust will erode its iron by its presence,
   Reducing thus the value of your essence.
If you write on some paper which is white,
   That writing can be read then at first sight;
If you write on what others wrote before,
   It cannot be deciphered any more,
For black on top of black creates a mess
   Which is illegible and meaningless.

And if to write a third time you turn back,   3400
    You'll make it, like an evil soul, pitch black.
Refuge in God apart, what else have we?
    Despair is copper, vision alchemy.
Lay down despair before Him, so you might
    Escape this deadly pain, and end your plight!

Sho'ayb told him these points, which caused the start
    Of a rose blooming deep within his heart.
That sinner's soul thus heard true revelation,
    And yet he said, 'I've seen no confirmation.'
Sho'ayb told God, 'This wretch will not repent!   3405
    He wants some proof of his own punishment.'
God answered, 'I'm the Veiler; I won't show
    The secrets to him; I'll give one clue though:
One sign that he receives my punishments
    Is that he fasts and prays like penitents,
And worships and gives alms, but it's a waste—
    Of mystic states he's never had a taste.
He does good deeds and acts of piety,
    But hasn't tasted true proximity;
His deeds are empty acts, as though he's lied,   3410
    A walnut with no kernel kept inside.
Spiritual savour is what makes fruit grow;
    There must be kernels in the seeds you sow—
Can kernel-less seeds still grow into trees?
    Soulless forms just exist in fantasies.'

Remainder of the story about the stranger berating the shaikh

He spoke about the shaikh as if insane;
    Distorted vision damages one's brain.
He said, 'I met him at a gathering;
    He's neither pious nor a mystic king,
And, if you doubt this, come along with me   3415
    To witness your own shaikh's depravity!'

He led him to a window: 'That's him drinking—
   Watch his depravity! What were you thinking?
A hypocrite: depraved once out of sight;
   A saint by day, a Bu Lahab by night!
"God's faithful servant" men call him by day;
   At night he fills his glass and drinks away!'
They saw his master with a glass of wine,
   So the disciple asked, 'Dear shaikh of mine,
Did you not say that Satan urinates   3420
   In every glass of wine, and celebrates?'
He said, 'My cup's so full in my heart's core,
   So no one can now pour in any more—
Look here! Is there room for another drop?
   Deluded men misread acts; you must stop!'
He didn't mean the wine that's visible;
   To see unseen things this shaikh's capable.
The glass is the shaikh's being, fool, beware!
   The devil can't direct his urine there.
He is pure light, with God's light he's filled up;   3425
   Becoming light has smashed his body's cup!
If sunlight on a piece of shit is seen,
   It stays the same and isn't made unclean.
'There's neither glass nor wine,' the shaikh then said;
   'If you want to inspect me, go ahead!'
He found some honey of a special kind,
   And realized his doubts had made him blind!
The shaikh told the disciple suddenly:
   'Go to the tavern to buy wine for me,
For I'm in pain, and thus compelled to drink;   3430
   I am so thirsty I have reached the brink.'
When helpless, even carcasses are clean;*
   Curse all deniers, as they're low and mean!
He went to the wine store immediately
   And sampled wine for him obediently,
But found no wine on which to spend his money—
   All of the jugs in there were filled with honey!
He said, 'Wine-tipplers, what has come to pass?
   I can't find wine here to fill up one glass!'

The tipplers sought the shaikh then hurriedly,　　　　3435
　　Beating their heads and weeping bitterly:
'Great shaikh, you visited our tavern once—
　　To honey our wine changed in consequence.
You changed our wine from its unlawful state,
　　So change our hearts now—grant us a clean slate!'
Even if only blood's available,
　　What God's slave drinks will be permissible.

Aisha* complains to the Prophet, 'Why do you pray anywhere and without a prayer rug?'

Aisha told off Mohammad critically:
　　'Prophet, both privately and openly,
Wherever you are, you perform the prayer,　　　　3440
　　Even though dirty people can step there,
And grubby little kids might urinate,
　　If they are playing there and cannot wait.'
'For the sake of great men,' the Prophet said,
　　'God makes unclean things pure and clean instead—
Each spot I place my head He'll purify,
　　From that bare floor to far beyond the sky!'
Stop envying the mystic kings, beware,
　　Or Satan's wretched fate will be your share!
Poison will turn to honey for those few;　　　　3445
　　Honey will turn to poison though for you.
The true man and his actions change this way—
　　He's now all grace; his fire is a light ray.
Each of *those birds** was a recipient
　　Of God's strength, so they'd kill that elephant;
Small birds destroyed an army, so you'd know
　　They gained their strength from God against their foe.
About those birds, if you have any doubt,
　　Find the tale in the Book* and read it out!
If you try to compete with God's elite,　　　　3450
　　I warn you that you're bound to taste defeat!

How a mouse pulled the rope of the camel's bridle and became conceited

A mouse got tied up in a camel's lead,
　　Which meant it travelled with it at great speed,
And since the camel didn't seem to mind,
　　It dreamt, 'I'm a mouse of a special kind!'
The camel sensed what that mouse dreamt about,
　　And said, 'Amuse yourself! I'll sort you out!'
After a while, the pair reached a deep river,
　　The sight of which made wolves and lions shiver.
The terrified mouse stood completely still.　　　　　　3455
　　The camel asked, 'Companion from the hill,
Why have you stopped? Why are you at a loss?
　　Step forward like a brave man—walk across!
Great mouse, my guide and leader, don't stop here
　　And give up. There is nothing now to fear.'
'The water is too deep,' the mouse complained,
　　'The fear of drowning leaves my frail heart drained!'
'Let me see just how deep,' the camel said,
　　And then stepped quickly on the riverbed.
'Look, mouse, the water reaches to my knees.　　　　3460
　　Why are you stricken with anxieties?'
'A dragon for me is an ant to you;
　　There's a huge difference between us two:
If it should reach your knees like you have said,
　　Then it is far above my tiny head.'
The camel said, 'Don't be so bold again,
　　Or else you'll burn with soul-tormenting pain!
Compete with your own species, and beware:
　　You've nothing that a camel wants to share.'
The mouse said, 'I repent! Please give a ride—　　　3465
　　Help me to make it to the other side!'
The camel, moved with pity, told it, 'Jump!
　　Climb on my back, then rest upon my hump.

This is not difficult for me to do;
　I could take millions of small mice like you!'

You're not a prophet—take the mystic way,
　From this pit to reach lofty heights one day.
Act like a subject, since you're not the sultan!
　Don't row the boat when you are not the boatman.
Since you're not perfect, don't start out alone.　3470
　Be pliant like good dough, not hard like stone!
God said, '*Keep silent!*'* so don't you forget.
　Be all ears, since you're not God's mouthpiece yet!
Request an explanation, if you speak.
　Before the King, like beggars, show you're meek!
Lust causes hate and pride—that's not disputed;
　And habit is what makes lust firmly rooted.
When habit makes a bad trait permanent,
　To those who hold you back you're violent:
You want to eat mud now, so you'll oppose　3475
　All men who hold you back, as if they're foes:
When pagans gather round an idol, they
　Will fend off men who try to block their way.
Since Satan had got used to leading, he
　Thought Adam his inferior heedlessly:
'Can there be someone who is my superior,
　That I should have to bow as his inferior?'*
Leading is poison but for spirits who
　Possess the antidote; such men are few:
Snakes in the mountains aren't cause for alarm;　3480
　The antidote's found there too, so stay calm!
When leadership controls your brain, you'll see
　Whoever thwarts you as your enemy;
If anyone should contradict your view,
　Hatred of him will soon rise up in you:
You'll scream, 'He's trying to dictate to me,
　Acting as if he has authority!'
If you do not have a bad disposition,
　Why do you flare up with such opposition?

You may have once seemed good to your opponent   3485
  And won his heart like this, for at that moment
Your bad ways weren't entrenched yet like sharp stakes—
  Through habit, ants of lust turn into snakes.
Kill lust's snake, so you can survive the trial,
  Or it will be a dragon in a while!
Each claims his snake's an ant, a trivial thing;
  About your true state ask a mystic king:
Till turned to gold, copper no flaws can see;
  Till made king, one can't measure poverty.
Copper, serve the elixir and you'll gain!   3490
  Endure, heart, your beloved's harsh disdain!
Mystics are the beloveds—can't you see?
  They strive to flee this world continually;
Stop finding fault with God's slaves, stupid fool,
  And don't accuse of theft the ones who rule!

The miracles of that dervish who was accused of stealing on a ship

A dervish once was travelling on a ship
  Without his own provisions for his trip.
While he slept, someone's purse had disappeared;
  Those who'd searched all the rest then gradually neared.
'Let's search this sleeping beggar,' one man said,   3495
  And so the purse's owner slapped his head:
'A purse was lost on this ship just today;
  We have searched everyone—don't run away!
Take off your jacket! Strip, so you can prove
  It wasn't you, and all our doubts remove!'
He prayed, 'God, Your meek slave might soon be killed,
  Accused of theft. May Your will be fulfilled!'
The dervish's heart then began to pound,
  And suddenly fish jumped up all around;
A million fish then from the sea took flight,   3500
  In each one's mouth a pearl which was so bright;
Millions of them rose up from the deep sea,
  Huge pearls held in their mouths triumphantly,

Each pearl the revenue of a whole nation;
   They sang: 'They're God's, free from association!'
The dervish threw some on the deck and flew
   Up in the air, ascending a throne too:
Like kings, cross-legged he sat on his throne
   Above the zenith, to which he had flown.
'You keep your ship; God will suffice for me.   3505
   This beggar won't stay in your company,
But who will lose out from this separation?
   I'm pleased with God, remote from His creation.
He won't blame me for theft mistakenly;
   And, for accusers, He won't shackle me.'
The other passengers screamed out, amazed:
   'To such a station how have you been raised?'
He said, 'Not for accusing mystic kings
   And bothering God just for trivial things,
But rather for revering His elect—   3510
   Great saints I didn't hassle or suspect!
Dervishes with sweet breath who've earned renown,
   For whom the chapter *Abasa** came down—
Their poverty is not life trapped in dirt,
   But "There is nothing but God" to assert.
How can I doubt God's special devotees,
   Whom He's entrusted with His treasuries?'
Suspect the self, not the high intellect;
   Your senses, not God's light, you should reject.
This cunning carnal soul needs to be hit—   3515
   Beat it instead of arguing with it!
If it sees miracles, it will agree,
   Then later claim, 'It was mere fantasy;
If that huge miracle were really true
   Why then did it not last and stay in view?'
It does remain in view for purest souls,
   Though it's not seen by sensual animals;
That miracle hates sensuality:
   When caged a peacock struggles to break free.
Don't say I am verbose, for what you've read   3520
   Is one small portion, one hair from your head!

Some Sufis verbally abuse another Sufi, saying 'He talks too much in front of the shaikh'

Some Sufis cursed another angrily
    Before the shaikh of their community.
They told the shaikh, 'We beg that you demand
    Fairness from him. Please make him understand!'
He asked, 'What is it that makes you irate?'
    'He has three habits, shaikh, which irritate:
He talks too much, as noisy as a bell;
    He eats more than a score of men as well;
He sleeps more than the Sleepers in the Cave.'   3525
    These reasons to their shaikh the Sufis gave.
The shaikh turned to the blamed man then, to say:
    'In every venture take the middle way—
The Prophet said, "*The best path's moderation*."
    A balanced nature leads to the best station;
If you should fail to keep that harmony,*
    Sickness will overwhelm you suddenly.
Do not exceed what you see in your friend,
    As that will cause division in the end.'

Moses's words appeared proportionate,   3530
    But Khezr found them too inappropriate;
Not tolerating doubting and debate,
    Khezr told him, '*This is where we separate!*'
Moses, you talk too much, so go away!
    Be mute and blind if you desire to stay!
If you remain here to debate all night,
    You'll still have severed all ties in my sight!'
If you should soil yourself while you are praying,
    'Go, clean yourself!' you'll then hear a voice saying.
If you don't go, your prayer will be in vain,   3535
    For purity has left you, empty brain!*
Go to your soulmates, who have the desire
    To hear your speech, and from it never tire!

The watchman's better than those fast asleep,
    But fish don't need a watchman in the deep:
Men's clothes need washing, but illumination
    Clothes naked souls with God's manifestation—
Step back from naked mystics carefully,
    Or from your body's garment now break free!
If you won't strip completely, timid man,   3540
    Follow a middle course then, if you can!

The Sufi excuses himself to the shaikh

The Sufi told the shaikh his point of view,
    Giving appropriate excuses too;
He answered the shaikh's questions, as one should,
    Like Khezr, with answers accurate and good,
Answers to Moses's interrogation
    Inspired in Khezr by the Lord of Creation:
He clarified all the obscurities;
    For all the problems he had found the keys.
From Khezr he had received inheritance—   3545
    He answered his shaikh with intelligence:
'Shaikh, though the moderate way is best to live,
    A mean is always something relative:
A stream won't even reach a camel's knee,
    Although to mice it seems a massive sea;
If someone can eat four loaves, eating two
    Is moderation from his point of view;
But it would be extreme if he should feast
    By eating all four like a greedy beast.
But what if someone easily could eat ten?   3550
    Eating six would be moderation then.
To eat a hundred loaves I'm capable,
    You just six rolls—we're not comparable;
You may be tired out by the evening prayer,
    While, after hundreds, I don't feel much wear;
One walks to Mecca, barefoot all the way,
    Another can't reach local mosques to pray;

One is prepared to sacrifice his soul,
   Another won't give up a mouldy roll!
For finite things, one can derive a mean,   3555
   As they have highs and lows which can be seen—
Both start and end must be observable
   For something's mean to be discernible—
There are no limits to the infinite,
   So how can one work out the mean of it
When its extremities no man has known?
   "*If all the seas were ink*" * this truth has shown.
If all seas turn to ink, still they can't write
   Enough for there to be an end in sight;
If all the forests turn to pens, still they   3560
   Can't lessen what God's speech has to convey.
The pens and ink will empty gradually;
   His boundless speech, though, lasts eternally.
Sometimes I look asleep, then those astray
   Imagine all I do is sleep all day;
My heart's awake, although I've closed my eyes—
   I'm working, but look lazy in disguise!'

'*My eyes sleep*,' was the Prophet's affirmation,
   '*My heart's awake to the Lord of Creation.*'
Eyes open, your heart sleeps now in their place;   3565
   Eyes closed, my heart is open to His Grace.
My heart has other senses than these five;
   In both worlds my heart's special senses thrive—
Don't look at me through your own failing sight!
   For me it's morning, though for you it's night;
For you it's gaol, but it's a park for me:
   Your hard toil is my rest and luxury;
Mud traps your feet, but makes my roses bloom;
   You mourn, while I rejoice with drums that boom.
I live on earth like you, but I can fly   3570
   Beyond the stars and planets in the sky;
My shadow's next to you, but I'm not here—
   My station's higher than thought's lofty sphere.

Since I've transcended all thoughts, I am now
  Racing beyond the questions 'why?' and 'how?'
I rule thought and don't follow its instruction:
  The builder has control of his construction.
Most men are slaves of thought, though, which explains
  Why, through depression, all life from them drains.
By choice, I give myself to thoughts, but still   3575
  I can jump far from them when that's my will.
While thought's a fly, I'm a bird soaring high—
  How can I be controlled by a mere fly?
I came down from the zenith too by choice,
  So those at lower stations might rejoice;
When I grow weary of their base traits, then,
  Like *birds with wings spread*,* I'll soar up again.
From my own inner essence these wings grew—
  I didn't stick my wings on with some glue.
Ja'far the Flyer's* wings were permanent;   3580
  Ja'far the Scoundrel's* wings were only lent.
To those who *haven't tasted*, it's pretension;
  It's truth to those *in the most high dimension*.*
Vile crows may think I'm bragging with cheap lies—
  Empty and full pots are the same to flies!

Since pearls grow from the things you eat, good man,
  Don't hold back—eat as much food as you can!
The shaikh, to fight off thoughts which were ill-willed,
  Vomited pearls until his bowl was filled.
This mystic master made pearls manifest   3585
  To those who with such wisdom weren't blest.
In you, though, food becomes impurity,
  So lock your throat and throw away the key!
For him in whom food turns to Glory's Light,
  All things he eats are lawful, every bite!

*In explanation of how there are some claims, the
truth of which is self-evident*

If you know my soul well, you'll recognize
   My pithy words are not pretentious lies.
If I tell you at midnight, 'I've come near,
   And, since we're kin, do not have any fear!'
You'll know for sure that these claims are both true,   3590
   For your own kin's voice is quite clear to you.
Kinship and nearness are the claims made here;
   You'll know they're true if you can clearly hear,
Because the sound of someone's voice can give
   Evidence that it is a relative;
That joy at a voice known immediately
   Will testify he's from your family.
But uninspired fools, who can't recognize
   A relative's voice from a passer-by's,
Will say these words are unreliable—   3595
   Ignorance claims they are deniable.

Speech from a sage filled with God's light is known
   As truth from what that voice sounds like alone.
In Arabic a man once made this claim:
   'I can speak Arabic.' This is the same:
His speaking Arabic proves that it's true,
   And so it is self-evident to you.
Literate people may each write this note:
   'I can both read and write,' as if to gloat.
Though technically this is another claim,   3600
   The note proves that it's truthful all the same.
A Sufi might say, 'In your dream last night,
   You saw me just as now I'm in your sight,
And in that dream I gave a long oration,
   Explaining what is self-annihilation—
Let it, like earrings, penetrate inside,
   So that my teachings serve as your mind's guide!'

Since you recall the dream that he has told,
  It is a miracle worth more than gold;
Although, in form, a mere claim it may seem,   3605
  Your soul says, 'It is true; I had that dream.'
And *the believer's camel that has strayed**
  Is just like these examples I've conveyed:
If you find truth where it does not belong,
  Why should you worry that it might be wrong?
When you tell someone thirsty, 'Hurry up!
  Drink quickly from the water in this cup.'
Will any thirsty man say, 'What a claim!
  Pretender, I can't trust you. What's your aim?
Show proof that water is contained inside   3610
  From that rare *gushing source*,* and you've not lied!'
Or if a mother tells her child, 'Come near!
  Since I'm your mother, you'll have naught to fear.'
Will the child say, 'I need some evidence
  Before I drink your milk—prove it at once!'
For every nation who seeks God, the face
  And voice of prophets show miraculous grace;
Thus, when their prophet shouts out to dictate,
  Inwardly each of them bows down prostrate;
Their inner ear has not heard such a shout   3615
  From a mere human, so they have no doubt—
If a strange voice should reach an inner ear,
  It will know God is saying, '*I am near!*'*

John the Baptist bows before the womb of the mother of Jesus

John's mother spoke to Mary secretly
  Before she gave birth of this mystery:
'I've seen that a great king is inside you,
  A prophet of God, *who is steadfast too*:*
When I encountered you by chance just now,
  The child inside my womb began to bow—

My baby bowed to yours respectfully,   3620
    And so I felt a strange new pang in me.'
'Yes,' Mary said, 'In me a strange sensation
    Told me about your embryo's prostration.'

A difficulty is raised by this story

The stupid men say, 'Leave this fable out,
    Since it is false; its accuracy we doubt,
For Mary during pregnancy had gone
    As far as possible from everyone:
That wonderful pure woman stayed away
    Until she gave birth—this is what texts say.
While she was pregnant, no one ventured near   3625
    And she did not go home—this much is clear.
When she gave birth to Jesus joyfully,
    She then brought him before her family.
When did John's mother see her then, to share
    What she had understood of this affair?'

The resolution of the problem

Those with true vision easily can view
    Remote things as though they are present too:
John's mother was to Mary visible
    And near, although that seems impossible.
With eyes closed you can see your distant friend,   3630
    If you can see through skin and comprehend.
Even if she did not see inwardly
    John's mother, still accept this tale from me,
Unlike those who hear stories but insist
    They aren't true, like a strict literalist:
'Kalila knew no language,' some men say,
    'How could he hear what Dimna would convey?*
But if these two friends did communicate,
    It wasn't with words men articulate.
How was that Dimna an emissary   3635
    Sent to the ox and lion? Answer me!

An ox can't be the lion's chief vizier;
  The moon can't fill an elephant with fear.
This book of fables is made up, we know,
  Because a stork can't share words with a crow.'
A story is a bushel which contains
  Meanings inside, as though they are wheat grains—
The wise man will take meaning's grains, but pay
  No heed to bushels, which will fade away:
The tale about the rose and nightingale*   3640
  Is rich in meaning, though it's just a tale.

On speaking with a mystic tongue and the comprehension of it

Heed well the moth and candle tale,* my friend!
  Learn from its message, if you comprehend!
Though speechless, it shows inner depths of speech—
  Soar high, friend, to where feeble owls can't reach!
A chess-player said, 'This is the rook's own space.'
  Someone asked, 'How did it obtain that place?
Did it inherit it or buy it cheaply?'
  Happy the message-seeker who dives deeply!
'*X struck Y*,'* a grammarian used to say,   3645
  'What had Y done?' an idiot asked one day,
'That X should strike him with such vehemence,
  Like beating slaves, blind to their innocence?'
'This is the bushel only,' he replied,
  'Take out its wheat and then throw it aside!
X and Y are examples of a rule—
  Though they are fictions, learn the grammar, fool!'
That man complained, 'I cannot understand
  How X hit blameless Y then with his hand!'
The teacher joked, 'That's what he had to do,   3650
  For Y once stole an extra W!*
X hit that thief as soon as he observed
  That he had sinned; it's what that Y deserved!'

Acceptance of worthless sayings by the hearts of worthless people

This fool said, 'Now the truth I can detect!'
    To crooked men, corrupt things are correct.
If you tell a cross-eyed man, 'There's one moon'
    He'll say, 'I see two, so don't speak too soon!'
If someone jokes with him, 'I can see two!'
    He deems it true—for such fools that's their due.
Liars attract lies to themselves—recite: 3655
    '*To wicked women bad men,*'* which sheds light!
Those with big hearts have power over all,
    While blind men always stumble, trip, and fall.

The search for that tree with fruit which gives eternal life

A wise man told this tale: 'There is a tree
    In India which hides a mystery:
Whoever eats its fruit will not grow old
    Or die.' This summarizes what he told.
A king heard this and found the tale impressive;
    He longed for that tree and became obsessive.
He sent a capable emissary,   3660
    An erudite man, to seek out that tree.
For years this cultured man then roamed about
    In India, where he sought this rare tree out.
This poor man went from town to town in vain,
    And searched in every island, hill, and plain.
Men laughed at him when asked about this tree,
    And said, 'Your search is sheer insanity!'
Many in ridicule would slap his face
    And say, 'Distinguished man, pride of your race,
How can the search by one with your fine brain   3665
    And pure heart be so obviously in vain?'
These false words were slaps also to his mind,
    And harder to bear than the other kind.

Sarcastically they praised him, 'Noble man,
   Head for this dangerous place now, if you can,
For in a forest there is a green tree,
   One lofty, broad, and bushy—you will see.'
The king's emissary searched each location,
   But people gave conflicting information.
For years he kept on searching everywhere   3670
   With cash from his king, who had sent him there,
But he grew weary in this foreign land
   And felt so weak that he could hardly stand.
He hadn't found a single trace or clue,
   Just rumours from men acting like they knew,
And all this disappointment snapped hope's thread,
   So what he'd sought he now ignored instead.
Finally, he decided he must go
   Back to the king; as he walked tears would flow.

The shaikh explains the secret of the tree to that seeker who had only imitative knowledge*

There was a mystic at a halting-place   3675
   When he arrived, tears rolling down his face.
He thought, 'With desperate need, I'll venture near
   Before I have to move away from here,
So that his prayer supports me when we part,
   Since I can't find the true aim of my heart.'
He walked towards the shaikh with tear-filled eyes;
   Tears dropped like rain from clouds in heavy skies.
He pleaded, 'Shaikh, have mercy now on me!
   This is the time for generosity.'
'Explain what is the cause of your despair—   3680
   What are you looking for that is so rare?'
He said, 'The king told me to come and find
   A bushy tree which is one of a kind;
Not only rare, its fruit is special too—
   Water of Life each one bestows on you.
I searched for many years, but found no trace;
   I found just ridicule in this vile place!'

The shaikh then laughed and said, 'Hey simple-brain,
    This tree is knowledge which the mystics gain.
It's the most tall, wide, and expansive tree;   3685
    It's Water of Life from God's boundless sea.
You looked for the tree's form, so in the end
    You picked no fruit of inner truth, my friend.
In fact, it's only sometimes called "a tree"—
    At other times it's "sun", "cloud", or "the sea";
From that one source a million things arise,
    With immortality its smallest prize.
Myriads of effects arise from it,
    And therefore countless names appear to fit:
Your father is a father just to you—   3690
    He has to be another man's son too;
He could be someone's foe, while to another
    He could be dearer even than a brother.
One man can have a million names like this;
    Watch just one side and the whole view you'll miss.
To seek the name whoever has selected
    Will soon feel, like you, hopeless and dejected.
Why cling to the name "tree"? You're obstinate!
    You'll thus stay bitter and unfortunate!
Look to the attributes, transcend the name—   3695
    They'll lead you to the essence, your true aim.'*
Disputes between men stem from names, my friend;
    Should they reach meanings, then peace would descend.

Four men argue about grapes, because each knows them by a different name

Four men received a coin and they were poor;
    One of them said, 'Let's spend it on *angur!*'
The second man, an Arab, screamed out, 'Stop!
    Don't buy *angur*, but *'enab* from the shop!'
The third, a Turk, said, 'Just ignore the rest!
    Don't buy *'enab*, for *uzum* tastes the best.'

'Stop all this talk!' the fourth, a Greek, then said,   3700
   'Because I want some *estafil** instead.'
They started quarrelling, each unaware
   Of what the other names meant, what they share;
They punched each other out of ignorance—
   Empty of knowledge, each of them a dunce.
A mystic knowing all their languages
   Could have united these four savages;
He would have said, 'With this coin I will buy
   Some grapes, which will each of you satisfy.
Submit your hearts sincerely now, as you   3705
   Will see one coin make all your dreams come true!
Your single coin will thus transform to four;
   Four foes will join as one and fight no more.
What each of you says causes separation,
   While what I say brings reconciliation;
Therefore, *keep silent*,* as God's told you to,
   So I can serve as tongue for all of you!'
Even if your speech sounds like it unites,
   Instead it causes arguments and fights.
Borrowed heat cannot warm you like a hearth;   3710
   Something innately hot has special worth:
Though you warm vinegar next to a flame,
   Drinking it makes you colder all the same,
Because it isn't hot intrinsically—
   Its nature's sour and cold originally.*
Instead if you pour grape juice in your cup
   And drink it down, it warms your liver up.
Thus, the pretence of shaikhs who truly see
   Is better than the blind's sincerity.
From the shaikh's speech comes union and elation;   3715
   Blind literalists cause only separation.

About King Solomon's time you have heard:
   He knew the language of each kind of bird.
Leopards and deer in his just realm were friends—
   They stopped their fighting and they made amends;

The dove no longer feared the falcon's claws;
  The sheep were not afraid of the wolves' jaws—
As mediator for each enemy,
  To all the world's birds he brought unity.
Since you're an ant, you hunt for grain all day—   3720
  Seek Solomon and don't remain astray!
The grain you hunt will end up trapping you;
  Seek Solomon and you will find grain too!
For bird-like souls there's no security
  In these times from each other's cruelty,
Although there's one with Solomon's high station
  Who'd bring peace and end all cruel exploitation—
'*There is no nation*', you must now recall,
  '*To which a warner wasn't sent at all.*'*
God said, 'There's not been one community   3725
  To whom I haven't sent a deputy.'
Their bird-like souls this mystic unifies,
  So they will end pretence, deceit, and lies,
And act more like a mother to her son:
  The Prophet said that Muslim souls are one.
Muslims through him attained this unity,
  Though previously each was an enemy:

The removal of disputes and enmity among the Ansar* through the grace of the Prophet.

Two tribes called Aws and Khazraj were at war;*
  It seemed that they would feud for evermore,
But, through the Prophet, their longstanding fight   3730
  Became effaced within Islam's pure light—
These foes became like brothers magically,
  Just like a bunch of grapes appears to be.
Believers are true brothers—unison
  Means each dissolves his body to be one;
The grapes appear like brothers on the vine,
  But, when you squeeze them, they become one wine.

Unripe and ripe are opposites in name,
    But, when unripe grapes ripen, they're the same.
Those grapes which never ripen properly   3735
    Were infidels from pre-eternity;
A grape like that is always shunned as well,
    Since it's condemned to be an infidel.
If I should tell what that grape hides within,
    A riot and dissension would begin;
What infidels hide one should never tell—
    Keep out of paradise the smoke of hell!
Unripened grapes with the capacity,
    Through mystics, will develop magically;
To ripened grapes they will transform so fast,   3740
    Leave spite and dualism in the past,
Then, as ripe grapes, their own skin they will flay,
    So they might form a unity this way.
If one's not joined, a friend becomes a foe,
    But one who's joined won't deal himself a blow.

May the shaikh's love be blest continually!
    It gives a million atoms unity;
What once was mud on some abandoned land
    Becomes a clay jar with the potter's hand.
Unity in our bodies made of clay   3745
    Is less than that of souls still in a way.
Analogies put forth for illustration
    Might just confuse your brains and cause frustration.
A Solomon now lives with us, but we
    Fail to see men in close proximity;
Men can be blinded by farsightedness:
    A sleeping man can't see his bedroom's mess.
We all delight in subtle conversation,
    Untying knots our favourite recreation;
Tying and opening our knots, like fools,   3750
    For answering questions we just make more rules,
Just like a bird which opens up its snare
    Then closes it, to master skills so rare—

She's thus deprived of open countryside;
　　With knots her whole life is preoccupied.
The snare does not grow flimsier one bit;
　　The bird's wings, though, are snapped apart by it.
Don't struggle with such knots forever, please!
　　Your wings will be snapped by your expertise.
A million birds have snapped their wings apart,　　　　3755
　　And yet from this world they could not depart.
In the Qur'an read all about that kind,
　　From *'They explored—a refuge could they find?'* *

Those men's fight over grapes which we've related
　　Was not solved, nor their rage eliminated,
Until that mystic Solomon came near
　　And made their dualism disappear.
As falcons hear the drumbeats from the king,
　　You too must heed them and stop arguing!
From all directions fly there to be free!　　　　3760
　　Replace your differences with unity!
Wherever you are, turn your face that way! *
　　He's not forbidden it—do not delay!
We are inept birds with the blindest eyes—
　　That Solomon we still can't recognize.
Like owls, we are the falcons' enemy,
　　And so we stay near ruins stubbornly.
Out of our wretched ignorance and blindness,
　　We hurt those privileged to receive God's kindness.
The birds which Solomon made radiant　　　　3765
　　Can't tear apart wings of the innocent;
Rather, they'd take to helpless birds some grain,
　　Since they're kind and their hearts no spite contain.
Their hoopoe longs to praise their king, and so
　　The path to Queens of Sheba it will show.*
Their crow is one in form alone; inside
　　She is a falcon which *turned not aside*.*
'Lak-lak!' their stork is always heard to shout;
　　With unity's fire, she sets fire to doubt.

On seeing falcons, their dove feels no dread—   3770
  Before this dove each falcon lays her head;
The nightingale, whose song makes your heart spin,
  Has a rose-garden hidden deep within;
Their parrot needs no sugar any more—
  Within she's found an everlasting store;
Their peacocks' feet are lovelier to view
  Than plumage other peacocks show to you;
Khaqani's birds' speech echoes all around,
  But where can Solomon's birds' speech be found?*
How can you know the squawks of birds, my son,   3775
  When you have never met King Solomon?
The wings of that bird which sings mystic songs
  To realms beyond both East and West belongs;
From God's throne comes each of its songs of love,
  And it returns majestically above.
A bird which flies without this Solomon
  Loves darkness like a bat and flees the sun.
Join with King Solomon, rejected bat,
  So you won't stay forever blind like that!
Walk one yard on the path which leads to treasure,   3780
  Then, like the yard, your step will serve as measure.
Though now you limp and hobble to your aim,
  You'll soon discover you're no longer lame!

The story about the ducklings nurtured by a domestic bird

Though you're a duck's child, a domestic bird
  Has nurtured you, but still you haven't heard.
Your mother's from that ocean—know your worth!
  Your nurse is the one who's attached to earth.
Your heart yearns passionately for the ocean;
  From your true mother it gained that emotion.
Your fondness for the world comes from your nurse—   3785
  Abandon her! Her views are always worse!

Leave the nurse on dry land and move beyond,
  Into Truth's ocean, like ducks in a pond!
Don't fear the water, though they've taught you to—
  Dive in the ocean with no more ado!
You can live on both land and water, duck,
  Unlike those land birds who must live in muck.
We've honoured Adam's children—God has planned
  For you to ride through water and on land:
Keep '*We've conveyed them on the sea*' in mind,   3790
  Leave '*We've conveyed them to the land*'* behind.
Angels have no way to reach land below,
  And of that ocean most men do not know.
In body animal, angel in soul,
  On both earth and the heavens you can stroll.
Human *like you*, but at a lofty station,
  Some men have been *inspired by revelation*.*
Although their earthly bodies landed here,
  Their spirits roam around the highest sphere.
We are all waterfowl, my mystic friends;   3795
  Our languages that ocean comprehends.
It's Solomon, while we're birds of a feather;
  We're travelling with Solomon forever.
Just like King Solomon, step in the sea—
  It will make David's chain-mail instantly.*
That Solomon now stands in front of you—
  He's blocked all eyes, but for the worthy few:
From slumber, ignorance, and needless fuss,
  Most feel fatigued when he's in front of us.
Thunder makes thirsty men's ears ring with pain,   3800
  Not knowing joy's clouds soon will make it rain;
The flowing stream is where they've fixed their eyes,
  Ignorant of the water from the skies:
To causes they ride aspiration's steed
  And not the Causer—veiled, they won't take heed.
The Causer some men can identify—
  On causes in this world they won't rely.

Pilgrims are amazed at the miracles of an ascetic whom they find alone in the desert

Once in the desert there was a fakir
    Immersed in worship like those men revere.
Pilgrims from many countries would pass by   3805
    And notice this ascetic looking dry—
His nature wasn't dry, just the location;
    He could survive the fierce winds and privation.
The pilgrims were stunned by his solitude,
    And by his good health and his fortitude:
He stood and prayed on sand that was so hot
    It could boil water poured into a pot,
As if he were in gardens that feel cool,
    Or on Boraq, or on the Prophet's mule,*
Or that his feet were on silk tapestries,   3810
    And desert winds cooled him like a sweet breeze.
Some pilgrims stood there in anticipation,
    For him to finish off his supplication.
Once he'd returned from his absorbing prayer,
    One of them, the most sharp-eyed person there,
Saw water dripping from his hands and face,
    His clothes damp with ablution's water's trace:
'From where does water come to this dry land?'
    Towards the sky above he raised his hand.
'Does it rain down whenever you can't cope,   3815
    Without wells, or *palm fibres** for their rope?
Faith's sultan, please reveal this mystery,
    So that your state might give us certainty!
Help us to understand the truth this way,
    So we might cut doubt's girdle straight away!'
He looked up at the sky and slowly said
    'Answer these pilgrims' prayer, so they'll be led!
I seek my sustenance from You above,
    Because You've opened Your door with kind love.

From Placelessness You've made this place appear,   3820
   "*Your daily bread's in heaven*" * You've made clear.'
A cloud approached once he had said this prayer,
   Slowly, like elephants which walk with care.
As if from skins, rain poured down suddenly,
   Filling all hollows which their eyes could see;
The cloud kept raining like a bowl upturned;
   The pilgrims stood there with mouths open, stunned.
Due to these marvels, one group zealously
   Cut off their girdles of uncertainty.*
Another group's faith was intensified   3825
   Due to this feat—*God knows best how to guide.*
The rest stayed sceptical, though it was clear—
   They'll stay inadequate. This book ends here.

EXPLANATORY NOTES

PROSE INTRODUCTION
[written in Persian prose; numbered by line]

14 *There is nothing . . . a fixed measure*: Qur'an 15: 21, where it is found in a list describing God's creation of the world and control over it.

16 *He has raised . . . set up the scales*: Qur'an 55: 7, where it is found in another such list describing God's creation of the world and control over it.

19 *He provides . . . whomsoever He chooses*: Qur'an 2: 212, where dutiful believers are contrasted with infidels who make fun of them.

24 *and they love Him*: Qur'an 5: 54, a verse frequently cited in discussions of the possibility of a relationship of love between God and Man, it is found in the context of a warning to those who turn their backs on worship of God, that God will replace them with better servants, those whom He loves and who love Him.

TEXT
[numbered by verse, or couplet]

4 *When he went on his spiritual ascension*: this alludes to the spiritual ascension of the Prophet Mohammad to the closest possible proximity to God, by the use of the same term: *me'raj*. Many Sufis have described their spiritual experiences as 'ascensions'. See further note to v. 2232 below.

6 *Blessed the day we opted to restart*: the Arabic term *esteftah*, which literally means 'start', is sometimes also used for a specific date in the Islamic calendar (15th of Rajab), and so some commentators have considered Rumi's use of this term as an indication that this restart of the *Masnavi* took place on that precise date.

7 *The date of its resumption . . . six sixty-two*: according to tradition there was a one year gap between the completion of Book One and the start of Book Two, because Hosamoddin was mourning the death of his wife. In the Islamic Hegira calendar 662 corresponds to 1264 CE.

10 *wine that never ends*: the reference to wine here is an allusion to the eternal wine served in heaven, according to Qur'anic descriptions (e.g. 47: 15).

16 *a piece of bread*: in the Muslim tradition the forbidden food that Adam ate is usually identified as grains of wheat (or barley), rather than an apple.

30 *Believers are like mirrors*: a saying of Prophet Mohammad, which Rumi uses here to assert that a true friend is like the clearest of mirrors, and thus reflects reality perfectly.

37 *I'll sleep just like the Sleepers in the Cave . . . Decius's slave*: a reference to the story about the seven companions who, together with their dog, are described in the Qur'an (18: 9–26) as hiding in a cave during the reign of the Roman tyrant Decius, and praying to God for protection. See further 'Sleepers in the Cave' in Glossary.

45 *With Alexander, find its rising place*: Qur'an 18: 83–90, from a passage describing the journey, from the setting-place of the sun to its rising place, of Zo'l-Qarnayn, who is often identified by exegetes as Alexander the Great.

52 *Like Moses's, your hand now shines so bright*: an allusion to the miraculous transformation of Moses's hand mentioned in the Qur'an (20: 22, 28: 132). God causes this transformation in order to strengthen Moses's belief.

54 *Mount Qaf*: in medieval Islamic cosmology, Qaf refers to a range of mountains that surrounds the world and marks the border with the spiritual realm.

59–60 *Abo'l-Hasan . . . All-transcendent station*: it is not clear which person called Abo'l-Hasan is being referred to here. In view of the reference to theological debates in this passage, it is possibly a reference to the theologian Abo'l-Hasan al-Ash'ari (d. 935), the eponym of the Ash'arite school and one of the most important Sunni theologians in history. He was trained as a Mu'tazilite, but devoted the latter part of his life to the opposing 'Sunnite' theology (for which see note to v. 61 below). This interpretation could only make sense here, if Rumi's intention is to illustrate the Sunni belief that God is both immanent and transcendent, by means of this highly unusual description of Abo'l-Hasan. The theological term for God's transcendence is used in v. 60.

61 *Mu'tazilite*: a member of the first school of Sunni systematic theology, which established the methodology adopted by the later schools. The Mu'tazilite school itself grew out of favour by the tenth century among Sunnis. They were criticized by traditionalist Sunnis for overstressing the value of reason and giving it precedence over revelation. Mu'tazilites have been mentioned in this passage because of their emphasis on God's transcendence and incomparability. See further 'mu'tazila' in the *Encyclopaedia of Islam*.

Sunnites: in this context it seems to refer specifically to members of one of the main schools of systematic theology. They were the main opponents of the rationalist Mu'tazilites, and held the view that God is both transcendent and immanent. See further 'ahl al-sunna' in the *Encyclopaedia of Islam*.

70 *There's no blame on the blind*: Qur'an 48: 17, from a passage exhorting the Arabs to fight in the cause of the truth. The blind, the lame, and the sick are exempt, and not to be blamed if they turn away.

74 *My idol's form's like Abraham . . . An idol-smasher in reality*: this is an allusion to Qur'an 21: 51–70, which describes how Abraham smashed his own people's idols.

79 *He's beautiful and He loves beauty*: a hadith which describes God.

80 *Good women for good men*: Qur'an 24: 26, where it is asserted that the good are meant for each other just as the impure are meant for each other.

99 *Pain led pure Mary to the date-palm tree*: an allusion to Qur'an 19: 23–26, which describes Mary's difficult experiences while she is pregnant with Jesus. By shaking the trunk of this tree, she can make dates fall off for her to eat.

113 Heading *In the time of Omar . . . the new moon*: this is based on a story about the Prophet Mohammad's companion Omar (see Glossary).

128 *The wolves are Prophet Joseph's enemies*: an allusion to Qur'an 12: 13–17, where Jacob fears letting Joseph venture out with his brothers in case a wolf should harm him. Later the brothers return weeping and claim that a wolf has devoured Joseph.

134 *Water of Life's cup*: see 'Water of Life' in Glossary.

143 *God's Greatest Name*: the greatest of God's names has power over all things and is a secret only known to prophets and elite saints. This is a familiar concept from the Judaeo-Christian tradition and early Sufi references mention the Prophet David in connection with knowledge of this name.

148 *Moses's pure hand*: an allusion to Qur'an 20: 22 and 28: 132. See note to v. 52.

157 Heading *There is no strength or power except through God*: an invocation which is recommended in many of the sayings of the Prophet Mohammad, especially when one is faced with extreme difficulties. The servant's use of this invocation expresses his belief that the visiting Sufi is insulting him by telling him how to do his job.

166 *Have opened up the gates*: Qur'an 39: 73, which describes the entry of the righteous through the gates of heaven.

173 *When angels tried . . . been appointed*: this alludes to the Qur'anic account (2: 30) of God's appointment of Man as His deputy, which was met with protests initially from the angels.

189 *God's light was sprayed on them*: part of a hadith of the Prophet Mohammad about the spiritual origins of Man.

190 *About His beauty mark I'll then confide*: in Persian Sufi poetry, God takes on the role of beloved and is consequently described using the stock images of beauty which the beloved must possess. The beauty mark (or mole) is often used to symbolize the essence of God.

206 *God give me strength!*: an abbreviated version of the invocation mentioned in note to v. 157 above.

224 *read aloud some prayers*: the original text specifies the first and the one hundred and first chapters of the Qur'an as the prayers that the Sufi read aloud.

255 *Serat's bridge*: pronounced 'serot' in Persian, this is the narrow bridge over hell mentioned by the Prophet Mohammad in eschatological hadiths.

One must successfully pass across it at the end of time in order to reach heaven and avoid falling off into hell.

272 *To wicked men come wicked women*: Qur'an 24: 26; see note to v. 80 above.

293 *the Resurrection*: this refers to the end of time when the dead are resurrected and the truth is revealed. Rumi uses this Qur'anic image frequently to represent the experience of mystical resurrection, or enlightenment, through which reality can be witnessed in this life.

296 *By the break of day*: Qur'an 93: 1, the beginning of a short chapter in the Qur'an which is believed to refer to the Prophet Mohammad's early life, and to serve as a reminder of how God always protected him and solved his difficulties.

299–300 *Abraham 'didn't love what sets'* . . . *'I don't love those that set'*: Qur'an 6: 76, in the Qur'anic account of Abraham's search for a deity truly worthy of worship—he worships in turn a star, the moon, and the sun, until he witnesses that each one of these is transient, at which point he declares '*I don't love the ones that set*'. This search leads him ultimately to worship none but the Eternal Creator.

301–3 *'By the night'* . . . *'He hasn't left you'* . . . *'He has not hated you'*: all these phrases are from Qur'an 93: 2–3, from the chapter mentioned in note to v. 296 above.

307 *Mansur's 'I am the Truth!'*. . . *claimed his own might*: Mansur al-Hallaj (see Glossary) is famous for his alleged utterance 'I am the Truth'. Rumi on a few occasions justifies this statement, arguing that it expresses greater humility than saying 'I am the slave of God', as one's own existence is not even acknowledged (the 'I' in 'I am the Truth' is God). In contrast, when Pharaoh said 'I am God', he was claiming divinity for himself (the 'I' is Pharaoh).

308 *The rod in Moses's hand* . . . *In the magicians' hands, though, it proved worthless*: a reference to the Qur'anic story (20: 62–76) about the help given by God to Moses, so that he could meet the challenge of Pharaoh to perform a miracle greater than the sorcery of his magicians. By magic they make their rods move about, while through God's help the transformation of Moses's rod into a snake is more astonishing.

309 *God's greatest name*: see note to v. 143 above.

334 *The people of the fire are not the same*: Qur'an 59: 20, from a passage exhorting Muslims to fulfil their duty to God, which will distinguish the people destined for heaven from those destined for the fires of hell.

349 *In size and strength* . . . *So Nimrod's realm my wings too can knock flat!*: this alludes to the story about Nimrod, who is killed by an army of flesh-eating and blood-sucking gnats sent by God. See further 'Nimrod' in Glossary.

350–2 *Though I look weak* . . . *will be killed instantly*: an allusion to the Qur'anic story (105: 3) in which God sends birds to throw down stones at a huge army attacking the Prophet Mohammad's tribe and intent on destroying the Kaaba. This defeat of the army from south Arabia, which even boasted an elephant, is traditionally believed to have taken place shortly before Mohammad's birth in the very same year, and thus serves as a sign that God provided help to pave the way for His prophet's future success.

353 *Moses came to the fray armed with a stick*: see note to v. 308 above.

355 *When Noah . . . Each wave in that huge flood sharp as a blade*: an allusion to the story of Noah's ark, which is repeatedly mentioned in the Qur'an (e.g. 11: 25–49).

356 *Mohammad . . . split the moon up in the sky*: an allusion to Qur'an 54: 1, which is usually interpreted as a reference to the miraculous splitting of the moon by the Prophet Mohammad.

358–61 *Moses too would pray . . . in Ahmad's time, deliver me*: Moses's request is an allusion to the Sufi belief that the Prophet Mohammad (also known as 'Ahmad') was privileged with the most complete knowledge of God. One of the consequences of this is that the saints who follow Mohammad can reach higher knowledge than the prophets who came before him.

367 *I was a hidden treasure . . . down to earth*: this alludes to a Sacred Tradition, a saying of the Prophet in which he presents a message from God in his own words. God tells the Prophet David that the reason He created the world was because He was a hidden treasure and wanted to be known. See further Nicholson, vol. vii (Commentary), p. 176.

369 *How many idols did the Prophet break . . . to make!*: the mission of the Prophet Mohammad is epitomized by his smashing of the wooden and stone idols which were housed in the Kaaba during his lifetime, in order to turn people towards the worship of the God of Abrahamic monotheism.

375 *Rostam faced trials, Zal got things on a plate*: Rostam and Zal are mythical kings from Ferdowsi's famous Book of Kings. Zal inherited the wealth of his royal family, but Rostam had to undergo many challenges before establishing himself as the greatest hero of all.

379 Heading *Shaikh Ahmad-e Khazruya*: Ahmad ebn Khazruya (d. 864) was an eminent Sufi from Rumi's native Balkh. Stories about his debts being paid off unexpectedly while he was on his deathbed were already part of his biographical tradition before Rumi's time.

382 *As He made flour for Abraham from sand*: this alludes to a story in which, at a time when Abraham had no food for his family, he followed God's instruction to fill a sack with sand and then the sand was transformed to flour.

386 *Like Ishmael . . . the power to cut*: an allusion to the story of Abraham's willingness to sacrifice his son in obedience to God. The son is identified in the Muslim tradition as Ishmael (*Esma'il*) rather than his half-brother Isaac (*Eshaq*), who plays this role in the biblical story.

387 *Since martyrs live on, joyful, free, and well*: an allusion to Qur'an 2: 154 and 3: 169, concerning the continued life of those who have been slain serving in the way of God.

423 *The Prophet split the moon . . . While Abu Lahab babbled out of spite*: the first hemistich alludes to the miracle of the Prophet Mohammad referred to in note to v. 356 above. The second hemistich refers to the Prophet's uncle Abu Lahab, who is mentioned in chapter 111 of the Qur'an and was his mortal enemy. See further 'Bu Lahab' in Glossary.

438 *Just like deaf men . . . were absurd*: an allusion to a story in Book One of the Masnavi (vv. 3374–409).

439 *We failed to learn from Moses's mistake . . . in Khezr's sake*: a reference to the story in the Qur'an (18: 65–82) about Moses's failed attempt to follow Khezr (see Glossary) as a disciple without questioning him about his actions.

470 *Show us how things are truly, their real state*: an allusion to the following prayer of the Prophet Mohammad frequently cited by Sufis: 'Show me things as they really are!'

476 *the order Be!*: the divine fiat; the way in which God is repeatedly described as granting created things existence, before which they are described as non-existents in a storehouse. See Qur'an 16: 40, 15: 21.

477 *your dog-soul . . . Of your pure heart*: the spiritual organ called 'the heart' is often described as a battleground for the commanding soul (here 'dog-soul') and the spirit, which pull it down to earth and pull it up towards God respectively. The Sufi strives to support the forces of the spirit to defeat the commanding soul, and thus turn it into 'the tranquil soul', which no longer holds the Sufi back from returning to God.

496 *Echoes and David's voice, so far apart*: this alludes to Qur'an 34: 10, where hills and birds are ordered by God to echo David's psalms. Rumi presents an exegesis of this verse in Book Three, which is discussed in J. Mojaddedi, 'Rumi', in A. Rippin, ed., *The Blackwell Companion to the Qur'an* (Oxford, 2006), 369–71.

511 *Did Sinai not fall crashing at My name?*: an allusion to Qur'an 7: 143, where Moses asks God to reveal Himself, and, in response, God reveals Himself to a mountain, flattening it. On witnessing this, Moses himself collapses and faints.

512 *For to the mountain . . . and made all look!*: Qur'an 59: 21, where God describes the power of His revelation by explaining how it could crush a mountain dramatically.

513 *Mount Ohod*: see Glossary.

520 *Poverty / Can almost seem like infidelity*: a hadith, or saying, of the Prophet Mohammad, which is usually interpreted by Sufis to mean that selflessness can reach such a profound degree that it ends up seeming like infidelity and heresy. For an example, see note to v. 307 above.

523 *A carcass . . . can have legitimacy*: a reference to Qur'an 16: 115, which specifically states that it is acceptable to eat unlawful food like carrion when compelled by circumstances to do so.

532 *sama*: see Glossary.

567 *those that set*: Qur'an 6: 76. See note to vv. 299–300 above.

578 *God is your purchaser . . . your customer*: an allusion to descriptions of God as our 'buyer' found in the Qur'an (11: 29, 111).

579–80 *Though Abu Bakr . . . in quality*: the Prophet Mohammad's companion Abu Bakr (see Glossary) is said to have spent 40,000 dinars for love of him. Rumi uses this allusion to stress that spiritual goals are the most important. Rumi is himself believed to have been a descendant of Abu Bakr.

609 *Some of you are believers . . . Some of you are unbelievers*: Qur'an 64: 2, in a passage describing what God has created and His awareness of everything.

623 *Eat!*: Qur'an 5: 88, in a passage in which God commands people not to forbid good things which He has made lawful.

633 *Reprieve me till the day that they're all raised!*: Qur'an 7: 14, in a passage where, after being banished for refusing to prostrate himself before Adam in heaven, Satan makes this request. The day when Mankind will be raised again is the Resurrection at the end of time (see further note to v. 293).

674 *They've cut his hands off!*: the punishment for theft according to Islamic law can be amputation of the hand, if certain strict conditions are met (e.g. the object stolen must exceed a specific value and there must be unimpeachable eyewitnesses).

682 *God's seal is on their hearing and their sight*: this is a Persian rendering of Qur'an 45: 23, which describes those who make desire their deity and are consequently led further astray by God.

689–90 *Placelessness . . . Dimensionless*: these terms signify the realm of Divine Unity beyond the dimensions of space, Man's origin to which he will return.

691 *Non-being*: in this instance 'Non-being' refers to subsistence in God after returning to Him (hence the capitalization), while being refers to the illusory existence of the self.

716 *An angel suffered thus a steep descent*: an allusion to Satan's fate after refusing to prostrate himself before Adam like the other angels. See further note to v. 633 above.

718 *We make him live long, then turn back to die*: Qur'an 36: 68, where it is presented among a list of the signs of God's power and will. Ageing and dying are presented in this Qur'anic verse as being made to turn back towards the beginnings of one's life.

719 *Water of Life*: see Glossary.

720 *Saqi*: see Glossary.

   when you're rid of 'you': when you have overcome the self.

722 *For you, reality . . . You still delight in niceties like rhyme*: an expression of Rumi's view of the relative importance of mystical experience and poetry writing. See also the Introduction.

757 *And chant God's name*: Rumi instructs here that one must perform the Sufi practice of *zekr* (see Glossary).

809–10 *The devil felt . . . but was cursed*: see note to v. 633 above.

812 *Bu'l-Hakam turned into Bu Jahl this way*: see 'Bu Jahl' in the Glossary.

820 *The saint is the Imam . . . From Ali and Omar's line comes this sage*: the point which Rumi is emphasizing is that mystic leaders are not necessarily from the family of the Prophet Mohammad (through his son-in-law Ali, for whom see Glossary), but can be from any line, even that of Ali's rival Omar (see Glossary). This statement is implicitly polemical against Shi'ites who believe that the only rightful successors of the Prophet are a line of his descendants called 'Imams', beginning with Ali and ending with the Mahdi (see note to v. 821 below). Both Sufis and Shi'ites believe that there must always exist mystical leaders, although they have a difference of opinion over their identity.

821 *Seeker, he is the guide and Mahdi . . . in front of you!*: Mahdi literally means 'the Guided One', but it is used as the equivalent of 'Messiah' in Islamic traditions, and is identified by the majority of Shi'ite Muslims as a descendant of the Prophet Mohammad who was born in 869 and will continue to live unseen until close to the end of time, when he will reappear and fulfil his Messianic functions. Furthermore, he is regarded by Shi'ites as the supreme intermediary between God and creation, from his birth until the end of time.

822 *Gabriel*: the Angel Gabriel, through whom the Prophet Mohammad received the revelation of the Qur'an.

823 *the niche*: Qur'an 24: 35, the famous Light Verse, which alludes to different gradations of light, and has attracted much mystical commentary.

855 *the Criterion*: the term used here for 'criterion' is *forqan*. This is a Qur'anic term, after which chapter 25 of the Qur'an has been named, and is often used to refer to the Qur'an as a whole. However, it may have been chosen by Rumi here because its root is the same as that of the terms for 'telling apart' which are also used here. The 'criterion' may therefore be the light in the hearts of mystics, which is the subject under discussion in this passage.

865 *The order 'Say!'*: this command, which is '*qol!*' in Arabic, occurs frequently in the Qur'an (e.g. 112: 1), where it is understood to represent God's command to the Prophet Mohammad to utter the words which immediately follow.

913 *That lightning flash*: Qur'an 24: 43, where God's power is illustrated through His control of clouds, rain, and lightning which can blind.

916 *Abraham's soul . . . a trace of fright*: this alludes to the story about Nimrod (see Glossary) having Abraham thrown into a fire. He was miraculously protected by God, who turned the fire into a comfortable rose-garden for his sake.

917 *When Ishmael fell . . . sharpened blade*: an allusion to the story about Abraham's willingness to sacrifice his son in obedience to God. See further note to v. 386.

918 *David's soul . . . melted just like snow*: an allusion to Qur'an 21: 80 and 34: 10–11, where it is said that God taught David how to make garments of chain-mail and gave him the power to make iron soften for this purpose.

919 *To Solomon . . . his faithful slave*: an allusion to Qur'an 38: 36, where Solomon is described as having been given power over the wind and demons.

920 *When Jacob bowed . . . his eyes again could see*: an allusion to Qur'an 12: 93–6, which describes the restoration of Jacob's sight by the placing of his son Joseph's shirt over his face as a sign (presumably through its smell) that he was still alive.

921 *While moon-faced Joseph . . . people's dreams*: an allusion to Qur'an 12: 43–9, which describes Joseph as being able to interpret dreams.

922 *And when the rod . . . how small was Pharaoh's land*: an allusion to the story about Moses and the magicians in the Qur'an (63: 71). See further note to v. 308 above.

923 *When Jesus found it . . . to the highest sphere*: an allusion to popular Muslim traditions about Jesus's ascent through increasingly loftier levels of heaven by means of ladders.

924 *And once Mohammad . . . split the moon*: an allusion to the story about the Prophet Mohammad's splitting of the moon, which is derived from Qur'an 54: 1. See further note to v. 356.

925 *By Abu Bakr . . . the name that he received*: the Companion of the Prophet and first caliph Abu Bakr is known by the epithet 'the veracious' (as-Seddiq).

926 *Omar learnt to tell true from false apart*: the Companion of the Prophet and second caliph Omar is known by the epithet 'the one who can discern' (al-Faruq).

927 *When to Osman's eyes . . . He gained two lights*: the Companion of the Prophet and third caliph Osman is known by the epithet 'the possessor of two lights' (Zo'n-Nurayn) because he married two of the Prophet's daughters.

928 *Ali dispersed pearls . . . God's own lion*: Ali, the Companion of the Prophet and fourth caliph (and his son-in-law, cousin, and first Shi'ite Imam), is known by the epithet 'Lion of God' because of his bravery.

929 *Jonayd saw his own army*: this is a play on words, because the name of the eminent Sufi from Baghdad Jonayd (d. 910) is similar to the word for army used here, *jond*.

930 *When Bayazid . . . "The Pole of Mystics"*: the eminent Sufi from Khorasan Bayazid Bastami (d. *c*.865) is known by the epithet 'Pole of the Mystics'. Regarding the meaning of 'pole', see further note to v. 1988.

931 *And when Karkhi watched over this deep stream*: this is a play on words, because the name of the eminent Sufi Ma'ruf Karkhi ('from Karkh'; d. 815) can also mean 'stream'.

932 *Prince Ebn-e Adham rode . . . the greatest king that day*: see Glossary.

933 *Once he'd traversed . . . much acclaim*: this is a play on words, because the name of Shaqiq Balkhi (d. 810), a disciple of Ebn-e Adham in Balkh, is similar to the word translated here as 'traverse'(*shaq*) which Rumi uses in the same hemistich.

947 *Whoever comes with good deeds*: Qur'an 6: 160, where those who return to God with good deeds are promised that they will be given ten times as much goodness in return.

977 *But for you*: part of a Sacred Tradition, or saying of the Prophet Mohammad in which he presents a message from God in his own words. God says in this tradition that were it not for Mohammad the purpose of creation would not have been fulfilled.

979 *Has there been one day?*: Qur'an 76: 1, which begins with the rhetorical question, 'Has there ever been a time when Man was something unremembered?'

1052 *Just like Ayaz he was Mahmud's attendant*: Ayaz and Mahmud are the protagonists in the most famous slave and master tale in Persian literature. Ayaz, the favourite slave of Shah Mahmud of Ghazna, won his master's love and was rewarded with the throne of Lahore.

1077 *David's Psalms*: the Psalms of David are considered by Muslims to be one of the four books of holy revelation (along with the Torah, the Gospel, and the Qur'an).

1078 *The Nile was purer . . . blood and strife*: this alludes to a story in the fourth book of the *Masnavi;* it relates that, while the Israelites drew pure water from the Nile, the Egyptians could find only blood. See 'Water of Life' in Glossary.

1079 *Martyrdom brings new life, believers claim*: see note to v. 387 above concerning Qur'anic statements about the continuation of a martyr's life.

1088 *heaven and its paths of grace*: Qur'an 51: 7. Later in this relatively short chapter, it is affirmed that God is the provider of livelihood and nourishment.

1091 *are still nourished*: Qur'an 3: 169, in a verse which asserts that martyrs do not die but continue to live and be nourished by God. See further note to v. 387.

1102 *Red is the best . . . the Great Sun*: the sun is a common image for God in Rumi's poetry, in whose eyes the greatest representative of God was Shamsoddin ('The Sun of the Religion'). Today, a red sheepskin still marks the place of the Sufi master in the ceremony of the Whirling Dervishes.

1103 *But land which joins with Saturn is instead*: Saturn is considered unlucky in Islamic astrology. See vv. 1713–18 of the translation.

1119 *Boraq*: see Glossary.

1173 *Return!*: Qur'an 89: 28, meaning 'Return to God!'—an instruction to the righteous on Judgment Day.

1194 *Here I am!*: according to a well-known saying of the Prophet Mohammad, this is God's response to the appeal, 'O Lord!'

1203 *robab*: a lute still very popular among Afghans, and traditionally believed to be Rumi's favourite instrument to listen to.

1204 *Esrafil*: the angel who, according to Muslim eschatology, signals Judgment Day at the end of time with a blast of a trumpet.

1207 *Or like the Merciful's breath . . . on its way to heaven*: this is based on a saying of the Prophet Mohammad and has been interpreted as an allusion to divine communication with Ovays al-Qarani, who became a follower of Mohammad's in the Yemen without having ever met him.

1209 *And also handsome Joseph's scent . . . from his son's head*: this refers to how Jacob is believed to have discovered that his son Joseph was still alive, through the scent on his shirt. See further note to v. 920 above.

1210 *gushing water*: Qur'an 67: 30, where the provision of gushing water in a drought is cited as one of the examples of God's gifts to Mankind and their need for them.

1213 *bow down to gain proximity!*: Qur'an 96: 19, in encouragement of those keen to get closer to God through worship.

1224 *A halter of palm fibres*: Qur'an 111: 5, where, as punishment, it is said that a halter of palm fibres will be placed around the neck of the wicked wife of Abu Lahab (for whom see Glossary).

1248 *Break Khaybar's gate like Ali if you can*: Ali (see Glossary) is said to have pulled down one of the gates of the settlement of Khaybar and used it as a shield, as he fought as the standard-bearer in a battle on behalf of the Prophet Mohammad's followers.

1277 *the tree of paradise*: this is based on a saying of the Prophet Mohammad about chivalry being a tree in paradise which can lead you there if you hold on to its branches that swoop over us on earth.

1278 *the firmest rope*: Qur'an 2: 256, where it describes the abandonment of false deities and the exclusive worship of God.

1280 *You're handsome Joseph, this world is your well*: this alludes to the Qur'anic story about Joseph. His jealous brothers decide to throw him down a well, rather than kill him (see Qur'an 12: 10–19).

1297 *Light on top of light*: Qur'an 24: 35, part of the famous Light verse, for which see note to v. 823 above.

1310 *When you threw then you did not throw*: Qur'an 8: 17, in a passage describing the Prophet Mohammad's actions in battle as being in reality God's actions. This is one of the most frequently cited Qur'anic verses in Sufi discussions of annihilation in God.

1323 *Borhan-e Mohaqqeq*: a disciple of Rumi's father, Baha Valad. He came from Balkh to Konya after Baha's death in order to supervise Rumi's education. See further the Introduction. The name 'Borhan' means 'proof', and is used with this meaning as a pun in the subsequent verse.

1325 *Salah*: Salahoddin was a goldsmith who became Rumi's deputy and the object of his praise and favour after the final disappearance of Shams-e Tabriz. This verse is the first of three consecutive verses which have been considered later interpolations by those who wished to give Salahoddin the prestige of having been mentioned in the *Masnavi*.

1336 *For Moses's sake . . . straight away*: this alludes to the Qur'anic story about Moses asking God to reveal Himself, which caused the mountain to be dramatically transformed. See further note to v. 511 above.

1338 *Nor are we, like the angels, dressed in green*: in some Muslim descriptions (including illustrations), angels are dressed in garments that are green, the symbolic colour of truth in the Islamic tradition.

1343 *This inner resurrection is supreme . . . a soothing cream*: this makes explicit Rumi's frequent use of the term for 'resurrection' (*qeyamat*) to refer to a spiritual resurrection rather than to the Resurrection at the end of time. See further note to v. 293 above.

1348 *When a dead donkey falls in a salt-mine*: salt is a symbol of purification and the means of spiritual resurrection.

1349 *The colour of God*: Qur'an 2: 138, where believers are described as receiving the colour given by God. It is therefore often understood as a kind of inner baptism.

1351 *Just like that saint who 'I'm the Truth' once said*: a reference to Mansur al-Hallaj. See further note to v. 307 above.

1375 *a barrier's there which can't be crossed*: Qur'an 55: 20, where it describes the way in which different kinds of water (salty and sweet) are kept separate, as one of a long list of signs in nature of God's favours to mankind.

1390 Heading   *Zo'l-Nun al-Mesri*: he was a major Nubian Sufi of the early ninth century and has been regarded by many as the first systematizer of the tradition.

1402 *You'll see hang on the gibbet poor Mansur*: a reference to the hanging of Mansur al-Hallaj in 922. See note to v. 307 above.

1403 *They kill the prophets*: Qur'an 3: 112, a reference to enemies of the prophets among the communities who received them.

1404 *We think you're bad luck*: Qur'an 36: 18, where it represents one of the reactions of disbelievers to whom prophets had been sent.

1407 *while you're with them*: Qur'an 8: 33, where it is explained that God would not rain stones down on those who did not believe in the Prophet Mohammad while he was still with them.

1414 *We had gone out to race*: Qur'an 12: 17, where it represents part of the explanation of Joseph's brothers to their father Jacob.

1429 *The Seven Sleepers' dog*: known as the 'Companions of the Cave' in the Islamic tradition, the Sleepers also had a dog with them in the cave. See further 'Sleepers in the Cave' in Glossary.

1435 *qebla*: see Glossary.

1441 *Whipped hard with Moses's cow's tail*: a reference to a Qur'anic version of the Old Testament story of the red heifer. The animal is referred to simply as 'Moses's cow' in the text (and it is yellow rather than red in colour according to the Qur'anic version; see 2: 67–73). God commands through Moses that such an animal be sacrificed and its tail used to whip a dead body, in order to make it come to life again.

1466 *Loqman*: a sage after whom chapter 31 of the Qur'an is named. See further 'Loqman' in Glossary.

1474 *The foe of false existence boasts Existence*: false existence is that of the self, while 'Existence' is abiding in God.

1487 *Iron became like wax in David's hand*: see the note to v. 918 above, concerning the Qur'anic allusions (34: 10–11, 21: 80) to the Prophet David's God-given ability to bend iron and make chain-mail out of it.

1514 *Loqman*: see note to v. 1466 above.

1545 *For blind men there's no blame*: Qur'an 48: 17, see further note to v. 70.

1549 *take away men's sight*: Qur'an 2: 20, which describes God's control over the fate of infidels, such as through lightning which almost blinds them.

1553 *as if by Saturn it's check-mated*: see note to v. 1103, and vv. 1713–18 of the translation.

1557 *the left side . . . the right side*: the exact phrases used here appear in Qur'an 18: 18, where they are used in the description of the bodily movements of the Sleepers in the Cave (see Glossary). However, Rumi seems to have in mind slight variants of these phrases which appear in an eschatological chapter of the Qur'an (56: 27–48), where they describe how blessings in the hereafter come to the right hand while damnation comes to the left hand. In consequence, people hope they will receive from the right side and not the left.

1563 *God's Friend*: Abraham is known in the Islamic tradition as God's 'Friend' (*Khalil*).

I don't love the ones that set: Qur'an 6: 76. See note to vv. 299–300 above.

1571 *sees by God's Light*: part of a popular saying of the Prophet Mohammad about the miraculous vision of the true believer.

1577 *Bu Bakr Robabi*: see Glossary.

1584 *by God's light*: see note to v. 1571 above.

1602 *Mercury's pen*: Mercury, the celestial scribe in ancient cosmology, here represents the Sufi master who will write on our hearts the truth about us, which we must confront.

1605 Heading *Belqis, the Queen of Sheba*: the monarch of Sheba mentioned several times in the Bible as well as the Qur'an (27: 22–44), but left unnamed in both these sources. See also 'Queen of Sheba' in Glossary.

1610 *split the moon*: Qur'an 54: 1. See note to v. 356 above.

1619 *The heavens were all torn apart*: Qur'an 84: 1, where it is part of the description of the Resurrection at the end of time. See further note to v. 293 above.

1623 *God does what He wills*: Qur'an 14: 27, where it is stressed that God will guide or lead astray whomever he should choose.

1626 *You raise up whom You will*: Qur'an 3: 26, in the context of a prayer to God, who can exalt or debase whomever He chooses.

1629 *I'm not like the four natures and first cause*: this refers to traditional theories about creation, according to which four natures, namely heat, cold, dryness, and moisture, are found in combination in each of the elements (fire, air, earth, and water) and are in flux. In the neoplatonic emanation theories of medieval Islamic philosophers, God is 'the first cause', from which everything else proceeds.

1637 Heading *If your water should have seeped into the ground*: Qur'an 67: 30, where it is linked to the question 'Who will bring you gushing water?', stressing God's omnipotence and Man's dependency on Him.

If water seeps in soil: Qur'an 67: 30, see paragraph above.

1650 *Sho'ayb*: see Glossary.

1665 *Or doves, like men who search, cry out 'Koo koo!'*: 'Koo' means 'Where?' in Persian as well as representing the cry of the dove.

1666 *How shall the stork call 'Lak lak!'. . . 'The Kingdom, God, is Thine'*: 'Lak' means 'is yours/thine' in Arabic as well as representing the cry of the stork.

1671 *Alast*: the Qur'anic Covenant of Alast (7: 172) is when Mankind testified that God is the Lord by saying 'Yes!' in response to His question 'Am I not (*alasto*) your Lord?' This is understood to have taken place when Mankind was pure spirit in the presence of God, before entering the world. See also Glossary.

1673 *Wisdom's our camel, though it be a stray*: a reference to a saying of the Prophet Mohammad: 'Knowledge is the stray camel of the believer', which has been interpreted as meaning that what seems like new knowledge from foreign sources originally belonged to Muslims, and should therefore be embraced rather than avoided.

1679–82 *God ordered Zechariah . . . Retain it in your heart and hide it there!*: a reference to Qur'an 19: 1–15, which corresponds with the biblical story about the aged Zechariah's desperation for a son and heir. God answers his prayer and explains to the doubting Zechariah that his silence for three nights will be a sign that God will bless him with the birth of John.

1707 *These are the Book's signs*: Qur'an 10: 1 (among a number of instances), where it refers specifically to the Qur'an's own verses, traditionally referred to as 'signs' (*ayat*). The same term is used to refer to natural phenomena which, through their extraordinary order and beauty, are also signs of God (e.g. 3: 190−1).

1719 *Remember God!*: Qur'an 33: 41, where it is a command to believers in addition to the command to praise Him. Sufis understand this as referring to their specific practice of *zekr* (see Glossary).

1720 *zekr*: see Glossary.

1742 *When I was ill you never once stopped by*: this is part of a saying of the Prophet Mohammad, which describes God as asking Mankind this question at the Resurrection (see further note to v. 293 above). They are bewildered by the suggestion that they could have visited God when He was sick, and so God explains that if they had visited the sick people whom they had ignored they would have found Him there. Appropriately perhaps for this context, a variant of this hadith identifies Moses rather than all Mankind as those being addressed by God.

1743 *through me both hears and sees*: this is part of possibly the best-known Sacred Tradition, or saying of the Prophet in which he presents a message from God in his own words. God affirms that his worshippers continue to draw close to Him through extra acts of devotion until they eventually see and hear through Him, and thus subsist through Him.

1745 *Fatema*: the highly revered daughter of the Prophet Mohammad and his first wife Khadija. She became the wife of the Prophet's cousin and disciple Ali, and the mother of the Prophet's grandsons Hasan and Hosayn.

1749 *He was not born, nor does the Lord beget*: Qur'an 112: 3, in a short chapter which asserts emphatically that God is one, eternal, and incomparable.

1756 *Above all else divorce is what I hate*: part of a saying of the Prophet Mohammad, which emphasizes how displeasing the separation of husband and wife through divorce is to God.

1772 *qebla*: see Glossary.

1790 *Who does what He should will*: Qur'an 14: 27. See further note to v. 1623 above.

1792 *that lote tree found at heaven's end*: Qur'an 53: 13−18, where, in a passage about the Prophet Mohammad's ascension to heaven, it refers to a lote tree marking the utmost reach of heaven and the limits of human understanding.

1794 *And may He bless your hand eternally*: this is probably intended as an allusion to the miraculous transformation of Moses's hand mentioned in Qur'an 20: 22, 28: 132. See note to v. 52 above.

1801 *zekr*: see Glossary.

1801 *And women's prayers though they still menstruate*: women are considered to be ritually impure when they are menstruating, and are therefore unable to perform the ritual prayer according to Islamic law.

1811 *If only I'd remained mere dust! Alas!*: Qur'an 78: 40, where it represents what the sceptics will be thinking once the Resurrection at the end of time actually starts to happen. See further note to v. 293 above.

1819 *the ones that set*: Qur'an 6: 76. See note to vv. 299–300 above.

1821 *Like angels, I've complained of forms like these*: see further note to v. 173 above.

1829 *Resurrection Day*: see note to v. 293 above.

1835 *gushing waters*: Qur'an 67: 30, where the provision of gushing water in a drought is cited as one of the examples of God's gifts to Mankind and their need for His gifts.

1841 *Heaven's reached through things you dislike . . . their desires*: a saying of the Prophet Mohammad.

1842 *Kawsar*: literally meaning 'abundance', this term is used in the first verse of chapter 108 of the Qur'an, so entitled. Kawsar is also the name for the heavenly fount of grace, which is what Rumi is referring to in this instance.

1860 *put it behind*: part of a saying of the Prophet Mohammad, which positions women behind men. Rumi often uses misogynist sayings and directs them instead at the carnal soul (*nafs*). The word '*nafs*' is a feminine word in the Arabic language.

1875 *Guide my people!*: the Prophet Mohammad is said to have made this prayer after his teeth were broken by a member of his own tribe, who had thrown a stone at him during the battle of Mount Ohod (see Glossary). A more complete version is cited in v. 1930.

1881 *Enmity born of his intelligence . . . due to ignorance*: a saying of the Prophet Mohammad.

1920 *Robabi*: see 'Bu Bakr Robabi' in Glossary.

   Iron I bend like David all the while: an allusion to Qur'an 21: 80. See note to v. 918 above.

1922 *God's hand is over their hands*: Qur'an 48: 10, in a passage where taking an oath with the Prophet is said to be the same as taking an oath with God, so the Prophet's hand represents God's hand.

1924 *The moon was split*: Qur'an 54: 1. See note to v. 356 above.

1930 *They know not, God; my people please still guide!*: a prayer of the Prophet Mohammad, which he made after his teeth were broken by an enemy from among his own Quraysh tribe. See note to v. 1875 above.

1946 *sama'*: see Glossary.

1958 *Call upon God!*: Qur'an 17: 110, where believers who weep and prostrate themselves in humility are instructed to appeal to God.

1960 *Find in the sky your daily bread!*: Qur'an 51: 22, which describes those who have lived righteous lives and are destined for heaven.

1984 *Sameri*: see Glossary.

1988 *the Mystic Pole*: the 'Pole' (*qotb*) is the title for the supreme Sufi saint of each age, who is the *axis mundi*, the central pivot of the universe and all its interests, towards whom all mystics are drawn. For Rumi's own descriptions of such a saint see vv. 2237 ff. in this volume.

2010 *Be silent!*: Qur'an 23: 110, where this represents part of God's response to the appeal for help and forgiveness at the end of time from those who used to deny revelation.

2012 *With Joseph, like a wolf you have behaved*: an allusion to Qur'an 12: 13–17. See note to v. 128 above.

2015 *the dog of Sleepers in the Cave*: see note to v. 1429 above, and 'Sleepers in the Cave' in Glossary.

2027 *I see by God's light*: part of a saying of the Prophet Mohammad (see note to v. 1571 above).

2061 *For Joseph can the wolf feel sympathy . . . as his enemy?*: an allusion to Qur'an 12: 13–17. See note to v. 128 above.

2062 *A dog can be a human in the end*: this alludes to the tradition that the dog of the Sleepers in the Cave (see Glossary), who is also mentioned in the Qur'an (18: 9–26), will go to heaven in the form of a human.

2064 *The moon was split*: Qur'an 54: 1. See note to v. 356 above.

2070 *Withdraw from them!*: Qur'an 32: 30, which advises the Prophet Mohammad to withdraw from the unbelievers.

2071 *He frowned*: Qur'an 80: 1, the first verse of a chapter so entitled, which tells how the Prophet Mohammad frowned and turned away from a blind man who had asked him a question. He did this because the blind man interrupted his attempts to convert one of the notables of Mecca to Islam.

2076 *Basra and Tabuk*: Basra is located in what is today south-eastern Iraq, while Tabuk is located in northern Arabia, and thus they are both outside of what were then already conquered Muslim territories.

2081 *People are like mines*: a saying of the Prophet Mohammad, suggesting that people cannot be easily judged from their outer appearance, which may conceal the treasures within them.

2099 Heading   *Galen*: see Glossary.

2115 *Placelessness*: see note to vv. 689–90.

2124 *And Satan still not bowing . . . claimed instead*: see the note to v. 633 above.

2144 *honour oaths he swore!*: Qur'an 5: 89, where it is a demand made of believers to honour their pledge to God.

   Keep your promise!: Qur'an 5: 1, where it is also a demand made of believers to honour their pledge to God.

2152 *Approach each dervish . . . don't stop circling round!*: this alludes to the importance of the complete Sufi. See further vv. 2224–57 of the translation.

2161–2 *God once told Moses off . . . friend of mine?*: an allusion to a saying of the
Prophet Mohammad. See note to v. 1742 above.

2166 *A special slave of mine fell ill . . . He is I*: an allusion to a saying of the
Prophet Mohammad. See further note to v. 1742.

2173 *Sayyed*: the most common title for someone who is a male descendant of
the Prophet Mohammad. Rumi actually uses another title (*sharif*) in the
text to indicate this status. The title *sharif* is often reserved for descendants of the Prophet through his grandson Hasan rather than his younger
brother Hosayn.

2188 *Jonayd or Bayazid*: a reference to two major Sufis of the ninth–tenth
centuries CE. See notes to vv. 929–30 above, and 'Bayazid' and 'Jonayd'
in Glossary.

2208 *Did what a Kharijite did to Ali*: this refers in particular to the assassination
of the Prophet's cousin and son-in-law Ali (see Glossary) by a Kharijite,
a member of a faction who seceded from his group of followers during
the Battle of Seffin against Mo'aviya (see Glossary).

2209 *monsters like Shemr and Yazid*: Yazid ebn Mo'aviya, the second Omayyad
caliph, succeeding his father, Mo'aviya (see Glossary). He is universally
reviled for having ordered the beheading of the Prophet's grandson
Hosayn and the massacre of his followers in Kerbala in 680. Shemr ebn-e
Ze'l-Jowshan was the member of Yazid's army who killed and beheaded
Hosayn.

2215 *amputee*: the punishment for theft according to Islamic law is amputation of the hand, if certain conditions are met (e.g. the object stolen must
exceed a specific value and there must be unimpeachable eyewitnesses).

2216 *in the Mohit . . . in the Vasit*: these names are presented as titles of canon-
ical compendia of Islamic law. *Mohit* and *Vasit* are words that are often
used in the titles of such voluminous works, because they suggest 'com-
prehensiveness' and 'breadth' respectively. Rumi does not appear to be
referring to specific books in this instance.

2232 *On the me'raj . . . the Throne and angels all the same*: on his ascension (*me'raj*;
see further note to v. 4 above), the Prophet Mohammad was accompanied
by the Angel Gabriel until reaching so close to God's throne that even
Gabriel could not continue further (see further Book One, vv. 1074–5).
Although he had many encounters along the way, his aim was to journey
as close to God as possible.

2245 *Hajj*: the major Muslim pilgrimage to Mecca, the central ritual of which
is circumambulation of the Kaaba (see Glossary).

2249 *Safa*: one of the hillocks in Mecca which pilgrims run between as part of
the rituals of the pilgrimage. This is spelt in Arabic like the word for
'purity', leading Rumi to use them together here as wordplay.

Omra: a shorter version of the Hajj, which can be performed at times other than the specific dates for the Hajj, but cannot substitute for it. This is spelt in Arabic like the word for 'lifespan', leading Rumi to use them together here as wordplay.

2258 *Companion in the Cave*: an allusion to the Companion of the Prophet Mohammad and first caliph, Abu Bakr, who had accompanied the Prophet on his escape from Mecca, during which they hid in a cave, while miracles diverted their pursuers (e.g. a spider spun a web over its entrance, and a bird brought her nest there, so as to give the impression that no one could have passed recently).

2269 *Life's Draught*: see 'Water of Life' in Glossary.

2277 *The sages you should heed*: the term translated as 'sage' here is 'Imam', which has many connotations, as well as being the generic Arabic word for 'leader'. In view of Rumi's discussion of 'the Imam of the age' earlier in this volume, the relatively neutral translation 'sage' has been used here. See further notes to vv. 820–1 above.

2279 *Still seek out their advice . . . But do the total opposite instead!*: this is the infamous advice given in a saying attributed to the Prophet Mohammad with regard to the opinions and advice given by women, but Rumi uses it here to refer to the urging of the carnal soul.

2294 *Serpents become mere sticks . . . Moses falls down drunk through you*: this verse alludes to two well-known Qur'anic stories about Moses, namely the transformation of his rod into a snake and back again (20: 17–21) and his falling in a swoon on witnessing the effect of God's revelation on Mount Sinai (7: 143).

2295 *Grasp it and do not fear!*: Qur'an 20: 21, where God tells Moses to pick up the snake to which his rod had been transformed, with the reassurance that it will change back into a rod.

2296 *your hand which has turned white*: Qur'an 20: 22. See note to v. 52 above.

2300–02 *It's like an army . . . not be cowardly*: an allusion to Qur'an 8: 44, which is interpreted as a reference to the Battle of Badr, in which the Muslims led by Mohammad were hugely outnumbered, but, through God's help, vanquished their Meccan enemies nonetheless.

2303 *God made jihads of both kinds*: jihad (pronounced *'jehaad'* in Persian), commonly understood as 'holy war', has been classified into two types in a famous saying of Mohammad: after the successful Battle of Badr, he tells his followers that they have returned from the 'lesser jihad' to 'the greater jihad', which is the war against one's own self and its desires (see further Book One, vv. 1382–98).

2304 *ease . . . hardship*: Qur'an 92: 5–10, where God says that while He will bring ease to those who are generous, He will bring hardship to miserly hoarders.

2308 *Zo'l-Faqar*: the most renowned sword in Islamic history. This scimitar with a V-shaped tip belonged to the Prophet Mohammad, and then to Ali, with whom it is usually associated.

2313 *God made the river . . . So that the giant Og would drown, the fool!*: a biblical giant killed by Moses, who is known in the Islamic tradition as Aaj (or Uj), the son of Anaq.

2341 *Dalqak*: stories in Books Five and Six of the *Masnavi* indicate that Dalqak was a court jester of a ruler of Termez in north-eastern Persia.

2372 *One even joined the Sleepers in the Cave!*: a reference to the story about the seven companions who, together with their dog, are described in the Qur'an (18: 9–26) as hiding in a cave during the reign of the Roman tyrant Decius, and praying to God for protection. See further 'Sleepers in the Cave' in Glossary.

2376 *It aided Moses . . . it swallowed Korah in one bite!*: Korah is a biblical figure who is also mentioned in the Qur'an (28: 76–82, 29: 39 and 40: 24). As a punishment for behaving arrogantly towards Moses and hoarding his own wealth, he was swallowed up by the earth.

2377 *Swallow, earth!*: Qur'an 11: 44, where it represents God's command for the flood to subside, so that Noah's ark would survive.

2380 *shrank from it*: Qur'an 33: 73, where it refers to the primordial trust accepted by Man to be God's vicegerent in creation, after the heavens and the earth had shrunk from such a weighty responsibility.

2394 *Placelessness*: see note to vv. 689–90 above.

2400 *Hu! Hu!*: 'Hu' is also the name for the essence of God which is chanted by Sufis during *zekr* (see Glossary), and induces mystical drunkenness.

2446 *God alone has bought us*: Qur'an 9: 111, where it is said that God has bought the believers' lives with heaven. This is in return for their complete devotion to him, even if that means being killed while fighting for His cause.

2463 *Beneath which rivers flow*: Qur'an 2: 25, among many occurrences, where it describes the gardens of paradise.

2475 *Harut and Marut*: a pair of fallen angels referred to in the Qur'an (2: 102). See Glossary.

2532 *Mansur's 'I'. . . Pharaoh's 'I' was a curse eternally*: see note to v. 307 above.

2539 *You didn't throw that time you threw!*: Qur'an 8: 17. See further note to v. 1310.

2543 *By the morning*: Qur'an 93: 1. It represents the whole chapter which it begins. That chapter recounts the favour and care God has shown the Prophet in times of difficulty.

2563 *The Gathering*: another name for the Resurrection (see further note to v. 293 above).

2584 *Are moths around the candle of His face*: in Persian poetry the Sufi lover of God is often compared with a moth circling around its beloved flame until it burns itself up.

2589 *They'll open the heart's book like Mercury*: see note to v. 1602 above.

2614 *Mo'aviya*: see Glossary.

2627 *He said, 'I was an angel at the start . . . with all my heart*: an allusion to Satan's original rank as an angel. See note to v. 633 above.

2652 *I spurned prostration . . . not dismissive*: an allusion to Satan's fate after refusing to prostrate himself before Adam like the other angels. See further note to v. 633 above.

2671 *Your trickery made Noah's people . . . they felt forlorn*: an allusion to the story of Noah's mission, which is frequently mentioned in the Qur'an (e.g. 7: 59–64). His opponents suffered the torment of drowning in the flood.

2672 *You helped destroy . . . fits of agony.*: a reference to the Aad (see Glossary), one of the vanquished nations referred to in the Qur'an (e.g. 7: 65).

2673 *You had a part . . . their abomination.*: a reference to the story about the vanquished community of Lot, which is mentioned a number of times in the Qur'an (e.g. 11: 77–82). They are destroyed by God's causing stones to rain down on them.

2674 *You shredded . . . much pain!*: see 'Nimrod' in Glossary.

2698 *An Indian . . . 'This makes men's faces look black!' he'd complain*: in medieval Persian literature, Indians represent black-skinned people, just as Turks represent white-skinned people in contrast.

2719 *to whom He taught the names*: Qur'an 2: 31, concerning God's bestowal of complete knowledge to Adam in the form of 'the names', during His establishment of Man as His vicegerent on earth.

2721 *We've wronged ourselves!*: Qur'an 7: 23, the response of Adam and Eve to God after they are blamed for eating from the forbidden tree.

2750 *When Prophet Adam's greed for wheat increased*: see note to v. 16 above.

2777 *So you would join the others . . . Follow the Prophet thus by reaching there*: it is considered meritorious to follow the Prophet Mohammad's recommended methods of worship, including prayer in congregation.

2827 *The common man's good deed is the saint's sin*: a frequently quoted saying in early Sufi literature, which makes the point that while good deeds are meritorious for ordinary men, for mystics they are still inadequate because the self may take pleasure in them.

2836 *A similar parable . . . in the Holy Text*: this refers to Qur'an 9: 107–10, which speaks of the building of a Mosque of Opposition for the purpose of causing dissension among Muslims. Exegetes provide a more elaborate story, which corresponds to Rumi's version in that the

Prophet Mohammad at first accepts the request of the 'hypocrites' (those pretending to be believers) to pray there as long as it can wait until his return from battle, but on his return he grows suspicious and destroys it.

2856 *He's a comrade in the cave!*: a reference to Abu Bakr as-Seddiq. See note to v. 2258 above.

2870–3 *Don't seek concern for your faith . . . to bring that Jew*: this refers to Abu Amer the 'monk', an enemy of the Prophet Mohammad who had fought against him alongside the Meccans and had then left for Syria. The people who had built the Mosque of Opposition wanted to bring him from Syria to Medina, to boost their cause.

2894–5 *Moses once from a bush . . . 'Lo, I am God!' from it he heard*: Qur'an 28: 29–30, the Qur'anic reference to the well-known biblical story of Moses and the burning bush. God speaks to Moses through the burning bush to inform him about his calling.

2898 *You lied!*: an allusion to Qur'an 9: 107, where God states that the builders of the Mosque of Opposition had lied.

2913 *The Mosque of Qoba*: this was a mosque built by the Prophet Mohammad on the outskirts of Medina during his migration, and the Mosque of Opposition is said to have been built facing it, with the aim of competing with and destroying it.

2914–15 *Like those who with an elephant . . . you should learn*: an allusion to the Qur'anic story (105: 3). See further note to vv. 350–2 above.

2917 *Companions*: the Companions, or contemporary followers, of the Prophet Mohammad. In Sunni Islam the Prophet's Companions are the first generation of his religious successors, and therefore the highest-ranking Muslims after him.

2921 *Each knows his own stray camel straight away*: an allusion to a saying of the Prophet Mohammad. See note to v. 1673 above.

2946 *Truth's like the Night of Power*: the Night of Power is when the first revelation of the Qur'an descended to the Prophet Mohammad. It is therefore considered the most auspicious night of the year, although its exact date (one of the last odd-numbered nights in the month of Ramadan) is uncertain. The highly poetic chapter 97 of the Qur'an celebrates this night.

2949 *discriminating, faithful sage*: part of a saying of the Prophet Mohammad, which describes the true believer in this way.

2956 *Thamud*: a vanquished nation referred to on several occasions in the Qur'an (e.g. 7: 73–9, 4: 23–31, 11: 61–8). They were destroyed as a result of their rejection and mistreatment of the Prophet Saleh, by either an earthquake (7: 78) or a mighty blast of noise (4: 31, 11: 67), or perhaps a combination of the two.

2957–8 *Turn your gaze back there! . . . Are there any flaws in sight?*: Qur'an 67: 3–4, where God tells the Prophet Mohammad to look repeatedly at the sky for confirmation that there are no flaws in His creation.

2982 *Suckle him*: Qur'an 28: 7, part of God's instruction to the mother of Moses to nurse him until she fears for his safety, at which point she should release him into the river and feel assured that God will protect him.

2991 *which leaves no doubt*: Qur'an 2: 2, where it describes the Qur'an itself.

2995 *In which are signs of truthful information*: Qur'an 3: 97, describing the Kaaba as containing evidence of its sacred past.

3031 *The Mosque of Qoba . . . was still unfit*: Rumi emphasizes the baseness of the Mosque of Opposition, by stressing that it was not fit to be considered alongside the Mosque of Qoba, even though that was merely an inanimate building. See further note to v. 2913.

3039 *They started . . . approved convention*: Islamic law manuals list all the rules and conventions about the performance of prayer. One of the conventions is to express silently one's intention to perform the prayer, before actually reciting it. Furthermore, once worshippers have formally started the prayer, they should not interrupt their recitation before its completion, as each of the Indians in this story does.

3040 *Did you make the call?*: this refers to the call to prayer, which, according to a strict reading of the regulations, must be given before the prayer in congregation is performed. It is for this reason that the Indian asks this question.

3044 *The prayers of all four men were spoilt this way*: each nullified his prayers by interrupting his recitations to speak to one of the others.

3048 *Have pity!*: part of a saying of the Prophet Mohammad encouraging pity for those who have fallen into difficulty.

3050 *Don't you fear!*: Qur'an 41: 30, where this represents the advice of angels to true believers in God, who can look forward to paradise.

3057 Heading   *Ghuzz Turks*: a Turkic tribal confederation, also known as 'Oghuz', who invaded the Middle East from Central Asia during the three centuries before Rumi's time.

3068 *Hud*: an Arab prophet after whom chapter 11 of the Qur'an is named, as it recounts (11: 50–60) his career as the prophet sent to the nation called Aad (see Glossary).

3085 *who spread it out*: Qur'an 51: 48, where it describes God as the creator of the world.

3088 *This one's my lord!*: Qur'an 6: 76–8, where this represents Abraham's premature declarations of faith in a star, the moon, and the sun, respectively, before he finally discovers that God is the only eternal object worthy of worship. See note to vv. 299–300 above.

3093 *like cattle, only more astray*: Qur'an 7: 179, referring to those who are unreceptive to God's revelation.

3097 *He is forgiving*: one of God's ninety-nine names is 'the Forgiving'.

3111 *the blissful life*: Qur'an 16: 97, where it describes the bliss with which believers who act well will be rewarded.

3122 *The saint's heart . . . God is found*: this alludes to a sacred tradition in which God says that though the earth and the heavens cannot contain Him, He can be contained by the heart of a true believer.

3124 *They fought the prophets*: Rumi often uses the terms saint and prophet interchangeably, and classes them together as God's representatives.

3127 Heading *Johi*: (Arabic: Joha) a legendary fool similar to the better-known Mollah Nasroddin, comic tales about whom are popular in the Middle East.

3145 *The Joseph . . . show your face!*: see note to v. 1280 above concerning Joseph's plight in the well, and Qur'an 12: 35–54 about Joseph's imprisonment in gaol.

3146–7 *You're Jonah . . . all must rise*: a reference to Qur'an 37: 142–4 (including a citation from the final verse in this passage), where it specifies that, had Jonah not been a devotee who praised God, he would have remained in the belly of the whale until the Resurrection at the end of time (see further note to v. 293 above).

3158 *Patience is heaven's bridge which must cross hell*: this refers to the bridge called 'Serat', which hangs dangerously over the flames of hell as it leads to the opposite destination, heaven. See further v. 255.

3170 *Aad*: one of the vanquished nations mentioned in the Qur'an. See note to v. 2672 above and Glossary.

3171–2 *A fox released . . . what has remained!*: this alludes to the story about the fox and the drum in the fables of Kalila and Dimna. A fox is attracted by the loud sound coming from a drum on which branches are beating in the wind, imagining that it must be a large animal that it might hunt. However, after tearing off its skin, it ends up disappointed to find that the object is empty rather than made up of flesh proportionate to its size and loudness. See further Nicholson, vol. vii (Commentary), 349–50.

3186 *God, we know naught . . . which You've kindly taught*: Qur'an 2: 32, where it represents the response of the angels to God's challenge to them to tell Him of 'the names' if they are aware of them. After they make this response, God tells Adam to inform them of these 'names', which represent the complete and perfect knowledge of God's vicegerent.

3221 Heading *Ebrahim-e Adham*: see Glossary

3245 *Throw it on my father's face!*: Qur'an 12: 93, this is Joseph's instruction for his shirt to be thrown on Jacob's face as a sign that he is still alive. See further note to v. 920 above.

3246 *In ritual prayer the most delight I take!*: this comes from a well-known saying of the Prophet Mohammad, in which he lists women, perfume, and prayer as the three things he likes the most.

3254 *He brings forth pastures*: Qur'an 87: 4, in a list of signs of God's power and ability to create.

3265–70 *that spirit/Which gives us life . . . perceived by few*: Rumi unusually distinguishes here the life-giving aspect of the spirit (*ruh*) from its divine, revelatory aspect. In this way, he can support his argument that the intellect is more hidden than the spirit, by explaining that he is referring only to its less lofty life-giving aspect, which can be detected from whether we move or not (i.e. are still alive). However, the divine aspect of the spirit is more hidden that the intellect, since the Prophet Mohammad's spirit was perceived by few, while his intellect was clear to everyone.

3273–5 *Like Khezr's . . . perceive, my friend?*: see 'Khezr' in Glossary. Rumi compares Moses to a mouse here as wordplay, because in Persian the word for 'mouse' is very similar in written form to his name.

3278 *God has bought them*: Qur'an 9: 111. See note to v. 2446 above.

3280 *to whom We taught the names*: Qur'an 2: 31. See note to v. 2719 above.

3320 *the two jarfuls and small pool*: in writings of Islamic jurisprudence, these are the minimum amounts of water necessary to be considered undefilable, and therefore appropriate for use in ritual ablutions. It implies therefore that the Sufi master cannot be harmed by any impurity.

3322 *God's Friend*: another name for Prophet Abraham. See note to v. 1563 above.

3336 *All but God's face must perish*: Qur'an 28: 88, where it is asserted that there is no deity but God and that only He is eternal.

3345 *At Adam's feet who was then the prostrator*: a reference to the angels prostrating themselves before Adam, as described in Qur'an 2: 30–34.

3354 *the gates*: heaven's gates, as referred to in Qur'an 39: 73.

3369 *Wherever you are, turn your face His way*: Qur'an 2: 144, where the Prophet Mohammad is instructed to face towards the Kaaba in Mecca.

3379 Heading *Sho'ayb*: see Glossary.

3431 *When helpless, even carcasses are clean*: see note to v. 523 above.

3439 Heading *Aisha*: a wife of the Prophet Mohammad, remembered for being very headstrong. She is the source of many Sunni hadith.

3447 *those birds*: Qur'an 105: 3. See note to vv. 350–2 above.

3449 *Find the tale in the Book*: this alludes to chapter 105 of the Qur'an. See further note to vv. 350–2 above.

3471 *Keep silent!*: Qur'an 7: 204, where God commands that when the Qur'an is recited it should be listened to with concentration and by keeping silent.

3477–8 *Since Satan . . . bow as his inferior*: a reference to Qur'an 7: 12, where Satan explains that the reason he would not prostrate himself before Adam is his belief in his own superiority.

3511 *Abasa*: 'He frowned', chapter 80 of the Qur'an. See note to v. 2071 above.

3527–8 *A balanced nature ... keep that harmony*: Rumi refers here specifically to keeping the four bodily humours in balance, in accordance with traditional Persian medicine. See further 'Humoralism' in *Encyclopaedia Iranica*.

3531 *This is where we separate!*: Qur'an 18: 79, where it represents Khezr's speech to Moses, after he had failed to resist questioning his actions.

3534–5 *If you should soil yourself ... empty brain*: an allusion to the fact that one loses the state of ritual purity after soiling oneself, and so must again perform ablutions before praying.

3558 *If all the seas were ink*: Qur'an 18: 109, where it is stated that the seas would all be exhausted before God's word could be written.

3578 *birds with wings spread*: Qur'an 67: 19, where it describes the flight of birds with an emphasis on their dependence on God to be able to stay up in the air.

3580 *Ja'far the Flyer*: Ja'far the Flyer was the brother of Ali, and the Prophet Mohammad's cousin. He was martyred fighting bravely for the Prophet's army, for which he was rewarded with the ability to fly in paradise.

Ja'far the Scoundrel: this does not seem to refer to a specific individual.

3581 *To those who haven't tasted ... in the most high dimension*: to 'taste' means to experience something directly and thus to know with the utmost certainty. Mohammad al-Ghazali (d. 1111) famously argued that, through the opportunity to 'taste' religious truths, the mystical experiences of the Sufis could provide certainty about them, whereas all other approaches and disciplines fell short in this regard.

3606 *the believer's camel that has strayed*: a well-known saying of the Prophet Mohammad. See further note to v. 1673 above.

3610 *that rare gushing source*: Qur'an 67: 30. See further note to v. 1210 above.

3616 *I am near!*: Qur'an, 2: 186, where God says that He is near whenever His devotees ask about Him.

3618 *who is steadfast too*: Qur'an 46: 35, where Mohammad is urged to be firm like the steadfast prophets of the past. Most exegetes have considered this quality as applicable to a select few of the prophets, including Jesus.

3633 *Kalila knew ... what Dimna would convey*: this refers to the main characters (two jackals) in the famous Sanskrit book *The Panchatantra*. It presents, in the form of accessible animal fables, practical advice for princes. The Arabic translation, which was named after these two characters, was popular in Rumi's time.

3640 *The tale about the rose and nightingale*: in classical Persian poetry the nightingale and the rose are stock images symbolizing the lover and the beloved, respectively.

3641 *Heed well the moth and candle tale*: see note to v. 2584.

3645 *X struck Y*: the text reads '*Zayd struck ʿAmr*', which is the generic example of a simple sentence used in books of Arabic grammar; that is to say Zayd and ʿAmr are the equivalents of X and Y, and not specific individuals.

3650 *For Y once stole an extra W!*: the text reads 'For ʿAmr once stole an extra W'. The Arabic name ʿAmr is written with a silent (and therefore 'extra') letter '*waw*', the equivalent of a 'w'. See note to v. 3645 above.

3655 *To wicked women bad men*: Qur'an 24: 26. See further note to v. 80 above.

3675 Heading *imitative knowledge*: this refers to superficial knowledge which is accepted blindly, such as by mimicking those who are considered authoritative models of religious behaviour.

3695 *Look to the attributes . . . the essence, your true aim*: in Muslim theological discourse, God is understood as having an essence and attributes which are distinguishable from each other (their exact relationship is the object of much discussion and debate). Thus Rumi is urging that one aim ultimately for union with God in His essence through His attributes, which are perceivable, rather than feel fulfilled with those attributes alone.

3697–3700 *angur . . . ʿenab . . . uzum . . . estafil*: the words for grapes in Persian, Arabic, Turkish, and Greek, respectively.

3708 *keep silent*: Qur'an 7: 204. See further note to v. 3471 above.

3712 *Because it isn't hot . . . Its nature's sour and cold originally*: this refers to traditional medicine in Persia, in which foods are classified according to whether they are intrinsically 'hot' or 'cold', rather than whether they happen to be hot or cold in temperature. See further note to vv. 3527–8.

3724 *There is no nation . . . To which a warner wasn't sent at all*: Qur'an 35: 24, an example of the Qur'anic sources for the universalist belief of Muslims that God has sent a prophet to every nation.

3729 Heading *Ansar*: literally meaning 'the Helpers', this title is given to the people in Medina, who helped the Muslims from Mecca (distinguished from them by the title 'the Migrants') to prevail over the pagan Meccans, by inviting them to their city and joining forces with them.

Two tribes called Aws and Khazraj were at war: the city of Yathrib (later called Medina) is said to have been suffering from a feud between the Aws and Khazraj tribes during the lifetime of Mohammad, and this was the reason why he was invited, as a trustworthy outsider, to act as the arbitrator and as the unifying leader for the whole community.

3732 *Believers are true brothers*: Qur'an 49: 10, where Muslims are instructed to make peace with one another as brothers. This part is believed to have been revealed in relation to the feud in Medina (see further note to v. 3729 above).

3756 *They explored—a refuge could they find?*: Qur'an 50: 36, in reference to the vanquished nations, who were helpless before God.

3761 *Wherever you are, turn your face that way!*: Qur'an 2: 144. See further note to v. 3369 above.

3767 *Their hoopoe ... to Queens of Sheba it will show*: an allusion to the Qur'anic story about Solomon and the Queen of Sheba (27: 22–44). At first, Solomon is not pleased with the hoopoe's absence, but then his bird explains that it had discovered a powerful queen while away. It is then sent back with an invitation for the queen, who eventually becomes a follower of Solomon. See further 'Queen of Sheba' in the Glossary.

3768 *turned not aside*: Qur'an 53: 17, where it describes the Prophet Mohammad's focus on God. Rumi's use of this Qur'anic citation here involves word-play, because the word for 'crow' and the word for 'turned aside' are spelt the same.

3774 *Khaqani's birds' speech . . . Solomon's birds' speech be found*: Khaqani (d. 1190) wrote relatively difficult Persian poetry and often referred to it as 'the speech of the birds' because it was difficult to understand. Solomon, however, could understand the language of the birds, among many other mysteries revealed to him by God. In this way, Rumi contrasts mystical knowledge with the less worthwhile intellectual knowledge.

3789–90 *We've honoured Adam's children ... to the land*: Qur'an, 17: 70, which describes how Man has been singled out among creation through such privileges.

3793 *like you ... inspired by revelation*: Qur'an 18: 110, part of God's instruction to Mohammad about what to say regarding his own status as a mere human who has been chosen to be God's messenger.

3797 *It will make David's chain-mail instantly*: this refers to the ripples and ring patterns that form on the surface of water. For the reference to the Prophet David, see note to v. 918 above.

3809 *Or on Boraq, or on the Prophet's mule*: see 'Boraq' in the Glossary. The Prophet also had a celebrated mule called Doldol.

3815 *palm fibres*: Qur'an 111: 5. See note to v. 1224 above.

3820 *Your daily bread's in heaven*: Qur'an 51: 22, where Man is told that in heaven is his sustenance and what has been promised to him.

3824 *Cut off their girdles of uncertainty*: in Persian literature, girdles are part of the dress of Christians and Zoroastrians, and so cutting off girdles is often used to symbolize abandoning one's old faith for Islam.

GLOSSARY

Aad one of the vanquished nations referred to in the Qur'an (e.g. 7: 69). They lived just after Noah's time and became proud because of their prosperity, which led them to reject the prophet HUD who had been sent to them. They were destroyed in the end by a roaring wind.

Abu Bakr Abu Bakr as-Seddiq ('the Veracious'), the first successor of the Prophet Mohammad as caliph, and thus considered by Sunni Muslims to have been the first of the four Rightly-guided Caliphs. He accompanied the Prophet on his migration from Mecca to Medina, during which he was his companion in the cave where they hid from the Meccans pursuing them.

Abu Lahab see BU LAHAB.

Abu Yazid see BAYAZID.

Alast the Qur'anic 'Covenant of Alast' (7: 172) is when Mankind testified that God is the Lord by saying 'Yes!' in response to His question 'Am I not (*alasto*) your Lord?' This is understood to have taken place when Mankind was pure spirit in the presence of God, before entering the world, and it is this event which the Sufi practice of SAMA' is intended to re-enact.

Ali 'Ali ebn Abi Taleb, often referred to as 'the Lion of God', cousin and son-in-law of the Prophet Mohammad who was brought up in the same household. He is presented in Sufi literature as the first Sufi saint, on account of being the disciple of the Prophet. In Sunni Islam he is revered as the fourth Rightly-guided Caliph, while in Shi'i Islam he is the first Imam, or religious and political successor of the Prophet.

Bayazid Abu Yazid al-Bestami (d. 874 CE), an eminent Sufi from what is now north-central Iran. He is a highly popular figure in Persian Sufi literature, in particular because of the many bold and controversial statements he is reported to have made, such as 'There is nothing under my cloak but God'.

Boraq the name given in tradition to the Prophet's fabulous mount during his Night Journey from Mecca to Jerusalem, which was followed by his ascension to heaven.

Bu Bakr Robabi a legendary early Sufi who took a vow of silence as part of his devotions.

Bu Jahl (lit. 'Father of Ignorance') the name traditionally given by Muslims to a mortal enemy of the Prophet in Mecca whose original name was Abu'l-Hakam, which implies that he became ignorant after having been wise (the cognate *hekma* means wisdom).

Bu Lahab (lit. 'Father of Flame'), an uncle of the Prophet who was his mortal enemy. He and his wife are condemned in chapter 111 of the Qur'an, which has also been named '*lahab*'.

Bu'l-Hakam see BU JAHL.

Ebn-e Adham Ebrahim ebn-e Adham (d. *c*.777 CE), a much celebrated ascetic precursor to the Sufis from Rumi's native Balkh. He is portrayed in hagiographies as a prince of Balkh who gave up his life of luxury for poverty and extreme asceticism.

Ebrahim ebn-e Adham see EBN-E ADHAM.

Gabriel the Archangel Gabriel, who revealed the Qur'an to the Prophet Mohammad, and guided him on his spiritual ascent.

Galen Greek physician and authority on medicine of the 2nd century CE, whose works came to symbolize Greek medicine and ethics in the medieval Middle East.

hadith a report which conveys the words and/or deeds of the Prophet Mohammad. These reports are the literary expression of the normative example of the Prophet, his '*sonna*', and as such are considered by most Muslims to be second in authority only to the Qur'an as a source of knowledge. Originally transmitted orally, they have been examined for authenticity, classified, and compiled into numerous collections for ease of reference. Their importance in Rumi's *Masnavi* is therefore representative of the Islamic tradition in general.

Harut and Marut a pair of fallen angels referred to in the Qur'an (2: 102). According to the exegetical tradition, they looked down on Man for his sinful nature, but when put to the test on earth themselves, they became prone to lust and tried to seduce a beautiful woman; that woman became Venus, while Harut and Marut were imprisoned in a well in Babylon forever as punishment.

Hosamoddin Hosamoddin Chalabi (d. 1284 CE), Rumi's disciple and deputy, who wrote down the *Masnavi* as Rumi dictated it (see further the Introduction).

Jonayd Abu'l-Qasem al-Jonayd (d. 910 CE), a Sufi who was widely recognized as the supreme authority of his generation. He lived in Baghdad, although he was born and brought up in Persia. In later tradition, his teachings are often described as representing a more circumspect 'sober' Sufism as distinct from the 'drunken' Sufism associated with BAYAZID.

Kaaba the approximately cube-shaped building in MECCA towards which Muslims pray and around which they circumambulate during the pilgrimage. According to Muslim tradition, it was constructed by Abraham and Ishmael for the worship of God, but was later turned into an idol temple. Mohammad's mission to establish Abrahamic monotheism is symbolized by his destruction of the idols at the Kaaba after the Muslim conquest of Mecca.

Khezr a figure usually identified with Enoch/Elias, and described in the Qur'an (18: 65) as someone who has been taught knowledge from God's presence. He is the archetypal spiritual guide in the Sufi tradition. The Qur'anic story about Khezr (18: 65–82) describes Moses as seeking to become his disciple in order to learn some of his special knowledge. Moses is warned that he does not have the patience required, but is finally accepted on condition that he should not question Khezr about anything. Moses fails to refrain from questioning Khezr, and, on the third such occasion, Khezr dismisses him.

Loqman a sage and ascetic, after whom Qur'an 31 is named. He is attributed in particular with various proverbs and fables and has often been identified with Aesop.

Mansur Mansur ebn Hosayn al-Hallaj (d. 922 CE), a controversial Arabic-speaking Sufi of Persian origin whose death on the gallows is believed to have been a major turning-point in the history of Sufism. He is famous for his alleged utterance 'I am the Truth', the most notorious of the theopathic utterances made by Sufis. Rumi's predecessor Faridoddin 'Attar, in whose eyes Hallaj was the most important Sufi of the past, writes that this utterance was the reason for his execution, but this is not supported by the sources stemming from the time of the events (see further 'Hallaj' in *Encyclopaedia Iranica*). Rumi on a number of occasions justifies Hallaj's utterance, arguing that it expresses greater humility than saying 'I am the slave of God,' as one's own existence is not even acknowledged (the 'I' in 'I am the Truth' is God).

Mecca city in western Arabia where the KAABA is located and the Prophet Mohammad was born. After the start of his mission, Mohammad and his followers were ridiculed and persecuted by the Meccans, and so eventually, in 622 CE, they migrated northwards to MEDINA. Towards the end of his life Mohammad led his army in a successful conquest of Mecca, during which the Kaaba was rid of its idols and reclaimed as a monotheistic place of worship.

Medina city to the north of MECCA to which the Prophet Mohammad and his early followers migrated in 622 CE after suffering persecution in Mecca. This migration marks the start of the Muslim, or 'Hegira', lunar calendar. Mohammad became the political leader of Medina, and from this base took control of the whole of western Arabia, including Mecca itself.

Mo'aviya the first ruler of the Umayyad dynasty, which succeeded the era of the four Rightly-guided Caliphs in approximately 661 CE.

Mo'aviya is a controversial figure, as he is reviled by Shi'ites, but accepted by Sunnis as a member of the revered class of Companions (see note to v. 2917) on account of his eventual conversion to Islam towards the end of the Prophet Mohammad's life. Shi'ites point to the fact that he was an enemy of the Prophet for most of his life and that he fought against ALI. Sunnis and Shi'ites agree that he made a major error in appointing his son Yazid as his successor as ruler.

Mount Ohod a mountain in the outskirts of MEDINA, where a famous battle took place between the Muslims of the city, led by the Prophet Mohammad, and their enemies from Mecca. The Prophet Mohammad himself was injured, breaking some teeth, and the Muslims were almost defeated because some of them stopped following his commands in the confusion, eager not to miss out on the booty. The moral of this story is that one should have faith in and always obey the Prophet.

Nimrod a powerful ruler mentioned briefly in the Bible, concerning whom numerous popular stories developed. One of these stories related that he had Abraham thrown into a massive bonfire. Abraham was miraculously protected by God, Who turned the fire into a comfortable rose-garden for his sake, while He had Nimrod killed by an army of flesh-eating and blood-sucking gnats, including one which entered his brain through his nostrils.

Omar 'Omar ebn al-Khattab, the second successor of the Prophet as caliph, and one of the four Rightly-guided Caliphs. He became a follower of the Prophet Mohammad after being one of his fiercest enemies among the polytheists in Mecca. The account of his surprising conversion relates that he had originally intended to kill the Prophet, but was moved on hearing the Qur'an being recited at his sister's house. Although his career as caliph was highly successful militarily, he is none the less portrayed as a pious ruler who lived simply and expressed concern especially to distribute alms to the poor as fairly as possible.

qebla the direction of the KAABA in MECCA, towards which Muslims pray, and, by extension, the Kaaba is the destination of the Muslim pilgrimage.

Queen of Sheba the monarch of Sheba mentioned several times in the Bible as well as the Qur'an (27: 22–44), but left unnamed in both these sources. In the Islamic exegetical tradition, she is known as Belqis. A hoopoe reports to SOLOMON about having seen a people, ruled by a very rich queen, who worship the sun. Solomon gives the bird a letter of invitation to take back to her. Eventually, the queen visits Solomon and is so amazed at his knowledge and miracles that she follows him in surrender to God.

Resurrection this refers to the end of time when the dead are resurrected and the truth is revealed. Rumi uses this Qur'anic image frequently to represent the experience of mystical resurrection, or enlightenment, through which reality can be witnessed in this life.

Rostam the heroic Persian king whose feats are recounted in Ferdowsi's *Shahnama* (*Book of Kings*).

sama the technical term for the practice of meditative listening to music, which is a characteristic form of worship for Sufis. This often includes dance (e.g. the Whirling Dervishes), and is designed to induce ecstasy in the participants. The same term can also be used to mean simply 'a concert'. See further ALAST.

Sameri the 'Samaritan'. He is identified in the Qur'an (20: 87–97) as the man who led the Jews to worship the golden calf in the time of Moses.

Saqi the cup-bearer. In Sufi poetry the Saqi can also represent the Sufi master or God.

Sho'ayb a prophet mentioned in the Qur'an (e.g. 11: 84–95), who was sent to the vanquished community of the Midianites, and has been identified with the biblical Jethro.

Sleepers in the Cave seven companions who, together with their dog, are described in the Qur'an (18: 9–26) as hiding in a cave during the reign of the tyrant Decius, and praying to God for protection. They slept there for some 309 years before waking up and returning to the outside world, though it seemed to them like a single night. Their experience is referred to in the Qur'an as a demonstration to sceptics of God's power both to protect His faithful servants and to resurrect men on Judgment Day. In the earlier Christian version of this Qur'anic story, they are known as the Seven Sleepers of Ephesus.

Solomon prophet and king, who is described in the Qur'an as possessing deep wisdom and having been granted power over nature, including knowledge of the language of the birds (e.g. 27: 15–44).

Water of Life a miraculous stream or fountain which grants eternal life. It is found usually in darkness and with the help of KHEZR.

zekr (lit. 'remembrance'), the remembrance of God by means of the repetition of His names or short religious formulas about Him. This repetition, which is the heart of Sufi practice in all its diverse schools, can be performed silently, under one's breath, or loudly in an assembly. It is also often performed in combination with SAMA'. Sufis are instructed to give total and uncompromising attention to God during *zekr*, losing awareness even of themselves performing the repetition.

The Oxford World's Classics Website

www.worldsclassics.co.uk

- Browse the full range of Oxford World's Classics online

- Sign up for our monthly e-alert to receive information on new titles

- Read extracts from the Introductions

- Listen to our editors and translators talk about the world's greatest literature with our Oxford World's Classics audio guides

- Join the conversation, follow us on Twitter at OWC_Oxford

- Teachers and lecturers can order inspection copies quickly and simply via our website

www.worldsclassics.co.uk

American Literature

British and Irish Literature

Children's Literature

Classics and Ancient Literature

Colonial Literature

Eastern Literature

European Literature

Gothic Literature

History

Medieval Literature

Oxford English Drama

Poetry

Philosophy

Politics

Religion

The Oxford Shakespeare

A complete list of Oxford World's Classics, including Authors in Context, Oxford English Drama, and the Oxford Shakespeare, is available in the UK from the Marketing Services Department, Oxford University Press, Great Clarendon Street, Oxford OX2 6DP, or visit the website at www.oup.com/uk/worldsclassics.

In the USA, visit www.oup.com/us/owc for a complete title list.

Oxford World's Classics are available from all good bookshops. In case of difficulty, customers in the UK should contact Oxford University Press Bookshop, 116 High Street, Oxford OX1 4BR.

THOMAS AQUINAS	Selected Philosophical Writings
FRANCIS BACON	The Essays
WALTER BAGEHOT	The English Constitution
GEORGE BERKELEY	Principles of Human Knowledge and Three Dialogues
EDMUND BURKE	A Philosophical Enquiry into the Origin of Our Ideas of the Sublime and Beautiful Reflections on the Revolution in France
CONFUCIUS	The Analects
DESCARTES	A Discourse on the Method
ÉMILE DURKHEIM	The Elementary Forms of Religious Life
FRIEDRICH ENGELS	The Condition of the Working Class in England
JAMES GEORGE FRAZER	The Golden Bough
SIGMUND FREUD	The Interpretation of Dreams
THOMAS HOBBES	Human Nature and De Corpore Politico Leviathan
DAVID HUME	Selected Essays
NICCOLÒ MACHIAVELLI	The Prince
THOMAS MALTHUS	An Essay on the Principle of Population
KARL MARX	Capital The Communist Manifesto
J. S. MILL	On Liberty and Other Essays Principles of Political Economy and Chapters on Socialism
FRIEDRICH NIETZSCHE	Beyond Good and Evil The Birth of Tragedy On the Genealogy of Morals Thus Spoke Zarathustra Twilight of the Idols

	Late Victorian Gothic Tales
JANE AUSTEN	Emma
	Mansfield Park
	Persuasion
	Pride and Prejudice
	Selected Letters
	Sense and Sensibility
MRS BEETON	Book of Household Management
MARY ELIZABETH BRADDON	Lady Audley's Secret
ANNE BRONTË	The Tenant of Wildfell Hall
CHARLOTTE BRONTË	Jane Eyre
	Shirley
	Villette
EMILY BRONTË	Wuthering Heights
ROBERT BROWNING	The Major Works
JOHN CLARE	The Major Works
SAMUEL TAYLOR COLERIDGE	The Major Works
WILKIE COLLINS	The Moonstone
	No Name
	The Woman in White
CHARLES DARWIN	The Origin of Species
THOMAS DE QUINCEY	The Confessions of an English Opium-Eater
	On Murder
CHARLES DICKENS	The Adventures of Oliver Twist
	Barnaby Rudge
	Bleak House
	David Copperfield
	Great Expectations
	Nicholas Nickleby
	The Old Curiosity Shop
	Our Mutual Friend
	The Pickwick Papers

	Travel Writing 1700–1830
	Women's Writing 1778–1838
WILLIAM BECKFORD	Vathek
JAMES BOSWELL	Life of Johnson
FRANCES BURNEY	Camilla
	Cecilia
	Evelina
	The Wanderer
LORD CHESTERFIELD	Lord Chesterfield's Letters
JOHN CLELAND	Memoirs of a Woman of Pleasure
DANIEL DEFOE	A Journal of the Plague Year
	Moll Flanders
	Robinson Crusoe
	Roxana
HENRY FIELDING	Jonathan Wild
	Joseph Andrews and Shamela
	Tom Jones
WILLIAM GODWIN	Caleb Williams
OLIVER GOLDSMITH	The Vicar of Wakefield
MARY HAYS	Memoirs of Emma Courtney
ELIZABETH INCHBALD	A Simple Story
SAMUEL JOHNSON	The History of Rasselas
	The Major Works
CHARLOTTE LENNOX	The Female Quixote
MATTHEW LEWIS	Journal of a West India Proprietor
	The Monk
HENRY MACKENZIE	The Man of Feeling